LOUIS RENAULT

Louis Renault *(Régie Renault)*

Anthony Rhodes

LOUIS RENAULT
A Biography

**with a foreword by
Lord Montagu of Beaulieu**

Harcourt, Brace & World, Inc.
New York

First American edition 1970

Library of Congress Catalog Card Number: 69-14841

Printed in the United States of America

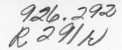

Foreword

BY LORD MONTAGU OF BEAULIEU

If I had to name a single figure as epitomizing the age of the motor-car in France during the first half of the present century, that man would be Louis Renault. France was of course the forcing-ground of the automobile, and if Renault himself was not in at the birth, he was well established as the creator of a new idiom by the turn of the century. Though he lost heart in racing after the tragic death of his brother Marcel in the Paris–Madrid Race of 1903, he had already pointed the way to lighter and more efficient competition machinery, while his determination to produce reliable cars at a reasonable price has led to his being slated as a conservative. The Renault of 1925 had much in common with its counterpart of twenty years earlier, but already in 1913 the company had accounted for one-fifth of France's automobile production. The policy of Billancourt in the interwar period may have resulted in cars that were dull and of no lasting historical merit, but Renault sailed through in complete solvency, whereas André Citroën's ambitious *traction avant* landed *le petit juif*, as Renault called him with a curious *tendresse*, in a financial collapse.

Nor did Renault's thinking end with the motor-car. His interest in aviation should not be forgotten, and before 1914 he was responsible for one of the world's first successful aeromotors, the start of a long line that was to lead to some most impressive light-power units which helped to win races like the *Coupe Deutsch de la Meurthe*. Further, his tragic and still controversial last days in the chaos of a freshly liberated France reflect the *malaise* of a generation, and the restlessness beneath the surface that goes back to the Stavisky Scandal and the *Front Populaire* of the 1930s. The stigma of 'collaboration', seen from a safe distance of twenty-five years, becomes a relative matter; are one's first thoughts to be for a country which seems in virtual and irretrievable liquidation, or for a labour force which may starve if the conqueror's orders are defied? Where would any of us stand, if confronted with this dilemma, and can one reconcile the character of a man who unstintingly turned his factories over to war production in 1914, when 'business as usual' was a favourite slogan, and yet made money out of the Nazis in the years that followed the subjugation of France? And can we reconcile either with the fact that the legendary *quatre chevaux,* the vehicle that was to rehabilitate Renault both technically and economically, was being surreptitiously evolved during the dark years?

Motoring history is a relatively new subject, if only because the sociological significance of the motor-car in all its aspects has only recently been recognized. Like every new science, it has its growing pains, from the tendentious to the owl-solemn and agonizingly factual, and only now are we beginning to realize that behind the assembly lines, the drawing-offices, and the circuits are men—men who devoted their lives to the new locomotion, and who translated their ideals, their foibles, their beliefs, and their enthusiasms into road-going machinery instead of paintings or sculpture. To deal with both men and machines in detail at the same time verges upon the impossible, because there is not the space in which to relate every change of specification to the human element.

In this book Mr Rhodes has sought to analyse and explain Louis Renault, the man—the *petit-bourgeois* Parisian consumed by a passion for machinery, whose absorption with his work made him a lone wolf, with all the consequences of such a path—alone in success, because his own judgement was safer than that of others, but also alone at a time when friends were needed. He has, rightly, regarded the cars as incidental, because they were in principle an extension of the man. I can testify to the painstaking work that has gone into tracing those still alive who had first-hand contact with this lonely colossus of industry, and I feel sure that this work will add to our understanding, not only of the whole Renault empire, but also of the great and sometimes enigmatical Republic against which the tale is played out.

MONTAGU

Beaulieu, Hampshire.
February 1969

Contents

List of Illustrations

LIST OF ILLUSTRATIONS

Acknowledgements

I am particularly grateful for help kindly given by the following: Mesdames P. Blanchard, J. Citroën, F. Lefèvre-Pontalis, and L. Renault; Messieurs M. Citroën, E. Daladier, P. Debos, P. le Grain-Eiffel (head of Commission Historique de l'Automobile Club de France), M. Griffon, S. Guillelmon, M. Hubert, le Comte H. de Lederkerke-Beaufort (Président de l'Automobile Club de France), F. Lehideux, le Ferron de Longcamp, J. Louis, P. Margot-Noblemaire, M. Pommier, C. Pouns, C. Renard (of la Régie Renault), J.-L. Renault, J. Seruys, M. Seruys and J. Thiroloix.

I should also like to thank the authors and publishers of the following works for permission to quote extracts:
Salvation, Vol. III of *Memoirs* by General Charles de Gaulle (Copyright © 1960 by Charles de Gaulle; Simon & Schuster, Inc.); *A History of the World War, 1914-18* by Sir Basil Liddell Hart (Little Brown); and *Renault* by Saint Loup (the Bodley Head).

Preface

At the beginning of the century there was little room in the French Panthéon for that new class of men who were about to dominate the planet, the industrialists. Statesmen, artists, legislators, generals, had their niches; but not the businessmen. Educated young men were still expected to enter 'the professions' —an attitude which as late as 1905 was expressed in Charpentier's opera *Louise*. Nineteenth-century French literature is full of it; in Balzac's novels, the comedies of Labiche, Georges Ohnet's *Le Maître des Forges*. For a country where literary incarnations have always been important, it is significant that in the French novel there is not a single example of an outstanding businessman. If they appear at all, they are ridiculed, and they completely lack the prestige of their American counterparts. If in 1900 some more tolerant observer had spoken favourably of the French businessman, it would have been about his common sense, honesty, reliability, tenacity, the duller virtues; such men were generally regarded as witless, lacking the heroic qualities. That this attitude is discounted in Europe today is primarily due to the influence of America.

By 1900, the Americans had realized that the steel-masters were not simply forging metal, but the future of the race; that a mechanical invention could have as much influence on the future of that race as the battle of Waterloo; and that more people were intimately affected by a novel means of production than by the latest theories of a philosopher. Sinclair Lewis savagely satirized this attitude of his countrymen in the novel whose hero is Babbitt, the businessman with the pet theory of the 'interchangeability of genius'. The great man, says Babbitt, whether a poet, legislator, general or industrialist, possesses a special type of brain, and how he employs it depends on the activity which at any given period in history appears to him most rewarding. According to this, if Henry Ford had been born in the Renaissance, when painting paid better than motor-cars, he would have become Raphael or Piero della Francesca; Edgar Allan Poe in the twenties would have been in charge of the New York police, Paul Verlaine head of the International Reparations Bank, and so on. Amiable nonsense it may sound; but Sinclair Lewis was speaking seriously. The American industrialist had become so important in his country that he now *was* the national hero; and he regarded himself as such, an outstanding human being, of the greatest value to humanity. Lewis shows him proudly telling the public about himself, his work, his family, the tobacco he smokes, anecdotes about his childhood, presenting 'a favourable image'.

The French industrialist, on the other hand, who had also become prominent in the general technical advance, was surprised, even embarrassed, by his new position. He was prepared to accept the doubtful compliment of being able to make money, but not the American 'heroism' that went with it. This was not due to any difference between the French and American temperaments; for French writers, statesmen and generals have never been backward in self-advertisement. But they have a tradition; installed for centuries in the *métier de grands hommes*, they feel at ease there. The French businessman, however, has never had the self-confidence to advertise himself in front of his sceptical countrymen, and his desire for anonymity is deep. There is still no proper term in French for 'Public Relations'.[1]

The man we are concerned with here, Louis Renault, was the greatest French industrialist of his time. At the height of his career, in 1935, he was created *Membre du Conseil de la Légion d'Honneur* (of which there are only fifteen members), the first businessman in French history to be accorded such an honour. With his many mechanical inventions, his vehicles and aeroplanes exported all over the world, his tanks which played such a large part in the First World War, he deserved well of his countrymen. But he refused to present himself to them in this light, with 'a favourable public image'; he did not understand, nor did he like, publicity. And this, perhaps more than anything else, accounted for his downfall.

---

[1] See *La Vie de Louis Renault* by J. Boulogne.

Part One

THE RISE

1 | The Coming of the Machine Age

Throughout history, civilized man has been much concerned with mobility, or attempting to achieve it. In recent times he has, with his technical inventions, carried on a continuous struggle with space and time, gradually increasing his ability to move more quickly on land and sea, and finally in the air. There are references as early as in the Holy Scriptures to the wonderful 'machines' the Egyptians used. In Chapter 2 of Nahum's prophecy is the passage, 'The chariots rage together in the streets, they jostle one another in the broad ways; the appearance of them is like torches, they run like the lightnings.' Some thousands of years later, at the end of the Dark Ages, the English monk Roger Bacon wrote: 'One day chariots will be constructed which will start and move without the impulsion of man or horse, or any other animal.' In the Renaissance, Leonardo made rudimentary designs for 'horseless carriages'; and Albrecht Dürer showed 'strange chariots moved by springs in the shape of apocalyptic animals'.

In the space of about thirty years (A.D. 1870–1900), all these prophecies were fulfilled, with almost alarming suddenness— alarming at least to the opponents of the Machine Age, who contend that to move in relative comfort at high speed has little to do with civilization. On the contrary, they say, the machine has enabled us twice in this century to damage our civilization with wars more destructive than any others in history. They talk also of the peacetime degradation of our cities, owing to the ubiquitous motor-car swarming noisily and dangerously in the narrow thoroughfares.

Typical of these opponents is Léon Daudet, who said that he knew of no more atrocious and inglorious death than that in a motor-car. 'A kind of explosion of the human body. There is something sinister about its very materialistic nature, the result of a sudden breakdown of metal, of man's ineffective control of

3

matter—which turns on him and revenges itself senselessly. . . .'
Medical men were worried for other reasons, principally for the
effect of petrol-fumes on the lungs. They contended that according
to Darwin's theory of the influence of surroundings, the human
body had gradually over the millennia become accustomed
to the smell of horse-dung. But it would not have time to adapt
itself to that of the carbon monoxide from the motor-car
exhaust—because its owners would be poisoned and dead long
before. . . .

On the other side, the advocates of the Machine Age had
equally good arguments. The American magazine *The Horseless
Age* said in 1896:

A pleasing prospect it is that rises before us in contemplating the
array of horseless vehicles! From the general displacement of the
horse in business and pleasure will come economy of time and practical
money-saving. In the cities and towns, the noise and clatter of the
streets will be reduced; a priceless boon to the tired nerves of this
overwrought generation. Then there is the humanitarian aspect. To
spare the obedient beast that since the dawn of history has been man's
drudge will be a downright mercy. On sanitary grounds, too, the
banishing of horses from our city streets will be a blessing. Streets will
be cleaner, jams and blocks less likely, and accidents less frequent, for
the horse is not so manageable as a mechanical vehicle.

To form an opinion about the merits and demerits of the Machine Age, we may first glance back across the centuries and see what
travel was like before the arrival of the internal-combustion
engine.

In Europe until the middle of the sixteenth century, owing to
the poor state of the roads, the only practical means of locomotion were by foot or horse. Riding was reserved for the nobility,
gentlemen and robbers; the rest walked. A lady rode on the pillion, clutching the gentleman or servant mounted in front, as
related in *The Canterbury Tales*. Queen Elizabeth I went mostly
in a litter (although she is said to have ridden on a pillion behind
the Lord Chancellor when she went into the City). One of the
first coaches, or 'waggons' as they were then called, belonged to
the Queen. It was little better than a cart without springs, and
must have been a painful means of conveyance. At one of the
first audiences the Queen gave to the French Ambassador, in

1563, she describes (according to Souvestre)[1] 'the aching pains she was suffering in consequence of having been knocked about in a waggon which had been driven too fast only a few days before'.

Here Queen Elizabeth was referring as much to the state of the roads as to the vehicle. Roads had been built by the Romans; but for over a thousand years after their departure they were in no sense national, simply tracks which were repaired locally by throwing in a few stones. It was easier to make a new track than to repair an existing one. One of the first laws in England about highways is significant. It ordained that all bushes and trees along them leading from one market town to another should be cut down two hundred feet on either side, 'to prevent robbers lurking therein'. No mention was made of upkeep of the surface. Money for upkeep was raised by such devices as selling Indulgences for breaches of the ecclesiastical law. As the fund available for this decreased with the decline of Catholicism, so did the condition of the roads. 'Waggons', such as Queen Elizabeth used, went pitching over the stones and into the ruts, dipping and rising like a ship in a rolling sea.

Conditions were much the same in France. At the time of François I (1494–1547), there were said to be only two 'carriages' in the kingdom: one for the king, the other for Diane de Poitiers. Very few people travelled in France in the Middle Ages, because the Roman roads were out of repair and hidden by an overgrowth of weeds and grass. Paris, as its Roman name 'Lutetia' denotes, was still a 'marshy city'. A *carrosse* such as François I used covered between ten and twelve miles a day, if it did not break down by pitching over the boulders or sticking fast in a quagmire. The few hardy travellers and explorers like Marco Polo on the caravan routes to the East were regarded as either lunatics or exceptional men. Respectable people stayed at home.

In North America at this time the situation was no better, because that continent possessed not even the remains of the roads and bridges of the Roman Empire. If a coach, in use about 1700, came to a stream too deep to ford, it was stood on its wheels in two parallel canoes and conveyed across; the horses swam. In contrast to Europe, where winter was avoided for travel, here it

---

[1] *L'Histoire de l'automobile* by Pierre Souvestre. Paris, Dunod, 1907.

was the best season owing to the frozen surfaces, at least in the northern and central part of North America.

The era of the stage-coach opened in the mid-seventeenth century. In England, it was used only on the better roads near London, and its speed did not exceed four mph. The enthusiasm of those romantics who still hanker back to 'the good old coaching days' may be modified by the following passage from the letter of a Prussian clergyman who travelled from Northampton to London in 1790. 'I can scarcely call it a ride,' he wrote to his wife.[1] 'It was a perpetual motion, an endless jolt from one place to another in a closed wooden box over what appeared to be a heap of unhewn stones and trunks of trees scattered by a hurricane.' Often, after joltings of this kind, passengers were so ill that they went supperless to bed.

Although coaches improved, and the speeds with them, travel remained a hazardous business until Telford and McAdam. In 1815 the latter used granite broken into small stones to give firmness to the road surface. Without these discoveries, none of the 'horseless carriages' of the late nineteenth century would have made any difference to the ease of travel.

Such was travel before the Machine Age.

The first man to apply a non-animal force to locomotion is said to have been the Italian Branco, who in 1629 'caused steam to strike the blades of a wheel, thereby giving it a rotational impulse'. He was followed by a Dutchman, Huygens, who attempted to force a piston to move in a cylinder by 'explosions'. These were simply gunpowder explosions, of considerable danger to all concerned; and yet the important ancestor of the gas or petrol explosion of today. A few decades later, the French Huguenot Denys Papin, who had taken refuge in Germany after the revocation of the Edict of Nantes in 1685, constructed a small boat whose wheels were moved by steam jets. But the seamen of Munden, where he had emigrated, were so suspicious of it that they smashed it.

The first 'powered vehicle' for land was made by the Frenchman Nicolas Cugnot in about 1769. It had a boiler from which steam issued to drive a piston; after ten or fifteen minutes the

---

[1] Letter quoted by Souvestre in his *L'Histoire de l'automobile*.

boiler 'lost its force', and it had to wait the same time before building up pressure again. It was a vast, unwieldy contraption on an oak frame, weighing over a ton and intended for drawing artillery; its radius of movement, during the spasmodic advances, was limited to about twenty yards.[1]

In 1786 an American, Oliver Evans of Pennsylvania, 'imagined' something of the same kind 'for turning mill-wheels and propelling vehicles'. He was considered by the Legislative Committee of Pennsylvania 'completely mad', although they gave him permission to construct the machine for the mills, but not for locomotion. He wrote, 'I am firmly convinced that the time will come when vehicles worked by steam will be generally used, as much for transporting passengers as goods, moving at 10–12 mph, and covering 200 miles a day on good roads.'[2] In 1804, he built a large paddle-boat; but there was no means of conveying it to the river, so he mounted it on wheels, 'which he put in motion by the machine'. This strange contraption, which he called *Eruktor Amphibolis*, then passed through the streets of Philadelphia, to the consternation of the passers-by.

A little earlier in England William Murdoch, a collaborator of James Watt, had constructed a steam-car which he tested at dusk at the entrance to the village of Redruth. Suddenly the engine broke away from the frame and careered across the road 'with the speed of a meteor', terrifying, among others, the local clergyman who happened to be reading in his garden. He thought he had seen the devil.

At the beginning of the nineteenth century in England two names are particularly important—Goldsworthy Gurney and Walter Hancock. The former built a steam vehicle with which he travelled by road from London to Bath. It used seventy-eight pounds' worth of coke and fuel. The enterprise was described in the *United Service Journal* (1828):

When he arrived at Melksham, a fair was in progress and the streets were full of people. Mr. Gurney drove the vehicle with the greatest care so as to hurt no one. Unfortunately, the lower classes of

---

[1] This machine is on show in the Conservatoire National des Arts et Métiers in Paris. A copy of reduced size is in the Science Museum, South Kensington, London.

[2] Quoted by Souvestre in his *L'Histoire de l'automobile*.

this town had been influenced against the new means of transport. And their feelings were inflamed by the postillions who thought that such a vehicle would adversely affect their employment. The crowd turned on him, cursing and throwing stones, and his driver had to be treated surgically. When Mr. Gurney saw that he could not continue, he drove his vehicle into a brewer's courtyard, where he persuaded the police to guard it for the night. The next morning he set out again for Bath. . . .

People were so suspicious of these vehicles that road-taxes in municipalities were levied whenever they passed, as much as £2 a time (ordinary stage-coaches paid 4s). The big industrialists were also hostile, for they were interested in the expanding railways and discouraged rivals. They persuaded Parliament to increase these taxes, on the ground that the 'horseless carriages' were a danger to public safety. In spite of this, Gurney went before a Select Committee of the House of Commons, where he stated that, over a period of several years, his vehicles had caused only one accident. The Select Committee proved to be surprisingly sympathetic; they announced that the taxes were excessive, because 'these carriages damage the road surface less than do the hooves of horses'.

The future for the 'horseless carriage' now seemed brighter. But then in 1834 a disaster occurred which was to retard the development in England for three decades. A steam-car operating between Glasgow and Paisley blew up in the street, killing five passers-by. The newspapers were full of letters condemning the outrage, and the road-taxes were immediately reimposed. Then, in 1861, the 'horseless carriage' received a serious set-back in England with the passing of the Locomotive Act, Section 3 of which provided that 'every locomotive propelled by steam, or *any power other than animal*, be driven and conducted by at least three persons; that every such locomotive shall be instantly stopped by any person with a horse or carriage signalling for the locomotive to be stopped'. The death-blow came a few years later when an even more stringent condition was imposed, 'that each such locomotive shall be preceded by a person walking at least twenty yards ahead, who in case of need shall assist horses in passing the same . . . and who will carry and display a red flag'.

This put an end to all experiments for swifter vehicles during the rest of the century, for the Locomotive Acts were not repealed until 1896. Meanwhile Frenchmen were experimenting with petrol-driven vehicles, and careering across open country by the end of the century at speeds of up to fifty mph.

In America the situation was quite different, and could not be compared with that of Europe, on account of the roads. There were a few good roads near the cities; but as yet no one dreamt of travelling across country by car as motorists did in France, whose highways were now the best in the world. A member of the Packard Motor Company, Mr H. B. Joy, tells how, on one of the yearly transcontinental tours in the United States which his firm made in 1900, he asked his Omaha dealer about the road west:[1]

'There isn't one,' the dealer replied.

'Then how do I go?'

'Follow me, and I'll show you.'

They drove west, he says, until they were halted by a wire fence at the end of the road. The dealer explained to Joy that he took down this fence, drove on to the next and repeated the process there, and so continued until he met no more fences, when he would follow two ruts on the prairie.

Later this apparent disadvantage was turned to good account by the Americans. Their cross-country roads, when built, were specially designed for the new form of transport. They were soon to have vehicles which were as swift and efficient as those of Europe, and which, owing to more modern methods of production, were cheaper.

---

[1] Related by Allan Nevins and F. E. Hill in *Ford: The Times, the Man, the Company*. Scribner, 1954.

2 | The French Genius

'France had her pockets full of seeds and let them fall carelessly behind her. Others came and picked them up and carried them away to their own countries, to plant them in chemically fertile soil, where they bore huge and scentless flowers.'

Le Coq et l'Arlequin, Jean Cocteau

In the decades that followed Cugnot's invention of the first powered vehicle on land, France retained her mechanical lead. Yet her inventions tended to remain, as might be expected of this intellectual race, more abstract than practical. M. Pierre Souvestre, the author of *L'Histoire de l'automobile*, the standard work on the early motor-car, writes, 'The period of French experiments corresponding with that in England and America over the same period [that is, late eighteenth and nineteenth century], was much less important in terms of results obtained. Apart from one or two rare exceptions, we tended to remain in the field of study and design. Practical application led to results in industry much later. . . .' The French are the creators *par excellence* of the prototype—the motor-car, the aeroplane, the submarine.

Some of these French experiments may be briefly referred to. Before even Cugnot, there had been Vaucauson who announced in 1748 his 'vehicle capable of moving on its own'. So mysterious did this sound to an equestrian society that Louis XV asked to see it. It proved to be no more than a hand-powered machine. The King was delighted and ordered one; he told the inventor, 'the pleb will take you for a sorcerer'.

One of the most important French inventions was Onésiphore Pecqueur's differential in 1828, which overcame the problem of turning corners. The first gas-machine, forerunner of the petrol engine, was developed by Etienne Lenoir in 1860. About this time Léon Bollée made important discoveries in joints for steering and the transmission of power. In 1866, Lotz ran a steam vehicle 'for passengers and goods' in parts of the country without a railway, which was called a *locomotive routière*. The nineteenth-century pioneers were much concerned with the problem of friction, of how the wheels would grip the earth when the vehicle was moving 'at speed'; one man invented a machine with claws which could be raised and lowered, gripping the earth.

The great year, as far as the petrol engine was concerned, was 1880 when the German Karl Benz invented his 'gas motor' with a two-stroke engine. As David Scott-Moncrieff says, in his story of Mercedes-Benz[1],

. . . every part of this vehicle had to be designed out of his own head and made with his own hands. He had to decide whether it should have three wheels or four, whether it should be driven by the front wheels or by the back; whether it should be steered by the front or rear wheels, how the power should be carried from the engine to the wheels or to one wheel, whether the engine should be placed in front, amidships or at the rear. . . . Benz had never seen a motor vehicle in his life; neither had he any knowledge of the form the few wholly unsuccessful experiments before him had taken. The genius of the man only comes home to us if we try to picture what our thoughts would be if we were given a gas engine and were told to attach it to some form of road vehicle . . . and we had never seen a self-propelled vehicle in our lives . . .

Sometime in the spring of 1885 the great event took place, and Benz tested his car on the ground surrounding his workshop. In the autumn of that year it covered one thousand yards at about eight mph on the public highway. Each time it was taken out Benz feared police intervention. He was determined that it should cover a good distance unaided, and he often took it out after dark.

In France, Armand Peugeot may well claim to have constructed the first motor-car. His family firm was founded at Vénisseux in 1849 for manufacturing tools, saws, farm implements and general hardware. As a young man he was sent to England to study business methods, and came to know what Souvestre describes as 'the superb factories of Leeds'. He was inspired by what he saw, and on returning to France he launched into bicycle construction. He knew of Benz's interest in gas engines, and began experimenting with one, finding that 'gas worked better

---

[1] *Three-Pointed Star*, revised edition published by Cassell in 1966.

at dusk and dawn, because in the full sunshine it was necessary to cover the tank and parts of the engine with wet or damp earth sods'; and 'because the motor secreted noxious odours, it was placed at the rear of the vehicle'. (Gas in those days could hardly be compared with our modern gasoline. At one point naphtha or camphor gas had been used, and the stench from the exhaust had proved overpowering.) In 1891, one of his vehicles accomplished the extraordinary feat of travelling from Paris to Brest and back at an average speed of ten mph. When one of his clients, the Comte de Cognard, crossed the St Gotthard Pass in a petrol-driven Peugeot, the firm's name was made. Peugeot may therefore be considered the first Frenchman to make the automobile a commercial proposition. In 1895 he sold two hundred vehicles. These, together with cars from Panhard and Levassor and other firms, made a grand total of five-hundred-odd motor vehicles now on the roads of France. They were still costly affairs, and only the rich could afford them in the early days. In 1900 Daimler sold the Prince of Wales his first vehicle; whereupon the Kaiser, not to be outdone by his uncle, ordered a bigger model. These potentates were followed by the King of the Belgians, the Shah of Persia and the King of Spain. Among monarchs, only Franz Joseph of Austria remained hostile to the new form of locomotion.

Louis Renault's other immediate predecessor was the Comte de Dion, perhaps the most picturesque figure in the history of the French automobile. This rich man was regarded in Paris merely as a gambler, duellist and *boulevardier*, until he became interested in machines in the early 1880s. In 1881, he discovered Georges Bouton and Trépadoux experimenting with small steam-engines at Clignancourt. They lacked capital and he offered them a partnership in a firm so that they could put their engines on the market. His Parisian friends regarded this as madness and he was soon known as '*le Comte mécanicien*'—particularly after he was seen slowly advancing along the road near *la porte Maillot* perched upon an extraordinary machine which vomited sparks and black smoke, to the delight of the children and disgust of the dogs.

His friends' mockery was typical of the attitude in those days. Although French motoring did not suffer from England's draconian legislation, there was still much opposition in the early 1880s. When a motorist nearly ran over the wife of the writer Hugués le

Roux, that author announced that if the police did not act against 'these mad dogs', he would go out with a pistol and shoot any motorist endangering the public safety. Typical also was a letter to the *Journal de Versailles* in 1895: 'Would it not be possible for all police stations to possess a number of carpets with nails projecting all over them, which could be placed in front of motor vehicles, to puncture their tyres, and thus make them stop. . . ?'

Undeterred by all this, de Dion and his partners went on with their steam-engines, for which they found a growing market. The method of ignition was still complicated—lighting a small coke furnace under the boiler and getting up steam before anything happened. The customers must have been courageous as well as enterprising, for the first question they asked when inspecting one was, 'Will it blow up?' In 1889, the Count became interested in Benz's gas machines, and suggested to his collaborators that they should start on petrol engines (Gottlieb Daimler had patented his first gas engine in Germany in 1888). They soon had a small four-stroke, $\frac{1}{2}$ hp petrol engine with a single verticle cylinder, 50 mm bore and 70 mm stroke; ignition was by sparking-plug and coil. In 1894 they fitted it into a tricycle, and found an even greater demand for this type of vehicle than for their steam-cars. Here the Count proved as good a businessman as a mechanic, revealing a flair for publicity worthy of a modern sales executive. He advertised this vehicle in the Press with coloured illustrations of young ladies in their underclothes, long frilly bloomers and corsets, being driven hilariously away from gesticulating parents in Dion-Bouton vehicles by dark, romantic-looking men in goggles.

Of Louis Renault's other French forerunners, Léon Serpollet, René Panhard, Emile Levassor and Alexandre Darracq must be mentioned. Levassor adapted Daimler's four-cycle engine, hitherto used only in boats, for road traction. Darracq had envisaged as early as 1890 what Henry Ford was later to develop on a mammoth scale in America, 'an enterprise which would allow him [Ford], by producing large quantities of vehicles, to lower their price'. But this, in Darracq's case, was only theory. Then in March 1899 a small advertisement in the *Petites Affiches* announced the foundation of a new firm, Renault Frères, with a capital of 60,000 Frs, 'whose object is the construction of self-propelled vehicles'.

3 | Louis Renault

'The nobility—corrupt! The proletariat—gross! But the bourgeoisie—ah, the point of transition and perfection!'

Maurice Barrès

Louis Renault was born in Paris on 15 February 1877, the fourth of six children. Their father, Alfred, of Saumurois origin, had moved there in the 1850s and established himself in a small drapery business in the Place des Victoires, where he later specialized in the manufacture of buttons. It cannot therefore be said, as it has been often of Louis Renault, that he 'started from nothing'. The fact that one of his elder brothers, Marcel, was sent to England 'to learn commerce and languages' alone disproves this. He had the perfectly conventional bourgeois upbringing, and was to retain all his life the bourgeois distrust, even fear, of the working-classes.

In those days one was born into a certain class and expected to die in it. A few businessmen had penetrated into the upper classes and the French aristocracy, but without much success—the art of knowing how to spend money has to be learnt from childhood up. Between 1885 and 1910 it was estimated that there were some seven to eight million bourgeois in France. This class was then notable for three particular features: respect for work; a certain decorum summed up by the stiff white collar and the top-hat; and the obligation of the *baccalauréat*. Despised by the nobility, scorned by the working people, who reproached it for its money-grubbing and superior airs, the bourgeoisie, the principal beneficiary of the French Revolution, had concentrated tenaciously on trade, and its higher branches had gained control of industry and banking. It was now engaged on founding the French industrial empire of the twentieth century. 'The bourgeois,' said a French sociologist, Emmanuel Berl, 'is a man possessing money and esteem – whose principal aim is to acquire more money and more esteem.' This was a fairly good definition of the Renault family.

Renault's father appears to have been a sound businessman who wanted his sons to enter the family firm and help expand it. He considered Louis, whose school reports were bad and who early showed an interest in mechanical gadgets, as the least satisfactory, and said, 'We'll never make a businessman of that greasy-fingered duffer.' He had no interest in machines, and when Louis spoke of motor vehicles, he told his son that they should have shafts in front, 'to give the feeling that a horse is really there'.

The mother was a Parisian, born Louise Berthe Magnien, a devout member of the *Tiers Ordre* (Order of Lay Sisters), and an annual pilgrim to Lourdes. 'My dear mother died,' she used to say, 'on the road to Lourdes. Would that I could too!' Her wish was to be fulfilled, almost literally, for she died in 1911 immediately after her return from that shrine. The grandchildren spoke of their surprise at seeing her 'in her coffin dressed as a nun'.

Louis was born at 14 Place de Laborde, but the family also possessed a small country property at Billancourt (a suburb to-day fully engulfed in the metropolis) where he spent his Sundays and half-holidays. He was allowed to play in the garden shed where, before he was ten, he had revealed a certain mechanical bent. He acquired an ancient boiler, which he repaired and soldered and put into service. He fitted a musical-box under the seat of a luncheon guest, the Abbé Baudrillart, with a trigger which set it off when the cleric sat down to table. He was probably not very different from any other small boy who likes watching a lawn-mower being mended, is fascinated by the gears of a water-mill, or delights in exploring the mysteries of a clock. Once he crawled on to the tender of a train about to leave Saint Lazare station for Le Havre and did not reveal himself until it was under way. The engine-driver could only take him on to the destination, where he handed him over to the stationmaster, who repatriated him to Paris.

His father died in 1891. Three of the other children, a boy and two girls, had died in childhood, and the elder brothers, Fernand and Marcel, now took over the family business. Louis was at the Lycée Condorcet preparing for the École Centrale exam, but he was already more interested in practical handicrafts than in solving written problems. After visiting the Automobile Exhibition of 1889 and admiring one of Serpollet's vehicles, he was bold enough in the holidays to go regularly to Serpollet's establishment in Montmartre every morning, and peer in through the door at the mechanics at work. They became so impressed by the silent, curious face of the child that they informed their employer. Serpollet had Louis brought before him, and asked what he wanted.

'To get up on your horseless carriage,' was the prompt reply.

Serpollet was a good-natured man, and he satisfied the boy's curiosity by taking him for a short ride in his vehicle. Louis sat up with him, and his excitement can be imagined as they went past the Gare du Nord, along the Boulevard Magenta to the Place de la République, at a speed which to Louis Renault seemed unbelievable. But near the Quai de la Rapée the vehicle swerved, and they saw one of the front wheels break away and roll off towards the river. Fortunately a mound of sand prevented the vehicle from following the same course. The wheel was retrieved, and, to the further delight of the youth, Serpollet allowed him to help attach it to the axle. Serpollet was impressed by his mechanical aptitude and said he could come to the factory whenever he liked. Several incidents of this kind—including the construction of a boat, which sank in the Seine—marked the opening of Louis Renault's career.

The time had now arrived for the Ecole Centrale. In the 1890s science was still regarded in French educational circles as a kind of branch of classical education, to obtain a further understanding of the True, the Good and the Beautiful. The laws of nature, the great scientific theories now being discovered, were regarded as interesting in themselves. It was still considered beneath one's dignity to apply them with the hands; as 'Art for Art's sake, so Science for Science's sake'. This was the exact reverse of Louis Renault's attitude. Such was his desire to be at the bench or in a workshop, that he decided not to take the Ecole Centrale exam. Instead, he applied for a place in the de Dion factory. But the de Dion establishment was thriving and did not want beginners. Undismayed, he set to work alone in the little workshop he had equipped on the family property at Billancourt.

His two brothers, Fernand and Marcel, had meanwhile been running the family business in the Place des Victoires, and they asked him to join them. A mechanic in those days, even if he was the Comte de Dion, enjoyed little prestige. The strange noises in the garden shed where Louis was turning at the lathe, and experimenting with a number of antiquated machines, filled the neighbours with disquiet. When he announced that he was making a gas engine they feared an explosion. A visitor to the house at the time, the fashion-designer Paul Poiret, wrote in a memoir,[1] 'The Renault son seldom appeared in front of visitors. Everyone knew he was busy in a workshop surrounded by crank-shafts and pistons, constructing his first engine. If by chance he did appear, he was covered with oil and grease—the dishevelled servant, the uncouth prisoner, of an ideal.'

Louis Renault did not want to enter the family firm and here he had the support of a member of the family by marriage, M. Richardière, who was at the Tribunal de Commerce and who introduced him to the boiler-constructor M. Delaunay-Belleville. Struck by the youth's technical knowledge, M. Belleville asked to see the generator Louis had made. He found it interesting enough to offer Louis a place in the firm. Much later, in a letter to Baudry de Saulnier (17 April 1906),[2] Renault describes why he accepted this offer immediately. 'You ask when and why I began to think about the automobile. Long before that, I had a weakness for anything mechanical . . . at about the age of sixteen I told my brothers that commerce did not interest me, and that I had decided to go in for mechanical things. This was why I entered Delaunay-Belleville, the boiler people, just before my military service. After this, I set about constructing for my personal use a voiturette from designs I had made during my military service...' He was able to work in this firm only a few months before being called up for military service.

He was now aged nineteen, a little under middle height, wiry and muscular, with dark brown eyes and hollow cheeks. With his small tooth-brush moustache he looked, to modern eyes, like Charles Chaplin; but unlike the comedian he was saturnine and taciturn. During his military service he took little interest in soldiering, except for the opportunities it occasionally offered to his inventive skill. The French military mind did not yet appreciate mechanical devices. In spite of this, he invented a successful

---

[1] *En habillant l'Europe*, Grasset, Paris, 1930.
[2] Quoted in Baudry de Saulnier's *Histoire de la locomotion terrestre*. Paris, L'Illustration, 1936.

device for economizing effort on the rifle-ranges. Before his invention, each target, a silhouette at which the marksmen aimed, was raised and lowered in the butts by a man who announced the score by waving a red flag. Louis Renault was shocked at this waste of manpower, and suggested that the manipulation of the targets and their marking could be effected by an automatic device worked by wires, and handled for all targets by *one man*. This proved to be a great success, and was later employed for the whole company.

During annual manœuvres, he drove a curious double-purpose vehicle of his own design; it could transport members of the staff and yet, thanks to a generating plant and dynamo which he drove off the engine, could be transformed at night into a searchlight. The official military view of motor vehicles then was that they might be of value for transporting general officers to visit one another rapidly behind the lines, but that, owing to the inevitable difficulties of terrain, they could never replace the horse in operations.

Apart from constructing these gadgets, Renault does not appear to have distinguished himself; he left the regiment as he had entered it, a *Simple soldat, 2e classe*, too boorish and unsociable to obtain promotion.

4 | **First Inventions**

By the mid-1890s the automobile industry in France was still confined essentially to expensive cars. A vehicle was made to order, and delivery often took several months. In this way, the order-form often became commercially as valuable as the commodity itself, and was sold several times between friends or prospective clients, increasing in value with each sale. The vehicle itself was, moreover, often regarded as unique; the notion of repetition (to be developed later into mass production) was unknown. Owners speculated on the value of well-known vehicles which had won races, and which were often dubbed like race-horses. It was supposed, for example, that the vehicle 'Indéfatigable' still had a great future. It had cost 25,000 Frs; but after its unexpected victory in an important race, it was sold for 35,000 Frs; two days later, for 45,000 Frs. A prospectus of the period comparing the costs of a horse and a car speaks seriously of the 'amortisation' in twenty years of a vehicle constructed in 1895.

Until 1900, motor-cars were only for the rich. Such a vehicle cost two hundred and fifty times the price of a suit of clothes; and four times the cost of a house to run. For the larger, faster models, the running costs were prohibitive. A 40-hp car could not be run under £600 a year. The owner of a Rochet-Schneider offered a firm of tyre-makers £300 a year to keep him in new tyres.

Automobile manufacturers confined themselves to making the engine and chassis, while specialist firms dealt with the equipment and coachwork, largely by hand. In Europe, it was not until the First World War that the automobile manufacturer took over most of the subsidiary work. Before this, it was assumed that the buyer would expect the body to be built to his own requirements and, as Mr C. Wilson in his book on Napier Brothers says, 'taste differed so widely in the matter of design and finish of the carriage work that the chassis price alone was fixed'. With the matter of the body settled, the buyer would indulge his fancy with additional extras. He would need lamps and a horn which, as a member of the firm put it, 'are charged extra, as most of our clients, having previously owned cars, already possess a number of such accessories and prefer not to have a new set provided and charged for in the price of the chassis; while those who do not already possess such accessories prefer to select the particular patterns which they fancy'.

Until about 1902 the bodywork, however expensive, was still primitive and driver and passengers often sat in the open. After only a few miles' travelling, the passengers' clothes were thickly coated with dust, and their hair so clotted with it that they always had to have a bath after a journey. The noise of the engine and gears was so deafening that they had to shout to one another, or sometimes stop if they wanted to talk. Any journey, even of a few miles, almost always included the chauffeur having to 'do something to the engine'. This generally meant that the chauffeur had to get under the car, and lie on his back in the dirt tinkering with nuts and bolts and taps an inch or two away from his nose, with oil dripping in his face. A suit of overalls had to be carried in every car together with a spare can of petrol. In 1902 Edith Wharton drove fifty miles in the Roman *campagna* with the American ambassador, and afterwards wrote in a letter 'His car was probably the most luxurious, and certainly one of the fastest, then obtainable. But that meant only a sort of high-perched phaeton without hood or screen, or any protection from the wind. Shaken to the bone, wind-swept, dust-covered, we were thankful to get back. . . . One sets out on a ten-mile journey here with more apprehension than would attend a trip across Africa.'

Another feature of the times, which seems curious today, was the attitude towards the aesthetics of vehicle construction. An article in *Figaro* (17 November 1896) said, 'One thing alone will prevent well-to-do people who have a feeling for elegance from buying these machines—their hideous shape. The horses have been removed and the eye is subconsciously always searching for them.' The newspaper accordingly opened a competition to artists for a design 'which would accustom the eye not to look for horses in front—to replace the present hideous shape of the automobile by something elegant as well as practical'. But this was, in the words of Souvestre the automobile historian, 'unfortunate because the artists, having a very sketchy idea of the mechanical requirements of an automobile, conceived fantastic

chariots which could not be constructed with the available
material . . .' The *Figaro* competitions, he said, went too far, 'de-
signing vehicles which could convey Fairy Queens to the Châte-
let, but not vulgar human beings. . . . Some attempted to construct a vehicle without horses, a *horseless* carriage, exactly the
same in appearance as a vehicle drawn by horses! Is this not the
negation of art, whose fundamental principle is to clothe every
product of human invention, whether a soup-cauldron, a cathe-
dral or an automobile with a shape appropriate to its function?
In trying to produce a Venetian gondola for the automobile, we
have achieved nothing but a lot of decapitated snails. . . .'

Some manufacturers had meanwhile thought of a lighter,
cheaper type of vehicle. One or two had attempted it, but with
unsatisfactory results, and they concluded that a reliable light
vehicle was a mechanical impossibility. The term 'strength of
materials', the use of metal alloys for specific purposes, was
in its infancy; no light frame could, it was believed, stand up to
the vibrations and strain 'at speed'. It was here that Louis
Renault first distinguished himself, revealing a remarkable
flair for adapting existing or embryo notions and inventions,
hitherto considered impracticable, to the requirements of the
future.

After finishing his military service, he was preparing to return
to Delaunay–Belleville, when one of the most important events
in his life altered his plans. During his time in the Army, he had
saved up enough money to buy a de Dion, $\frac{3}{4}$-hp tricycle. He drove
it about, and felt that it was 'uncomfortable and inelegant', that
it should be capable of carrying two people, seated more comfortably than one person on a saddle. He therefore constructed,
purely for his own pleasure, a small two-seater car in his little
workshop at Billancourt. His intention was that it should be
much lighter than the average car, and would therefore not need
a powerful engine. Just before his twenty-first birthday, he removed the Dion-Bouton engine from the tricycle and fitted it
in the front of a small four-wheel vehicle. He had constructed all
its members, the chassis, axles, and so on, at his lathe and forge.
The relative weakness of a cycle engine in the heavier frame set
him thinking of how to economize its energy.

Transmission in the early engines was effected by a belt or
chain to a central axle, from which another chain imparted the

drive to the rear wheel, with a variable gear multiplication according to the pinion engaged.[1] Transmission was noisy and wasteful of energy, and gave the vehicle a constant vibration. Louis Renault began experimenting with a new form of transmission designed to economize energy before the motive force reached the back axle. This proved to be his first, and greatest, invention, the direct drive by cardan shaft and bevel pinions. Behind the engine were the clutch and gearbox. The latter, instead of having sliding pinions, as in the existing system, drove direct through the clutch, and had on either side a lay shaft or eccentric carrying two pinions that could be engaged faceways with their opposite numbers by operating the relative eccentric. Direct drive was for the speed most often used, top gear, and the gearbox came into operation only for subsidiary speeds. It provided three speeds, the transmission employing a universal jointed shaft to the back axle. With this, Louis Renault had invented a drive system which, with barely no alteration in principle, became standard for the next thirty years (until the arrival of synchromesh). Other features were a conical clutch, a narrower chassis in front, suspension entirely on four springs, and ball-bearings throughout.

He also built the coachwork, including the petrol tanks, in his Billancourt workshop. The gear mechanism was cut for him by the firm of Durand, rue Oberkampf, where he made an important acquaintance, a sixteen-year-old draughtsman called Serre, who was to become one of his closest associates.

The vehicle was made in two and a half months, being completed on Christmas Eve, 1898; it weighed 550 lbs. and could do 30 mph. A notable feature was its silence, unusual at the time. Another novelty was its lightness; no car had ever before been constructed largely from bicycle parts. On Christmas Day he took some friends for a short ride, and they were much impressed. However, he had designed it for his own amusement, and he now prepared to work at the firm of Delaunay–Belleville. But the vehicle proved so efficient and convenient, as good on hills as the Dion–Bouton tricycle, and carrying two passengers instead of one, that

---

[1] To appreciate the inconvenience of this, a vehicle of the period may be examined in the Conservatoire des Arts et Métiers in Paris, or in the Montagu Museum at Beaulieu.

some of his friends asked him if he would repeat it for them. Louis Renault returned to his lathe.

When the results proved equally successful, and further orders came in, he considered selling the direct-drive invention to a cycle firm that was experimenting in light cars. But something must have told him that his invention was valuable for, after bargaining with the firm, he withdrew the offer, and instead took out a patent for 'direct drive by cardan shaft and bevel pinions'. This decision was to make his name and fortune.

Firms interested in constructing light bodies had, at this time, given little thought to the stresses and strains in frames and mechanisms. Here the self-taught Renault had first revealed his sure mechanical flair. Later, in his great days as owner of the biggest automobile firm in Europe, many stories are told of how he would come unexpectedly into a workshop, pick up and examine a piece of metal or shaft, and tell by its 'feel' whether it would stand up to the stresses and strains.

His two elder brothers had always criticized his decision to become a mechanic; but they were shrewd businessmen, and quickly saw the commercial possibilities of the vehicle. Louis needed capital, so they suggested that each of the brothers should put 20,000 Frs into a joint enterprise. It was at this point, in March 1899, that the announcement already referred to about Renault Frères appeared in the *Petites Affiches*.

The new firm took a stand at the Salon de l'Automobile on 12 June 1899. Here the public could view the well-known makes, Peugeot, Dion–Bouton, Panhard, Serpollet, Mors, and so on. Here too, equally on view, were the great names of the motoring world in person: Charron, victor of the Paris–Bordeaux race on a Panhard-Levassor (1899); de Knyff, victor of the Tour de France on a Panhard-Levassor (1899); the Comte de Chasseloup–Laubat, holder of the kilometre speed record. To stimulate further interest, some of the earliest models were displayed, aged steam-engines at which the public laughed, comparing them with 'the moderns'. The first days were more of a social than a technical occasion. The general public wanted to see the well-known vehicles rather than the new inventions. Indeed, inventions now seemed unnecessary; had not Jenatzy, on an electrical vehicle, attained the giddy speed of sixty mph? But on the third day, the more mechanically minded began to take an interest in the small stand with the ¾-hp light vehicle possessing a new form of drive. The chassis was cheaper than any of the others, costing about £300. Orders were received with surprising regularity, and when the exhibition closed Renault Frères had collected sixty. Such a demand could not be satisfied in the small hut he had been using as a workshop. A bigger building with assistants and more mechanics was required.

On the Ile Séguin at the bend in the Seine opposite Billancourt stood an old boathouse belonging to the Cercle Nautique de Billancourt, which had gone bankrupt. The Cercle Nautique sold it for a small sum to the Renault family; and with the help of some workmen, Louis Renault transported it and re-erected it as a workshop in the garden. The whole operation cost little as Louis did most of the manual transportation himself; he was simultaneously carpenter, joiner, engineer and roofer. The main cost lay in the equipment and machinery. With the help of M. Richardière he bought a steam-engine with a third of the Renault Frères capital, and another third was spent on lathes and cutting machines.

He also constructed a cement furnace, and installed a number of accumulators along the wall. When he set to work on his orders with his assistant, Edouard Richet, whom he had met during his military service, almost all the Renault Frères capital had been exhausted. But by the end of 1900 they had sold two hundred vehicles, and the capacity of the works had to be doubled. Louis Renault's discovery had heralded something new in automobile construction. Henceforth, there was a slump in the production of luxury cars. Louis Renault was the first French car-manufacturer to realize the possibilities of providing light vehicles for a wider public than the rich clients who bought the Comte de Dion's vehicles.[1]

Here too, in connection with the Comte de Dion, whose two-cylinder Dion–Bouton engine he had been using, he had a stroke of luck. In 1901 the Comte's chief designer, M. Viet, drew up

---

[1] We are here speaking of Europe. In America, Oldsmobile was already very active in light-car production. But in America, the bad inter-city roads still ruined the cars. Their light cars were much cheaper than the European counterparts. 'Yours in Europe last longer,' said an American visitor. 'But I can buy three in America for the price of one here.'

plans for a four-cylinder engine. But the Comte did not believe in a multi-cylinder engine, and he turned the plans down. Viet left the firm and accepted a position with Louis Renault. It was Viet who produced the first Renault four-cylinder engine, in the vehicle which a few years later won the Paris–Vienna race and established the reputation of Renault Frères. We must now speak of these inter-city races which were of great importance in the early history of the firm.

5 | The Heroic Period

'The Germans undoubtedly were responsible for the motor-car, but it is to the French that we owe the sport of motor-racing.'

The Gordon Bennett Races.
Lord Montagu of Beaulieu

At the turn of the century, while motor vehicles in England had only just been permitted by Act of Parliament to use the Queen's highways and American cross-country roads had not yet been perfected, the French were organizing races between cities and rushing across the countryside at speeds of anything up to sixty mph. This era of the great inter-capitals races, 1895–1905, is generally referred to in France as 'the heroic period of the auto-mobile'. The term implies a certain exclusiveness; but after 1900, these races were no longer the preserve of the rich, of sport-ing aristocrats like de Dion or the Comte de Chasseloup–Laubat, whose struggles for the kilometre speed record with Jenatzy were famous. The whole of France took an interest in the races, which were widely reported in the Press. On account of the danger to the onlookers, they even became the subject of impassioned Parlia-mentary debates; and at one point, when the Kaiser, not to be outdone in 'heroism', insisted that Germany should have them, they assumed an international importance. All forms of propul-sion were permitted provided they were mechanical—steam, electricity, compressed air, gas, petrol, and so on.

Not until the aeroplane crossed the seas was the same kind of enthusiasm ever again generated in the public. Those who recall the Atlantic flights of Alcock and Brown, or later of Lindbergh, will have some idea of how the public reacted to their motor-racing heroes in the 'heroic period'. Foremost among these were the Renault brothers, who took part in races which were often suicidal, because it was the best way to attract public attention to the firm. For nearly five years they won, or distinguished them-selves in, all the big events, international and French; and it was only the death of Marcel in the last, the Paris–Madrid race (1903), which ended their participation. Originally, these races took place between French cities. But in 1900 the American Gordon Bennett presented a trophy to be raced for internationally between European cities: Paris–Berlin, Paris–Vienna, Paris–Madrid, and so on, within the framework of these more important races.

That France still led the world in the production and export of motor vehicles (her best clients were England and America) was revealed by the entries for these races. The Paris–Bordeaux race of 1895 was open to any firm, native or foreign, and it described itself as 'International' but the entries consisted entirely of French vehicles—Panhard, Mors, Dion, Darracq to mention a few. The only exceptions were Daimler and Benz, both of whom were represented by French firms. The first mention of Renault Frères in this connection is in 1899, in the Paris–Trouville race.

Marcel Renault had now left the family drapery firm to the direction of his elder brother, Fernand, and joined Louis in the more exciting motor-car business. Unlike his brother, Louis, Marcel was not an expert mechanic; but he had common sense, a quick eye for a business opening and physical courage. He realized that the best way to publicize the motor-car was by feats of spectacular driving; and for this he was prepared to risk his own neck. With his large, spade-shaped beard, he soon became one of the best known racing-drivers in France.

In the Paris–Trouville race, Marcel and Louis both did well in the voiturette or light-car category, at an average speed of twenty-one mph. In the general classification, which included the big cars, they were still well down the list; but that a light car should have *completed* the course, beating many of the heavier entries, was an indication of things to come.

Next year, in the Paris–Toulouse–Paris race, Louis Renault competed with a supercharged engine, unaccompanied by a mechanic. It was a hot day and near Fontainebleau the tube of the grease-pump broke. He was unable to mend it, so he bought a funnel and a soup-spoon from a local tinker. The grease-tube passed near the driving-seat, and he continued the race driving with one hand and feeding oil with the spoon and funnel into the tube with the other.

Another problem in those days was fuel replenishment; regular petrol stations did not exist. Having ascertained beforehand where he could refill, the racer had to ensure that he could reach the place. With the primitive tyres, too, it was common to have a dozen punctures in a race of this length. On this occasion Louis Renault had eight. At one point, to avoid a cyclist, he ran over a pile of stones, putting his front axle out of alignment. All he could do was to dismantle it and carry it to the local smithy to be straightened.

As a result of these misadventures, he did not arrive at Toulouse until after nightfall. He had no lights, and on the outskirts of the town he hit the cart of a wine-drayman, was pitch-forked into the road on his head and lost consciousness. The cartman was half-asleep and continued as if nothing had happened. Louis Renault remained prostrate in the middle of the road for nearly an hour, and if any other vehicle had come along, the last would probably have been heard of Renault Frères. When he regained consciousness and staggered into Toulouse he found his brother Marcel, who had arrived earlier on another Renault. The next morning they left at the same time on the second stage to Limoges, arriving back in Paris the following day.

The race was won by a big car, a Mors, but the Renault voiturettes (three had been entered) were first in their category; and they were the only voiturettes to complete the course. One of the advantages possessed by Louis was that, being a mechanic, he could repair axles, crankshafts, and so on during the race. Famous drivers like de Knyff knew something of machinery, but they were not in the Renault category. Again and again during these races, Louis Renault found himself dismantling the differential, changing a half-axle, stopping up an oil-leak with cotton-wool, or fitting new couplings for broken springs with insulating-tape.

Next year (1901) in the Paris–Berlin race, Louis Renault was first in the light-car class and seventh in the general classification. The latter achievement, which was widely reported in the Press, proved that the small Renault vehicles could combine speed, handiness and reliability, especially when speed had to be picked up rapidly and checked before and after corners. They also did better on hills. The year closed with a host of orders at the Salon, and the capacity of the Billancourt works had to be doubled again. Even after these victories, Louis Renault revealed his distaste for personal publicity at the Salon de l'Automobile. He preferred to walk around unnoticed in the crowd, and peer under the bonnets of his rivals' exhibits.

Although the publicity value of these races for the trade was great they were now being criticized on account of the number of accidents, which increased with the speed. If the competitors were killed this could be regarded as their own fault. But in the Paris–Berlin race a small boy was knocked down at a corner and later died in hospital (then as now spectators always selected a dangerous turning, in the hope of seeing an accident). The next day the newspapers of both countries came out forcibly against the racing. *La Petite Républicaine* said, 'With the guilty support of the public, a veritable act of human folly has been perpetrated since yesterday morning on the main roads between Paris and Berlin . . . at this moment seventy-one dangerous madmen are driving over open country at speeds of express trains. These maniacs who crouch over the wheels of their mechanical carriages at fifty mph knock down human beings, cyclists, cattle, anything in their path. . . .'

Charles Jarrott, one of the competitors, gives a slightly more favourable picture—at least from the driver's point of view. 'The enthusiasm of the crowd was terrific. We were absolutely smothered with flowers thrown by the villagers in both countries; nothing seemed too good to offer us in the way of refreshment at the various control points—champagne, food, cigars. . . .'

Nevertheless, it was with some difficulty that the next intercity race, Paris–Vienna, was organized the following year. Both Switzerland and Bavaria, through which the drivers would have to pass, were now hostile to the sport. Austria welcomed the idea, however; her motoring-clubs offered prizes, and the Government used the occasion to make propaganda about Bosnia and Herzegovina, where the racers and their friends were invited to undertake excursions afterwards. Finally, a compromise was reached. The cars would cross Switzerland without racing, as tourists; Bavaria would be avoided.

The course had been specially selected because it introduced a new element—mountainous country. The earlier races, to Bordeaux, Toulouse, Berlin, had been run over comparatively flat land; but the Arlberg Pass into western Austria is, even today, a

29

difficult ascent. The Renault brothers believed that, for this very reason, the course would reveal the further advantages of light cars. They had by now formed a team of seasoned drivers and mechanics, Serre, Richet, Vauthier, Szisz, in addition to themselves. The start took place outside Paris at the Fourche de Champigny at 4 a.m. on 28 June, and there were 210 competitors. The stages were: first day, Paris–Belfort 259½ miles; second day, across Switzerland without racing; third day, Feldkirch–Salzburg 231½ miles; fourth day, Salzburg–Vienna 212½ miles. The vehicles were divided in categories according to weight: heavy cars 1,430 lb. to 1 ton; light cars 880–1,430 lb.; voiturettes under 880 lb. The Renaults wished to keep in the light or 880–1,430 lb. category; but Louis Renault wanted to test his new four-cylinder 3.8 litre engine, and the danger was that this might make the vehicle too heavy for the light-car class. By stripping every superfluous detail he managed to keep the weight under 1,430 lb. Developing 35 hp like a heavy vehicle was something quite new in racing.

The decisive day was the third, when the vehicles were confronted by the formidable 5,912 ft Arlberg. The cars had to negotiate a gradient of 1 in 7 on a tortuous road, often without parapets, beetling over 1,000 ft precipices. Radiators were soon boiling, and some mechanics had to alight and put a shoulder to the wheel to help in the last shuddering two mph movement to the top. Some vehicles had to turn about and go up in reverse. Others had to dismantle all superfluous weight, in the form of doors, seats, spare-wheels, petrol-cans, and so on, and leave them by the road; then they had to return on foot and carry them to the summit on their backs. Louis Renault's mechanic, Szisz, had to lean forward in front of the engine as they climbed, ceaselessly filling the radiator with water as it boiled away.

The descent was even more dangerous, because motor-car brakes had never been put to such a test before. Manufacturers had been concerned primarily with making cars *go*—not with stopping them. The competitors flung themselves down the vertiginous slopes; their brakes caught fire, and in some cases gave way entirely. All they could then do was to hurl themselves into the cliff-side to avoid the precipice. One Austrian competitor was found suspended from a salient rock by his braces, while some four hundred feet below in the valley his car lay in pieces.

The Renault brothers had their share of adventures. Louis Renault negotiated the Arlberg without mishap; but not far from Innsbruck he saw a closed level-crossing too late, hit the first gate, taking it with him, and smashed into the second one. He broke a wheel and twisted his front axle; the bonnet was dented and the radiator leaked. Instead of abandoning the race, however, he and Szisz dismantled the broken parts and set off with them for the nearest village, where they found a smith who straightened the axle. But the wheel had lost six of its spokes. Louis Renault accordingly replaced the spokes with cross-bars from a chair, and set off again. Luck was certainly against them because when they arrived at Innsbruck one of the referees stopped them; while Renault was being questioned about some details in the race, the Baron de Caters, who was behind, failed to stop owing to faulty brakes and crashed into his rear, smashing Renault's back axle. This too was repaired; but these incidents had cost him the race, and he reached Vienna well down the list of arrivals.

The story of Marcel, driving the other light Renault, was very different. He drove brilliantly over the Arlberg, and he was well placed at the end of the difficult third day. In front of him, when the competitors set off on the last day, were only six cars in the general classification, all heavy vehicles. The route was by no means flat, at least in terms of the great northern European plain where the earlier races had been held; but he hardly expected to make much impression on them. Until now, he had been content with heading his category, ensuring that he finished the course. That day something made him decide to take risks and push his vehicle to its limit. It seemed in excellent condition in spite of the Arlberg ascent, and after what he had seen there he suspected that the engines of the heavy cars in front must be feeling the strain.

In those days vehicles travelled in a cloud of dust, so that just before and during the passing of another car the chauffeur was driving almost blind. It was here that most of the accidents occurred. The driver's aim was to get ahead and throw the dust back in the eyes of his competitor if he could. Marcel put his foot down, and to his surprise during the morning passed five of the leaders. In his own words (related by M. Souvestre), this is how, not far from Vienna, he came upon the leader.

I had done many kilometres, negotiating helter-skelter turnings and kerb-sides at full speed, relying only on my faith in our machine, when I suddenly saw the hoped-for cloud of dust ahead. It grew larger. I waited some time behind it, then decided to go into it. I confess that for several minutes I seemed to be in a thick fog with only the hazy outlines of my adversary to guide me. Then I made out the silhouette of the driver, and both my mechanic and I let out a whoop of joy like wild animals as we drew alongside. A minute later we were in front. . . .[1]

Marcel's average speed for Paris–Vienna was thirty-nine mph which, considering the crossing of the Arlberg, was a remarkable feat. At times he must have been travelling at nearly seventy mph. What impressed the public in Vienna most, however, was that he had travelled faster than the Arlberg Express, then regarded as the fastest train in Europe. The race was a complete Renault triumph. Apart from Marcel being first in the general classification and therefore, theoretically, driver of the best car in the race, Renault cars took second and third places in the voiturette class. All finished the race under their own power; whereas many more celebrated drivers, such as the Baron de Forest, arrived at the finish in the Prater drawn by two horses from the Municipal Sanitary department.

In 1903 the Paris–Madrid race was organized with greater difficulty than the Paris–Vienna. The Automobile Club de France suspected that some of the vehicles, the Mors, Panhard and Dietrich of the 80–100 hp class, were now capable of speeds of over 90 mph. Manufacturers naturally tried to keep their speeds secret; and in one year since the Paris–Vienna race the law of geometrical progression in speed was making itself felt. The cars went much faster; but the roads on which they travelled were exactly the same. Although the Route Nationale 10 to Bordeaux was the fastest in France, it still belonged to the age of carriages, and its curves were designed to deal with nothing faster than a galloping horse. Its hump-backed bridges dated from the seventeenth century, and if its gutters did not harm springless carriages, they were dangerous to car wheels.

The Spanish authorities had readily agreed to the race and arranged elaborate festivities in Madrid for those who completed

---

[1] *L'Histoire de l'automobile.*

it. It was the French Government, under pressure from socialists in Parliament as well as from certain public bodies and the Press, which objected. Until the last moment it appeared that the French part of the course would have to be omitted, and that the race would cover only the Irun–Madrid distance from the Spanish frontier. But then, after many representations from the Automobile Club de France, authorization was obtained from Paris. The race was to last three days. The first day was Paris–Bordeaux; the second, Bordeaux–Vitoria; the third, Vitoria–Madrid. There were 314 entries.

The start took place at Versailles on Sunday 24 May at 4 a.m.; but such was the enthusiasm of the crowd that they had begun assembling there the day before. This was the famous *Belle Epoque* and, after an evening at the music-hall, the public liked waiting up during the hot summer night for the dawn start. The cafés were invaded by people in cycling costume. Supplementary trains to Versailles set out from the stations of Saint Lazare, Montparnasse and the Invalides. In the avenue of the Bois de Boulogne and on the roads to Ville-d'Avray motor-cars in hundreds and cyclists in thousands were on their way to the start, mixed up with charabancs, horse-drawn *fiacres* and *calèches*. The lights of the cars and the lamps of the bicycles gave the whole thing the appearance of a torch-light tattoo. It was afterwards calculated that more than a hundred thousand people spent the night in the open-air near Versailles, sleeping on benches or wherever they could lay their heads. Small fortunes were made by itinerant food and wine vendors. The local inns were full, the price of hard-boiled eggs increased hourly, and all the bread in Versailles was sold out before the start; by 4 a.m. there was not a slice of ham or cup of coffee left.

Amid a blaze of fire caused by the multi-coloured flames of several hundred exhausts, in an aroma of petrol, acetylene and alcohol, over six hundred strange creatures clad in black leather and goggles strode about beside their vehicles, nervously puffing at their last cigarettes and sipping from small glasses of cognac. The competitor who caused the most interest was the only female in the race, the famous Amazonian Madame du Gast, who was driving a Benz, wearing her celebrated corseted leather armour. A hideous cacophony, the back-firing of dozens of differently designed engines, the varied horns and cries of the spectators split the air and woke up the local inhabitants. One hundred and sixty policemen on foot and sixty mounted police tried vainly to keep some order in the unruly, half-intoxicated mob. Marcel Renault must have had a presentiment of what was in store, because he said some days before that he would have preferred not to compete this time. But the future of Renault Frères was at stake, and they required services of their best driver.

At 4 a.m., the hour of the start, Louis Renault and de Knyff objected that it was still too dark. The starter granted a quarter of an hour's respite, while the three hundred competitors, who were to leave at one-minute intervals, waited in the half-light surrounded by the staccato din of their exhausts. In front was a solid phalanx of spectators, all hoping for thrills. The general hubbub of the crowd was at last cut by the level voice of the time-keeper counting off the remaining seconds to each driver, who leant forward to catch his words in the half-light of the dawn, soon to brighten into the full blaze of a summer day.

Along the highway to Bordeaux about a million people lined the route; and in spite of earlier fears, the Government had taken inadequate security precautions to control them. The police and soldiers especially enrolled proved powerless to control the seething mob of careless, ignorant spectators, shrieking encouragement and refusing to leave the highway until the racing-cars were actually bearing down upon them. If a vehicle crashed, everyone flocked to see it and took photographs, and people crossed to and fro over the road like so many chickens. Here and there cattle strayed on the road, and children played in the gutter. One of the drivers who got to Bordeaux, Jarrott, wrote afterwards to a friend[1], 'I remember long avenues of trees top-heavy with foliage, gaunt in the nakedness of their trunks; a long, never-ending white ribbon stretching away to the horizon; and myself holding a bullet directed to that spot on the sky-line where earth and heaven met; fleeting glimpses of villages and dense masses of people—mad people, insane, reckless people holding themselves in front of the bullet, to be ploughed and cut and maimed to extinction . . .'

Louis and Marcel Renault were driving their light, 1,430 lb.

---

[1] Quoted by Souvestre.

four-cylinder vehicles[1]; and even on the tremendously fast roads
of the great French plain it was soon clear that they were more
than holding their own. Louis was said to have touched 90 mph
in the early hours. He had been luckier in the draw than Marcel,
who left well down the list. In those days before tar-macadam the
luck of the draw could make a great difference on account of the
dust. In spite of this, Marcel passed many cars during the morning; and it was not until after Poitiers, near Couhè-Verac, that
disaster came. He attempted to pass a cloud of dust containing
the famous Léon Théry. Théry, who had good visibility, saw the
turning ahead, but Marcel did not. Within a second, he was no
longer on the road but crossing a ditch at 80 mph. His front wheel
caught in it, and the car did three somersaults before landing a
hundred feet away on its back with the bonnet facing Paris.
Underneath, unfortunately not thrown out in the somersault, lay
Marcel Renault. Maurice Farman, who was following, stopped to
give first aid. Marcel seemed to have no open wounds, but his
ribs were broken. He was taken to hospital where he did not
regain consciousness, and he died the following morning. A reason
later adduced for this accident was that Louis Renault had fitted
what would be, by our standards today, an excessively high top
gear for the dead straight French roads. The Renault light racer,
while capable of 90 mph once it was 'wound up', took a long time
to regain speed when it was checked; hence the driver's reluc-
tance to suffer a check while passing another car, even on a
bend.

Meanwhile Louis Renault, well ahead and unaware of what had
happened, had taken the lead after Chartres, and he was the first
to arrive at Bordeaux. His time was 5 hrs 33 mins, at an average
speed of 61 mph. He was first in the light category and second in
the general classification (Gabriel on his heavy Mors was first—
5 hrs 13 mins, at an average speed of over 65 mph). Louis Renault therefore appeared well placed for the second, more
mountainous, day in Spain; and it seemed likely that he might
repeat his brother's Paris–Vienna triumph.

But this was not to be. Marcel Renault's accident was only one
of many. Throughout the afternoon as survivors struggled to the

---

[1] The innovation in Renault's light racers was mechanically operated
side-valves in an L-head of a 6.3 litre engine.

finish of the first stage at Bordeaux, they brought tales of
crashes, deaths and injuries to drivers, mechanics and spectators.
At the Bonneval level-crossing, a vehicle driven by the Englishman Porter overturned, caught fire and his mechanic was burnt
alive. Near Angoulême, Tourand, attempting to avoid a little
girl in the road, drove into the crowd and killed three spectators,
two of whom were soldiers who had tried to keep the girl back.
At Libourne, Loraine Barrow, an Englishman driving a Mercedes,
ran over a dog and hit a tree. His mechanic was killed instantly
and he himself died fifteen days later. Stead overturned and broke
both arms. Madame du Gast, who was immediately behind,
stopped and managed to extricate him before the petrol, which
was flowing all over him, caught fire. She kept the crowd away
until an ambulance arrived—thereby losing all chance in the race
herself. The Mercedes driven by Terry, an American, caught fire
and his mechanic was roasted alive. Of those who finished the
course and arrived at Bordeaux intact some had to be lifted out
of their vehicles and carried on stretchers.

During the night of 24/25 May the French Government telephoned the Prefect of Bordeaux and ordered the race to be
stopped. The next day the most stringent measures were taken
to prevent competitors slipping over the frontier and continuing
to Madrid. They were not even allowed to drive back to their
respective homes, nor go to the railway station under their own
power. Guarded by gendarmes, drawn by horses, their vehicles
were escorted to the railway platforms and thence transported by
train. These measures hardly affected Louis Renault, however,
because, when he learned of his brother's fatal accident, he
immediately withdrew all his cars from the race.

That was the end of the 'heroic period'. Public opinion,
voiced in the newspapers, supported the Government's action,
and one of the punning headlines was *'Du cent et du sang'*. Although two years later, races were permitted on closed circuits,
at La Sarthe or Le Mans, in which Renaults still distinguished
themselves, never again was the founder of the firm to take the
wheel of a racing-car. After the race, the Automobile Club of
Great Britain announced that its members would take no more
part in inter-city Continental races. Henry Ford in America
also condemned them.

·   ·   ·   ·   ·

It may well be asked what the murderous races of the heroic period achieved for the automobile. Their supporters maintained that this insistence on speed brought a number of technical improvements, even safety measures, for the benefit of the public. The adversaries of speed contended, on the other hand, that the races tended to convert what was essentially a utility vehicle into nothing more than an instrument of sport, and a dangerous one at that. The public, they said, were attracted, as in the Roman arenas of old, by watching other human beings risk their lives.

There is something to be said for both points of view. Undeniably, after one of these great inter-city races, with all its attendant publicity, orders flowed in to the motor-car manufacturers. Renault's Paris–Toulouse success, only a year after the foundation of the firm, had brought in five hundred orders; and the sales profits far exceeded any prize money. The manufacturers clearly found it profitable to invest heavily, as the large number of entries by Panhard, Mors, Dietrich for the Paris–Madrid race proved—at a cost of hundreds of thousands of francs.

That the races were of value to France as a nation is also undeniable, for national prestige as well as business. In 1905 when the inter-city races were abandoned the world automobile industry seemed exclusively French. In competition with thirty internationally well-known French firms entering for the races the Germans could muster only Mercedes and Benz, the English only Napier, and the Americans Pope Toledo. All other non-French makes put up a mediocre performance. In the Paris–Berlin, for instance, the first seventeen in the general classification had been French.

Nevertheless, the French public now began to realize that the motor-car was essentially a utility vehicle; the purely speed races, henceforth on closed circuits, never again drew the same crowds or excited the same enthusiasm. Moreover, the vehicle manufacturers soon found the races too expensive; the publicity value for a given financial outlay began to diminish. Louis Renault, for obvious family reasons, took the same attitude, and entered cars for races only occasionally, in order to reaffirm periodically that his firm could still construct a first-class racing car. He now became concerned with something more important

—creating the greatest car firm in France, founded upon sound, low-priced, utility vehicles.

A comparison here with America is instructive. As early as 1899 the Americans had attempted to run races on the French inter-city lines, but, for the reasons already stated about the condition of their cross-country roads, they could not be as successful as the French who then had the best roads in the world. Although the *Chicago Times Herald* sponsored a Chicago–Milwaukee race, the American public showed surprisingly little interest in the new sport. Only six competitors arrived for the start, three finished, and the race was won by a Duryea at an average speed of five mph. Undeterred, Frank Duryea decided to take an improved version to compete in Europe a few years later. The French had been so long at the head of affairs that they scoffed at the idea that anyone could even compete with them. To their surprise, Duryea defeated some of their best racers, including the big Panhard. Although races had been going on for well over a decade in France, in three years the Americans had produced a vehicle apparently superior to anything French.

6 | Early Methods

Louis Renault had intended after his military service to continue as a mechanic in the Delaunay–Belleville factory. He was still happiest in his overalls, at the bench or lathe. The notion of becoming an 'industrialist' had never entered his head. Without social ambition, he hoped one day to own a small house in the country with a workshop attached, where he could spend his weekends. This wish was to be fulfilled, but not in quite the way he intended. His rise from overalls to millions was to be so rapid that he hardly had time to indulge this partiality.

In the early days, he still regarded the firm as essentially a family affair, to be run on the same lines as the button business— he, Louis Renault, in charge of the technical side, while his brothers, who had commercial experience, would deal with the accountancy, which interested him less. One of the axioms of his hey-day (related by Maurice Druon) was, 'Men and things—they alone are real. It is pointless to reign over an empire of account-books.' But this was not to be. Marcel had been killed in the Paris–Madrid race; and now Fernand, who had never been strong, was coming to the office much less. Whether he liked it or not, Louis soon found himself 'reigning over the account-books'. Like most men of his class, he was much concerned with conserving the family patrimony. To hand on to his descendants more than his forebears had handed to him was a question of honour. Likewise, to spend more than he earned was not only unwise, it was almost sinful. In any case, he always regarded money not as an end but as a means, for continually improving the factory. With the increasing demand for voiturettes it seemed to be growing independently of its creator. No sooner had a new improvement been introduced than another was necessary, and the factory was always having to be expanded.

In those days most French businesses were 'family structured', in a way not generally associated with modern capitalist economics. They were united economically in the sense that business and household purse were one—just as national treasuries were once inseparable from the king's personal fortune. In such firms it was customary for each of the partners, and often for any of the relations who wished, to leave their disposable funds with the business, as we today would deposit money in a bank. An interest of 5–6 per cent was paid on these current accounts, while the depositors went to the cashier whenever they needed money, even if it was only petty cash for daily expenses. Each had his own account-book, duly kept up with all the other records by the overworked accountant. This system was particularly popular in France, where the word '*Maison*' for a business has retained its commercial connotation almost down to today. The primary concern was to live well within one's means, avoiding the use of credit, to amortize expenses rapidly and build up reserves, and to finance expenses out of these reserves, without recourse to our system of stock and bond issues.

It was also the golden age of individual production, when the work of one man differed in a dozen details from that of his mate at the neighbouring bench, and machine work still had something of craftsmanship about it. Every car Louis Renault constructed in 1904 differed from its predecessor, with some improvement or innovation he had devised. It was the type of work he loved, for he was a craftsman himself. Wearing the same overalls as his employees, working beside them, he treated them in an egalitarian, even familiar, manner. He would go round the factory, stop at a lathe and ask the workman how many crank-shafts, cylinder-heads, or back axles he was producing a day. On being told, 'Eight, M. Renault,' he would take off his coat and, in his shirt-sleeves, show the man that by employing different techniques, twelve could be produced. If the man produced twelve on the morrow, his pay would be doubled. Devoid of any undue sense of personal importance, he asked no more from his assistants than from himself, hard work and the highest standards.

His French biographer, M. J. Dauvergne,[1] tells how one evening after the factory had closed, Louis Renault had gone up to the design office, where he liked to brood alone over the day's plans and achievements. With pencil, compass and T-square, he would sit at a stool before the drawing-board, sketching in alterations or suggestions until late in the night. Often, he

---

[1] *Vie de Louis Renault.* Paris, Table Ronde, 1954.

forgot his dinner. On this occasion, he found one of his best engineers at the drawing-board doing the same thing, having also forgotten his dinner. Looking over his shoulder, Louis Renault asked the man what he was working on. When the engineer explained, he said, 'Give it up, my man, it's no good! Instead of wasting your time on that sort of thing, look at this new half-shaft I've just designed.'

But the man said defiantly, 'I'm sorry, M. Renault, your ideas don't interest me at the moment. I'm working on my own.'

'Your ideas are rubbish!' Irritably, Louis Renault picked up the man's papers, threw them on the floor and placed his own designs on the desk. Whereupon the engineer only pushed these aside, picked up his own, and put them back on the desk.

'If you do that,' said Louis Renault, pointing to a large bottle of ink, 'I'll break that over your head.'

'All right,' said the engineer coolly, 'in that case, I'll chuck this ink-well in your face.'

The two men stared at one another like warriors. Then suddenly in the empty office late at night, they started roaring with laughter at their puerile behaviour. . . . They were still discussing plans at midnight.

At once mechanic, draughtsman, fitter, driller and turner himself, Louis Renault was respected rather than loved by his workmen. 'Hard, he is,' they said. 'A real slave-driver. But you can't refuse him anything. Because he works harder than you do.' A loosely fitting nut or bolt would catch his eye immediately. What was disconcerting, too, was that he was always turning up in parts of the factory where he was least expected. At no time in his career, according to his family, did he sleep more than five hours a night, and he would often wake up and write down ideas. If he left the factory at 11 p.m. he would be telephoning one of his subordinates at the man's house by 6 a.m. the next morning with ideas for the coming day; and by then he would have bathed, breakfasted and probably taken a walk, for he was a great believer in exercise.

On one occasion he was going through the machine-shop with Serre, one of his closest collaborators who had joined the firm in 1903, in animated discussion about some new project. They happened to stop near a workman at a particularly noisy milling-machine; Renault went on expatiating, but having to raise his voice so that he was almost shouting. The man had seen the *patron* approaching, but he continued quite unperturbed at his work. Renault stared at him, but the workman only smiled as if to say, 'Work comes first in this place, doesn't it?' At last, unable to control himself any longer, Renault leant over angrily and shrieked in his ear, 'You noisy bastard! Can't you stop for a moment? So we can hear ourselves speak!' The workman responded with hoots of laughter, nodded his head amiably—and went on working. The two directors had to move on. Incidents such as these between Renault and his staff were common in the early days.

At this time, too, there was no hierarchical order in the firm. None of Renault's collaborators had a clearly defined job or a specific responsibility. There was no 'Head of the Project Department', no 'Assistant Assembly Manager', no 'Sales Manager', let alone a 'Vice President'. His collaborators were expected to carry on their tasks without the help of titles, being known simply by their surnames, 'M. Serre,' 'M. Hugé,' and so on. The patron himself was 'M. Renault'. If anyone had addressed him as 'M. le Directeur', he would have looked over his shoulder to see if someone else was being referred to. The older workmen were known to him likewise by their Christian names, 'Pierre', 'André', 'Jacques'.

This worked well enough in the early days, but with the more dynamic methods arriving from America, it had to be revised. Complications were caused, for instance, in relations with other firms, who wanted to know exactly what position the M. Serre, M. Hugé or M. Lefebvre who were negotiating on behalf of Renault Frères occupied in the firm. Was he a man of importance, a departmental head, or a nobody?

The divisions of work and individual responsibility seem to have been deliberately ill-defined, so that Renault's subordinates never knew exactly what they were expected to do—except that it should be more than they were doing. It was an ingenious way of keeping them on the alert. Such a state of uncertainty existed in the firm that even the oldest, most trusted hands used to go to work each morning not knowing if they would still be there in the evening. 'Working for him,' said one of them, 'was like being with a volcano. Now, a volcano's a fine sight! Brilliant flames and all that. But if you get too close, you may get a boulder on your head.'

Louis Renault's physical capabilities helped to inspire respect in his staff; with his wiry, muscular frame he could undertake the most strenuous tasks of any of his workmen. There were two things about his appearance, we are told, which impressed at first glance. The hands, with the coarse, overworked fingers of the man at the lathe and machine-bench, dexterous and immensely powerful; the great spatulate fingers moved incessantly in conversation, conveying his thoughts better than his halting words. When he was impatient or annoyed, they came down with a thump on the table. And then the eyes, scintillating with an extraordinary violence, liveliness and native intelligence. One had only to look into them to be mesmerized. His nephew by marriage, François Lehideux, who later occupied a high administrative post in the firm, says that when Renault was talking about something that excited him, he would shut his eyes, 'giving an impression of extraordinary conviction'.

Salaries in Renault Frères were on a similar haphazard basis. Louis Renault would mention casually that André or Pierre in the die-stamping department should be paid a certain sum from tomorrow—or from next week—or from the month after. Then Serre would come up and say, 'Look M. Renault, old André does a good job. He deserves a bit more.' 'Very well,' said Renault; and the word about old André would somehow percolate down to the accounts department.

For his closest collaborators Renault chose fellow mechanics without academic education, preferably men of a somewhat saturnine temper to whom he could say, 'Now don't look so gloomy! It's not as bad as all that. See, I have the answer.' These men soon learned how to handle him. If one of them had a solution to a given problem by which he set great store, he knew it would be fatal to suggest it. Renault would immediately point out its disadvantages, and turn it down. He had to approach him with two, three or even four alternative suggestions, and announce them in reverse order of importance, keeping the true solution till last. Renault would immediately dilate on the defects of the first suggestion; nor was the second, he would say, much better; nor the third. But the fourth—ah, did the man not see that this was obviously the answer!

His was the true mechanic's flair, for he had no academic training in the calculations for strength of materials. His knowledge came from increasing experience, a natural mechanical bent and a gift of observation. He did not believe in formulae and figures, sharing something here with his fellow motor-car constructor Bugatti, who joked about pages covered with figures, and the integral calculus which he compared with the notes of written music. This lack of scientific training enabled Renault to take extraordinary technical liberties, because nothing seemed impossible to him. He thereby often achieved solutions which no ordinary engineer would have dared attempt; the instinct of such a man is to use his flair for assessing everything visually and tactilely. He had wooden models of new parts made, and enlarged or diminished according to the impression they offered to his senses. His flair lay in making quick decisions which generally proved to be right. He would walk round the workshops and pick up an axle on which a man was working, balance it in his hand and say, 'It'll break *here*.' Almost always, when put to the test, the material fractured in the place indicated.

M. Pommier[1], who was later in charge of his estate at Herqueville, tells how Louis Renault once wanted a large barn renovated. This involved installing a steel girder to support the weight of the second floor, which was being added. Pommier suggested that they should consult the design department of Billancourt.

'No,' said Louis Renault, 'you're a qualified engineer. I employed you for that. You work it out yourself. In any case, the size for a 30-metre run with that weight above would be about 25 cm by 45 cm width, I should say.'

Pommier was surprised that he should state the dimensions of something which required a complicated equation with bending-moments, the coefficient of the metal, weight, and so on. But when he had calculated the dimensions, they tallied almost exactly with those suggested by Renault.

As this shows, Renault was essentially an empiricist. 'You think the quickest way from A to B is a straight line,' he used to say. 'Well, often it isn't. Mostly it's a zig-zag.' He believed in a course adapted to the situation as it developed. 'The great thing is not to worry how to get somewhere,' he used to say, 'but to leave, to set off. You can't see every difficulty ahead on a journey

---

[1] M. Pommier now holds a high administrative position in the present nationalized Renault firm.

from Paris to Toulouse, can you? So don't try to deal with them before they arise.'

It seems surprising that his closest collaborators could say of this man who built up one of the greatest industrial empires of Europe, 'He had the attitude of a grocer towards his till—not of a financier.' By this they meant that he refused to have anything to do with the credit facilities which modern commerce puts at the disposal of businessmen, and of which the expanding Billancourt factory could have availed itself. Louis Renault distrusted these devices; he was concerned only with the 'cash in the till'. The rules of business which he was to follow all his life may be summarized briefly.

(1) Never take a sou out of the business which has given it birth. Instead, use the sou to nourish its mother.

(2) A business must be self-sufficient, requiring no outside help. To accept loans or credit is to run the risk of interference by others, to mortgage the future, and be hampered in developing one's own ideas.

(3) Never owe anything to anyone. Creditors must be paid on the 30th of each month, by cash or cheque.

He once said that the manufacturer who retains all his wealth in cash and machines 'has the possibility of using time better'. Firms with these resources are better placed to act or, more important, *not* to act; for they can afford to await the favourable moment. In general, he believed, delays in action operate for the benefit of the powerful firm and against the weak one. It is this capacity 'to hold out to the last quarter of an hour', he said, which often makes the difference between success and failure.

Such was his distrust of borrowing that he even refused the well tried *traites en circulation*, a credit device which had been used by French businessmen since the days of Napoleon and the foundation of the Banque de France. This enabled a purchaser without ready cash to give the seller his *traite*, or signed certificate, guaranteeing that he would settle on such and such a date. The *traite* had to be endorsed by the Banque de France, who would have investigated the record and reputation of the signatory. Any French bank would then advance the money to the creditor. Renault would have none of it. To go to a banker was to him as disagreeable as going to a doctor, and he despised 'money made from money'.

Much later, in the 1931 economic crisis, he was forced by Caillaux of the Senate, to adopt the *traite* or the small firms he did business with would have gone bankrupt. Like everyone else after the financial collapse of that year, even Renault had not the spare cash himself at the time; and as his clients dared not lose the custom of so important a firm, he knew he could let them wait. In face of his stubbornness, Cailloux passed a bill through Parliament forcing him to conform and use the *traites en circulation*. It is still known as *la loi Renault*.

The corollary to this is that if, after some crisis such as the flooding of the Seine a few years later, the till is empty, the firm is bankrupt. This flooding of the Seine was the worst natural disaster Paris had known since 1685. But such were the resources of Louis Renault that even after this catastrophe, which caused all other firms affected to live for months on credit, he was still able to maintain his principles. The esplanade of the Invalides was a sea of mud, and people were going up and down the Rue de Lille in canoes. The Boulevard Hausmann was a canal, and the Eiffel Tower stood in a lake; the bears in the Jardin des Plantes were swimming. There were six and a half feet of water in the Renault plant at Billancourt, and his firm lost six hundred chassis and thousands of pounds' worth of machinery. But Renault and his 'grocer's till' faced the disaster without having to borrow a sou from the banks.

It is indicative of the patriarchal manner in which firms were then run that Louis Renault's own income and that of the firm were so closely identified as to be indistinguishable; capital in the factory at Billancourt and that in the private property he later bought at Herqueville, were both regarded as Renault Frères investments. He probably had no idea what his personal income was. In the words of André Maurois, 'This type of man has little interest in money as such. He reinvests every year all his profits in his business, machines and new construction.' Such was his innate respect for property that he was careful to make the firm his own tenant. Renault Frères paid rent for the factory to the landlord, Louis Renault, who could officially evict them at any moment he liked. Here was the deep peasant conviction that everything man-made could be destroyed or overturned; but nothing short of an earthquake could shake the land.

That he must have made money by 1907 is proved by his private life. He had a mistress, a boat on the Seine, and several motor-cars. This may sound fashionable, but it was not; he had nothing to do with Parisian society. M. Saint Loup, in his well-documented study of Louis Renault,[1] said he was so timid in the presence of women that he could think of nothing to say other than to ask them to sleep with him.

His mistress was an actress called Jeanne Hatto, with whom he lived in blissful domesticity for over ten years. She was a plump and appetizing blonde who came from the Jura, where her parents, appreciating her musical talents, had given her singing lessons. She sang at the Opéra Comique; and, in spite of Renault's repeated proposals of marriage, she refused because it would 'ruin her career'. When he first saw her, he immediately bombarded her with bouquets and took a house outside Paris at Viller-le-Bacle for weekends with her. She appears to have been a simple, good-hearted woman, who developed a real affection for him and did much to smarten him up, making him clean his finger-nails and buy presentable suits. She also made him take spelling and diction lessons. Under her influence he developed a taste for gypsy music, of which he made a collection on gramophone records (played on a machine he had made himself). She also introduced him to painters, such as Fix-Masseau who became a close and lifelong friend. His first interest in painting, in Greuze, Boucher and Carpeaux, was encouraged by her. She even tried to interest him in the theatre. But its artificial atmosphere, both on the stage and in the foyer during the interval 'meeting friends', was distasteful to him and he only went on sufferance. 'We are not put into the world only to amuse ourselves,' he once said of the stage.

The fact that she lived with him so long but refused to marry, may have been partly due to his Boetian manners and dislike of social life. It was about this time, when his name was becoming known, that his reputation for boorishness was established. A member of the Guignarand family recalls that he and various friends belonged to a Parisian tennis club of which Louis Renault

---

[1] *Renault*. Bodley Head, 1957.

was also a member. 'The rudest man I've ever known,' he said. 'If Renault had booked the court for a certain hour and we, who were playing in the hour before, required a few more minutes to finish the set, he refused to allow a second of overtime. He hustled us off the court according to the letter of the law.'

At the weekends, he would bring down a few of his cronies, Serre or Hugé—associates in the firm who had, like him, only one interest in life, machines—and they would continue what was virtually the conversation they had had in the factory at work. When Jeanne Hatto brought her friends, who were generally theatrical people, Louis Renault found himself at a disadvantage and said little. Literary people filled him with apprehension. 'We read to escape thinking,' he said once. Reading a page or two of a book set him thinking on his own; he continued to read the printed word in front of him with unseeing eyes, because his mind was reading what he was thinking. All his life he seldom went to clubs or met the leaders of other professions, and his mind was never broadened by the clash of liberal discussion. To the end, he demanded the right to think and judge for himself, as an independent human being. His mind was critical and non-conformist, and he refused to recognize any intellectual authority, whether a priest, professor or 'expert'. He was not religious and would smile if he heard excessively devout people talking; on the other hand, he respected religion and disapproved of jokes in bad taste about it.

In family matters he does not appear to have been any less intractable than with his workmen. The first indication of this was revealed in his treatment of a young woman called Suzanne Davenay. After Marcel's death in the Paris–Madrid race, Louis Renault learned to his astonishment that Marcel had left his share of the firm to this lady, a mistress of long standing. In the five-year existence of the firm, the 20,000 Frs originally contributed by each brother had swollen to about a million. Louis Renault was determined that Suzanne Davenay should know nothing of this; he had no intention of compromising the future of the firm by allowing a third of its assets to fall into the hands of an inexperienced woman. He accordingly paid her a visit and explained that since Marcel's death he had become very concerned about her future. He said he would like to make some provision for her, so that she should have no financial worries—for Marcel's

Louis Renault working on his direct drive system in 1898 *(Régie Renault)*

A 'tool shed' at the bottom of the family garden. Louis Renault's first workshop *(Régie Renault)*

1899 at Billancourt. A family photograph of the first Renaults. *From left to right:* the 1897 de Dion quadricycle with Marcel Renault in the passenger seat; the ¾-hp 1898 voiturette prototype, driven by Louis Renault; and the first 1¾-hp model, introduced in 1899, driven by Paul Hugé
(Régie Renault)

1898—Voiturette with 1¾-hp de Dion engine *(Renault Ltd)*

1899—Voiturette with 3½-hp engine and saloon coachwork *(Renault Ltd)*

The entrance to the Renault Frères offices and workshops at Billancourt in 1905 *(Régie Renault)*

Aerial view of the Régie Nationale des Usines Renault, 1969 *(Régie Renault)*

Paris–Vienna 1902. Marcel Renault doing the lap of honour round the Prater *(Régie Renault)*

Paris–Bordeaux 1903. Marcel Renault and his mechanic Vauthier *(Régie Renault)*

Szisz and Marteau in the French Grand Prix car in 1907. In this 100-hp car they won the first ever French Grand Prix in 1906 (Renault Ltd)

1909—Two-seater saloon with
spider seat, 8-hp
(*Renault Ltd*)

1924—Skiff body on 40-hp
'Sport' chassis, 6-cylinder
(*Renault Ltd*)

1925—40-hp, 9-litre 'Sport'
chassis with open four-seater
body used by Garfield and
Plessier at Montlhery to break
seventeen records, including
500 miles at nearly 104 mph
(*Renault Ltd*)

1926—40-hp, 6-cylinder
chassis with special
leather-panelled saloon body
driven by Garfield, Plessier
and Guillon to obtain the 24
hours World Record at
average of 107.9 mph. First
car to exceed 100 mph for 24
hours (*Renault Ltd*)

The chassis assembly shop in 1907 (*Régie Renault*)

sake. She replied that Marcel had provided for her in his will; she understood she had inherited a part of the factory.

For a man known throughout his life for his taciturnity, Louis Renault must have revealed a remarkable forensic skill on this occasion. A motor-car factory, he explained to her, was worth very little. Its short hey-day was over; the motor-car would prove a transitory vehicle in the history of locomotion. He emphasized the financial risks for anyone taking part in the direction of a motor-car firm. Bad times were coming, and the 20,000 Frs invested by each brother would soon be reduced. He recommended her to remove her money while there was still time. He himself knew something about mechanics, and was prepared to take the risk, but she—what did she know of universal joints and differentials? He would guarantee her, legally, the rent of a flat in a fashionable part of Paris, and sufficient income to take regular holidays on the Riviera, if she would hand over her share of the firm. Moreover, the factory would present her with one of its latest models, and maintain the car for her. All this he offered if she would accompany him to a notary and sign an agreement transferring her shares to him on these conditions.

Twenty-four hours later these blandishments had had their effect, and Louis Renault came into possession of the second third of Renault Frères, a share which was to represent at its height many billions of francs. It is only fair to add that he continued during Mademoiselle Davenay's long life paying the income he had promised, increasing it regularly to allow for devaluation. The other third still remained in the hands of his brother Fernand.

A factor often not taken sufficiently into account in a successful career is the physical one. Renault was a man of the rudest health, who attached great importance to exercise, swimming, walking, playing tennis (later skiing), less for the sport itself than to keep fit. He had a mania about fitness and was never ill. Only his stomach sometimes gave him trouble and he devoured a quantity of aspirin. He congratulated himself on this, saying, 'If I had had a good stomach, I should have eaten and drunk too much. So I can count myself lucky.' He was a frugal eater, and generally drank only water, no spirits, and very occasionally a small glass of Bordeaux or champagne. He did not smoke. He adored fruit of all kinds, particularly grapes, of which he would grab fistfuls from the table between courses. Every morning he did exercises for twenty minutes before breakfast.

He was gradually becoming aware of the meaning of the financial power he wielded, and began to reveal the tenacious qualities of the class from which he had sprung. The French bourgeois has always been noted for his instinctive distrust of officialdom, and a tendency to rely on his own resources. Even today, in the Welfare Society, the French bourgeois and peasant regard the State as a powerful, impersonal and on the whole hostile organization. Generally speaking, the small Frenchman has the feeling that he lives from hand to mouth, has nothing to fall back upon and is ever at the mercy of accident, bureaucratic heartlessness or sudden dismissal. This perhaps explains why Louis Renault gradually began to collect all the financial threads into his own hands, why in the future he always distrusted governments as well as collaborators.

That he now knew how to use his growing financial power was revealed about this time when he sued certain firms for infringing his patents. In 1907 he learned that some of these firms, foreign as well as French, were illegally using his direct-drive system. M. Richardière, who was now working in the firm, knew something about the legal niceties of patents and he pointed out to Renault that the firms infringing his patents were extremely powerful; to sue them would be expensive and they could, through influence and bribery, subvert the course of justice. Renault asked him if he knew a man called Cottereau. When Richardière confessed he did not know anyone of that name, Renault explained that Cottereau was a small Dijon businessman who had recently set up a local motor-car firm. He was illegally using the Renault direct-drive. They would sue him. Richardière objected that they would not get much out of him, and he would probably go bankrupt if they sued.

'Exactly!' said Louis Renault. 'Sue him.'

This was his way of attacking the big firms. He too realized that a frontal attack on them would be dangerous; but by first winning the case against a small man a precedent would be established. And this is what happened. He sued Cottereau, who was condemned on first instance, and again on appeal. The wretched man then went bankrupt. The inviolability of the

Renault patent was thus established in the courts, and Louis Renault now turned to the big firms who had infringed it. When the Cottereau proceedings were brought to their notice, they were glad to settle out of court. Soon, firms in France, England, Germany and the U.S.A. were all paying Renault for the use of his direct-drive. A further indication of his character is revealed in the way he patented the direct-drive. It was not registered in the name of 'Renault Frères' but of 'Louis Renault, Inventor'. And so it remained, in the case of almost all his inventions, for the next twenty years. The Motor Car Company of England had infringed his name when they imported two Renault voiturettes and put them in a race masquerading under the name of M.C.C. Triumph cars. Renault brought a successful action to restrain them. In his *Lost Causes of Motoring*[1], Lord Montagu describes how a Scot called Alex Govan designed and built a light car, the Argyll. Unlike others, who took a horsed carriage and fitted it with a motor, Govan based his ideas closely on those of Louis Renault—although Renault, it would seem, did not take him sufficiently seriously to start proceedings for infringement.

In the early days these patents were one of his main sources of income, and he hired an expert, M. Saives, whom he put in charge of them. The two men became highly skilled, not only in protecting Louis Renault's patents, but also in purloining those of others. They discovered that all patents could be adapted and used if the actual letter of the law was not infringed. If Louis Renault wanted to use someone else's patent. Saives would analyse it technically, and they would try to devise a solution. If, however, they concluded there was none and that infringement could not be avoided, they considered the personality of the inventor; they found out about his character, domestic habits, political affiliations, above all about his bank balance. If he was a poor man, they used his patent without more ado; it was unlikely that he could afford the money required to win a case. On the other hand, if he was powerful, Louis Renault would negotiate with him, bargaining for the lowest price.

Renault found he was forced to adopt these questionable procedures on account of the equally astute methods used by other firms. The American firm of Budd, for instance, was one of the

---

[1] Cassell, 1960.

first to construct coachwork in welded steel, for which it took out some ten thousand patents, each of which was not, properly speaking, for a new invention. The aim was primarily to embarrass potential competitors by forcing them to take circuitous and complicated courses such as Renault and Saives adopted and thereby retarding their progress, or, by forcing them to pay the royalties.

The *Motor-Car Journal* of 20 May 1911 has the following entry: 'Dashboard Radiator Patents. M. Louis Renault, head of the well-known firm in Paris, has brought an action against a French motor-car manufacturer for infringement of his dashboard radiator arrangement in connection with the thermo-syphon system of water circulation. The courts have decided in favour of M. Renault, but an appeal against the judgment has been lodged. Much interest is being shown in the matter, as it is indicated that similar actions are to be brought by M. Renault against other motor-car companies which are using the dashboard radiator in several of their models.'

Renault was now inventing prolifically, and every month a fat letter went off to the Government patent office. One was a device for increasing the gas pressure in the cylinders; another for ignition without a magneto, working with a single distributor. He invented a method for advancing and retarding ignition; a separable multi-piece sparking-plug, and a new form of clutch-cone engagement. His hydraulic shock-absorbers are the ancestors of those we use today. He patented a starter worked by compressed air from the engine. He had several different patents for carburettors, air intakes and petrol mixtures. The chassis arrangements of almost all the cheaper French makes were standardized on the original Renault layout. This consisted of a front-mounted engine, clutch, gearbox, cardan shaft and universal joints, with a differential and a bevel-gear rear axle. Before this standardization, the chassis and drive arrangements varied greatly. Thousands of francs were now earned from them annually. By 1906 engine design had crystallized on Renault lines with a type which was to remain fundamentally the same until after the First World War. Engines were of L-head type, the cylinders cast in pairs; ignition was by high-tension magneto, the cooling by thermo-syphon. The sliding-type gearbox had a quadrant change.

As the orders poured in, the factory at Billancourt, which had originally covered two acres, had to be expanded. Here, too, Renault was unscrupulous. He would offer a modest sum for a shop or private house in the neighbourhood which he wanted to buy for his expansion. If after every blandishment the owner refused to sell, he would be subjected to what was, virtually, a siege. Renault vehicles would be driven up and down outside his house all day and night, revving up, 'testing'. When Renault Frères started making aeroplane engines in 1907, these even more ear-splitting machines proved invaluable for evicting owners; after two weeks of agony they were only too pleased to sell. By 1908, Renault Frères stretched around the big bend of the Seine opposite the Ile Séguin, and he had his eyes on the island too. The factory was now divided into three groups of buildings. The largest occupied the space bounded by the Rues Point-du-Jour, du Cours and Saint-Cloud. The second group was between the Avenue du Cours, the Rue du Point-du-Jour and the Rues Théodore and Gabrielle. The third group stretched down to the river.

Renault used much the same methods for enlarging the private property he now acquired at Herqueville some eighty miles north of Paris, in a bend of the Seine near Rouen. He built a country house here, bought three farms with their surrounding lands, planted trees (one of his hobbies) and developed the property. Those familiar with the French peasant and his feeling for land can imagine the interminable discussions, arguments and tergiversations which took place before the deals were settled. There were often 'triangular operations' with a third party, a piece of land which was not wanted being acquired for use later as a counter in the bargaining for the coveted patch. He would approach a peasant whose hectares marched with his and offer him a small price for what he wanted. When the owner refused to sell, Renault flattered him about how well the man ran his property, at the same time pointing out its disadvantages—the poor site, infertile soil, the absence of trees, proper irrigation—which would not worry *him* as he had other plans for its employment. He quoted figures about potato and milk production, revealing a surprising knowledge of agriculture. The land, he suggested, would be more suitable for a factory. If the man still refused to sell, a different kind of assault was launched. He, Louis Renault, had been commissioned by the Government to build a factory near by; the smoke and chemical exhausts would blow far and wide, ruining the land and vegetation. If the peasant still remained obdurate he would tell him he knew the Government would shortly expropriate the land for a derisory sum. Generally after a few days or weeks of this treatment, the man's resolution faltered and he sold.

When Renault became the owner of Herqueville, he bought up so much land around that he was soon owner of the parish. In a most arbitrary way he had the mayor's office pulled down because he had other plans for that area, and he offered to build in return a much better one elsewhere, installing the mayor at his own expense. This skill in acquiring land was revealed again when he bought his town property in what is now the Avenue Foch. The Parc Monceau was the fashionable area then, and the Porte Dauphine area regarded as very inferior. He constructed a building with several floors so that he could let a part of it and thus bring in an income. In those days of grand houses flats were considered very risky affairs; but he made an excellent investment.

Louis Renault was no more generous in his treatment of his own family. His brother Fernand's health had deteriorated rapidly, and he had now given up coming to the factory entirely. Both brothers realized he had not long to live. Louis Renault had not forgotten the episode with Marcel's mistress, Suzanne Davenay, and he did not intend that the third part of the firm should be left to another woman, Fernand's wife, and her children. He therefore took advantage of an accommodating suggestion Fernand had made some months before. His brother had admitted that he was doing almost nothing in the firm; it was only fair that Louis should have the main share of the profits. Louis thanked him for this and offered what he described as 'something in return'. He would buy his brother out entirely, at a handsome price. He said that he foresaw certain risks, particularly for minors (Fernand had a son and two daughters) in running an expanding concern. He offered a low price, suggesting that with this Fernand could take a house on the Riviera at Cannes which would benefit his health. Fernand refused. Whereupon Louis Renault raised his offer, pointing out that he was running the firm entirely on his own; it was only fair that he should own a business for which he was now alone responsible.

Once again, faced with this combination of blandishment and threat, the victim finally succumbed. Fernand did not even discuss it with his wife. To her he said later, 'Louis was *hard, hard* with me. You know what he is like when he wants something. But then, has he not the right to be hard? It was he who really built Billancourt.'

Louis Renault had bought the balance of the firm just in time. Three months later in 1908 he followed Fernand's coffin to the Passy cemetery.[1] He was now in undivided control of a rapidly expanding automobile firm that was soon to be the first in France.

---

[1] After the death of Fernand Renault Frères ceased to exist. La Société Louis Renault took its place.

7 | The Rising Industrialist

The decade before the First World War was a relatively quiet one in the otherwise turbulent life of Louis Renault. Yet for this very reason it was one of the most important in the growth of his factory, and of French industry in general—when a man might toil to some purpose and enjoy the fruits of his labours. For after the war, the Exchequer took a large part of the profits. But Renault had made his fortune by 1914. Later he told one of his closest collaborators, M. Hubert,[1] that the annual profit of the firm by 1913 was three million francs (and they were then gold francs). How in a decade did his firm become one of the biggest in France? The answer depends partly on the man, partly on the favourable economic conditions in that legendary *Belle Epoque*.

Charles Fohlen, in his studies of French industrialists at the turn of the century, said there were two distinct types. Firstly, there were men like Pouyer-Quartier, found particularly, he claimed, in Normandy, who regarded their factories a means, not an end—simply a way of becoming rich and rising in the social scale. Secondly, there were men concerned only with the success of their undertaking, to which they sacrificed everything, identifying themselves with it, using their profits only to invest further in an ever-expanding concern. To this second category belonged Louis Renault.

Although in 1904 France led the world in automobile construction, with more than thirty thousand vehicles produced annually, Renault's contribution was still not a hundredth part. There was still no convention in motor-car design because no tradition had yet been established. In the words of Ian Nickols and Kent Karslake in *Motoring Entente*[2], 'each maker had his "system" or basic design, some of which were eminently practical while others were hopelessly unsound, and the ordinary would-be motorist, or even his technical advisers, had little or no means

---

[1] M. Hubert later became his general factotum—what we would call today 'his P.A.'

[2] Cassell, 1956.

of distinguishing the sheep from the goats'. There was only one real way of proving the reliability of a new method or model—by racing. All constructors were therefore racers. The fearful victory of Paris–Bordeaux in that year, with its attendant notoriety, following the even greater victory of Paris–Vienna, had swelled the Renault order-books.

Yet in 1904 Louis Renault was still not thinking of commercial competition on European lines with such firms as, for example, Mercedes-Benz, although the Germans were already becoming France's principal rivals. He was concerned solely with perfecting his inventions. Not until his concentration on the lighter, cheaper models began to pay dividends did he foresee that competition within the next ten years would increase enormously, and that he must take steps to face it. Here, he may be contrasted with another French manufacturer, then bearer of a greater name, Panhard, who continued to manufacture exclusively luxury vehicles. Men like Panhard argued that they did not need to bother their heads about small, inexpensive models when they had a continuous demand for luxury vehicles, chassis at £1,000. Nor did they want to make motoring a popular pleasure. But Renault thought he saw a new market, at first perhaps only for enthusiasts like himself or younger sons with limited pocket-money, but later for a completely different class of society and pocket-book. When the municipality of Paris approached Panhard about providing the city with a fleet of taxis, he refused; the price would be too low. This was an opportunity for Renault, who immediately offered to produce them at the required price. It was now that he entered commercially on the national, and later international, scene. By 1906 he had supplied Paris with fifteen hundred 2-cylinder taxis for the figure of 3,800 Frs each (about £450); he had already realized that to reduce the price would serve him well in the future. The next year his taxis were on the streets of London. The *Motor-Car Journal* (23 August 1908) has this entry: 'Although only a few months ago the "Red Renault" taxis practically had the field to themselves in London, this state of affairs is being rapidly altered and several British cars are making their appearance . . . among them the Siddeley.'

Now that the vast economic possibilities of the automobile were everywhere acknowledged, and it was clear that there would soon be world markets, Louis Renault laid plans for greatly increased production. Yet he still mistrusted any mechanical part that was not made by hand at the bench; he objected to anything savouring of mass-production, because he could not be sure of its quality. The firm was now producing four models: a 2-cylinder 10 hp, the popular private car (the chassis for about £200 may be contrasted with Ford's T model at £180 complete); the 2-cylinder 8 hp taxis equipped with Renault's special device for automatically registering the cost of a journey, depending on distance and speed, soon to be known as the taximeter; a 4-cylinder 14 hp, developed from the vehicle which had won the Paris–Vienna race; a 4-cylinder 35 hp based on the Paris–Bordeaux winner, capable of 72 mph. After 1906 he produced his one expensive model, the 4-cylinder 20 hp with elaborate coachwork (still not supplied by himself) and a fourth forward gear, which was soon employed by the Government departments. When Edward VII visited Paris for the *Entente Cordiale* he was driven through the city in this vehicle.

Renault also foresaw the importance of buses for public transport. By the end of 1906 his first bus, a 20 hp weighing five tons, with twenty-one seats, moving at 8 mph, was in service in Paris. The city streets were soon being cleared, too, by his sanitary vehicles. In the same year, he began selling two, three- and five-ton delivery vans for use all over France. Even before this, when he had seen the milkman delivering his horse-drawn wares in the early morning at his house in Billancourt, he had realized the possibility of a milk-van, and began constructing it.

His first great advance therefore was made with commercial rather than private vehicles; and in this domain he was always to lead France. His figures for the first ten years tell the tale better than words.

1899......	71 vehicles (voiturettes)	
1900......	179	,,
1901......	347	,,
1902......	509	,,
1903......	780 chassis of different types	
1904...... 1,100	,,　　,,　　,,　　,,	
1905...... 1,200	,,　　,,　　,,　　,,	
1906...... 1,600	,,　　,,　　,,　　,,	
1907...... 3,000	,,　　,,　　,,　　,,	
1908...... 4,500	,,　　,,　　,,　　,,	

Aware now of increasing European competition, he realized that the lead he had established in these fields could not last unless he was continually improving his models. If in 1904 the price of the cheapest Renault was £270 (chassis), by 1905 twenty-two European makers were producing cars at competitive prices. The public now wanted inexpensive cars, and it required all Louis's dexterity and industry to compete with men who knew how to use his inventions or produce their own; or to face the sales methods of a man like Darracq who had entered the motor-car industry not as an engineer, but as a businessman. Darracq knew more about advertising and marketing than Renault, whose sales methods were still relatively primitive. Instead of trying to persuade the public, Renault's attitude was roughly, 'I know more about motor-cars than the public; they must take my word for it'. Even when he began to appreciate the importance of publicity, he did not know how to frame an advertisement. Until quite late in his career his publicity managers had difficulty in dissuading him from filling the space in the newspaper with a mass of technological details about his vehicles—his new brake-bindings, his new transmission, universal joints, and so on—which meant little or nothing to the general public. A suggestion that one advertisement should depict a beautiful young girl in the driving-seat, accompanied by the slogan 'Buy Renault! It keeps you young' filled him with suspicion. But once he had become convinced of the importance of advertisement, he left it to the department concerned and did not interfere. Later, he allowed large sums to be spent on publicity, but as one of his publicity managers, M. Girard, said, 'I could do what I liked with the money. But if I so much as put a nail in the wall of my office or altered the partitions I was for trouble. That would have been altering the factory. No one was allowed to do that except M. Renault.'

Competition with foreign firms increased greatly after 1905. French manufacturers realized that they could not stay indefinitely in the lead, even after the Paris–Vienna race; in any case Mercedes–Benz, whose cars were equipped with honeycombed radiators, mechanically operated inlet valves, gate gear-changes and pressed-steel frames, was now ahead in design. So important, for example, had Mercedes become that Baudry de Saulnier, the acknowledged French authority on motor-cars, was writing, 'We

would like to remind our readers that the house of Mercedes has inaugurated a complete revolution in the automobile industry. It has become more or less compelled to take over the control valve, the honeycomb radiator with fan, the magneto make-and-break ignition, the pressed-steel chassis, and the ball-bearing. . . . Today, many manufacturers find it the best recommendation for their product to refer to its similarity with the Mercedes type. These are facts which may not flatter our national vanity, but which are hard truths, and whose existence cannot be denied . . .'[1]
Attempts were therefore made to incorporate some of the German features either by buying, or without infringing, the patents. In the German competition Renault played a curious role. As early as 1904 Mercedes-Benz were ahead in Germany, partly due to Karl Benz having imported a shaft-driven Renault from Paris. In face of the opposition of the other directors Benz had built a shaft-driven Benz prototype. It was badly done (for the Renault patent could not be infringed directly), but he realized that it was the drive of the future. He then engaged a team of French technicians and fitters.

By 1907 international competition was intense; the 6-cylinder engine had, for instance, been envisaged, but it was still generally regarded as too heavy and impractical. Renault was not in favour of it; he wanted the working parts of an engine to be as few as possible, and he contended that a 6-cylinder engine would lower the thermal efficiency. But he watched the other countries closely, particularly England where S. F. Edge, working for Napier, was developing the 6-cylinder engine. It proved to be much quieter than a 4-cylinder, and was a great success. Against general opinion, the English had produced something which put them temporarily ahead of every other manufacturer. Competitors hastily followed suit. By 1908 there were eight French, ten American, three Belgian and one German firm all making 6-cylinder cars. Renault's was a 9.5 litre 50–60 with pressure lubrication.

The importance of Renault's light car was not lost on the other manufacturers, in particular Panhard, who tried to compensate for his original error and invaded the voiturette class, as did Darracq. They had some success, but Renault with his patents

---

[1] From Baudry de Saulnier's *Histoire de la locomotion terrestre.*

and earlier start always managed to keep a little ahead in this field. Darracq spent thousands of pounds on producing something inferior to Renault's original model.

In 1908 there was cut-throat international competition over valves. There was great prejudice against overhead valves, particularly in England: they were regarded as noisy and suitable only for racing cars. Charles Y. Knight had arrived from America with his sleeve-valve, and it seemed that not only overhead valves but poppet valves in general were on the way out. Such leading makers as Daimler in Germany, Panhard in France, Minerva in Belgium, staked everything on the new Knight valve. Some manufacturers began feverishly experimenting with other alternatives to the poppet valve. Napier in England patented a double-sleeve valve, Wolseley a piston valve, Darracq a rotary valve invented by the brilliant C. E. Henriod, and Louis Renault a single-sleeve combined with an overhead poppet valve. In 1909 *The Autocar* reported: 'The general impression at the *salon* is that the French under Renault are feeling their way in the matter of engines with new valve systems.' Darracq made the mistake of basing everything on C. E. Henriod's rotary valve, which did not come up to expectations, and, in 1911, having almost bankrupted his company, Henriod had to resign.

The price of raw materials from abroad also affected vehicle design. In 1907 a boom in America so raised commodity prices, particularly of copper, that costs rose faster than sales. The boom collapsed in October of that year with a panic on the New York Stock Exchange. The collapse spread to Europe where several big banking firms failed. Although copper was down to its old price by the end of the year the slump hit the motor-car industry, particularly in France, where some smaller firms went out of business. The French car industry was saved largely by the light car which was less affected than the expensive models. This was a lesson Renault never forgot; luxury vehicles might make large profits but their sales depended on too many extraneous factors. At the same time he also learnt to his cost how the political situation can affect sales. When the Kaiser suddenly sent a gun-boat to Agadir Europe seemed on the verge of war for several months, and no one bought, or thought about, a motor-car. From this developed his suspicion of politicians, whom he regarded to his dying day as meddlesome and dishonest.

61

On the alert for every form of mechanical advance, Louis Renault built his first aeroplane engine in 1907, an 8-cylinder in B form, air-cooled, 60 hp. In that year some Clermont-Ferrand businessmen offered 100,000 Frs for the first aviator to land on the Puy de Dôme, a 5,200 ft mountain with an acre or so of flat land at the summit. For three years no one had dared attempt this; but on 7 March 1911, after a flight in the mist and by compass, a Maurice Farman powered by a Renault engine succeeded. A few months later the same machine showed its tactical manœuvrability in a military competition at Rheims before the High Command. (When war broke out France had five squadrons equipped with the Renault engine, its horse-power having been increased to 80.) In the same year it gained the world record for height.

By 1909 Renault cars were being sold in several parts of the world, including America and Russia. The 'Renault Selling Branch' in New York aimed at selling in that year '1,200 to 1,500 vehicles if we can show the undoubted quality of our wares'. They entered a 4-cylinder 35 hp in the 'New York 24 Hours Race', in which it distinguished itself at an important moment in American motor-car history; for it was in this year that Ford produced his T model, of which more were to be sold than any other car in history. In 1908 King Edward VII bought a 3-litre, 4-cylinder 14/20. By 1910 Renault had an agency in Madrid, and in 1912 a stand at the Tokyo fair.

A comment on his progress at this point is provided by the interest shown in his firm by Basil Zacharoff, the armaments financier. He used to drive down to Billancourt in his Rolls-Royce to be shown around the works, for which he expressed the greatest admiration. He invited Renault to England, and took him to Birmingham to see the Vickers works. This firm became interested in the Renault aeroplane engine, and Zacharoff even suggested investing money in Renault. Louis Renault naturally refused, and later, when war came in 1914, he said (according to M. François Lehideux), 'Now I can see certain individuals wanted war. They were planning it.'

In these last years before the war, he became aware for the first time of labour troubles, if only on a limited scale. The Trade Unions were now a power to be reckoned with. When Renault had begun his career, there were only two classes of any real importance in France, the aristocracy and the bourgeoisie. The power of the proletariat had been destroyed once and for all, it had been thought, by Thiers in 1872. The First International, whose aim had been to prevent workers from working, to ferment strikes and attack property, had been banned in 1876. When its offspring, the Second International, was formed in 1889 the bourgeoisie was prepared to bring in certain social measures under the heading of 'paternalism' in order to canalize its powers. Philanthropy and social measures were to be granted by the rulers, and anything increasing the power of the workers was to be resisted. With considerable difficulty the Trade Unions extracted a maximum working day for women of eleven hours and for adolescents under sixteen of ten hours. When the eight-hour day was mentioned one of the big industrialists, the iron-master Schneider, described it as 'economic Boulangisme'. 'For me,' he said, 'a healthy worker can easily do ten hours and he should be allowed to do more if he wants.'[1]

All this was repugnant to Renault with his preference for individual worker-owner relationships, and his dislike of the masses. The first strikes took place at Billancourt in 1912 when he tried to introduce piecework. In those days, the administrative staff did not belong to the Unions and so they went on working in their offices. They were pelted through the window by the workers with a hail of nuts and bolts—to the consternation of Louis Renault who could hardly believe his eyes. In the Place Nationale at Billancourt the workers were charged and dispersed, not without some bloody heads. Renault's attitude of familiarity with individual workers changed almost overnight; he felt, he said later, as if friends to whom he had been kind had forsaken him.

His attitude to the masses is reflected in a well-known book published at that time, and to which he attached great importance, *Crowds: A Study of the Popular Mind* by G. le Bon[2] about

---

[1] The situation was much the same in America; although the American workers had demanded an eight-hour day somewhat earlier. An *Association for the eight-hour day* had been formed in Chicago, as early as 1886. However, it was doomed to die a quick death. On 1 May 1886, sixty thousand workmen went on strike. The police were called upon to break it up, and in the process four men were killed and twelve wounded.

[2] Benn, 1947.

the credulity, insensitivity and hysteria of the mob. He read and re-read it, underlining in pencil the passages he considered important, and showing them to his friends. His personal copy is still extant. A few of the underlined passages reveal his attitude:

Possessing little reasoning power of its own, the mob is always violent. Thanks to its recent organization (Trade Unions) its power has much increased. Its dogmas, which we shall soon see treated as universal truths, possess all the power of the old traditional dogmas—that is, a tyrannical and sovereign force protecting it from every kind of opposition. The Divine Right of Kings will soon be replaced by The Divine Right of the Masses . . .

or:

By the sole fact of being part of an organized mass or group, a man descends several degrees in the scale of civilization. Isolated, on his own, he may be a cultivated person; part of a mass, he becomes a creature of instinct, an automaton no longer directed by his own will, a barbarian . . .

or:

Among special characteristics of the mass we may note—irritability, impulsivity, incapacity to reason, absence of judgement and critical faculty, inflamed sensibility and other qualities normally associated with beings belonging to inferior forms of evolution, such as the savage, the child, the woman . . .

or:

If the mob is feminine, the most feminine of all is the Latin mob. He who relies on it may rise very high, very quickly; but he is climbing a Tarpeian rock from whose height he will soon be pitched headlong . . .

Lastly perhaps a comment on his own role:

The masses display a docile respect for strength and authority; they are little impressed by kindness, which they regard only as a form of feebleness. Their sympathies have never been with good-natured masters, but with tyrants who have crushed them . . . [This is sheer Machiavelli.]

We now know that these strikes were only the forerunners of the far graver ones that occurred after the war. But when they were over Renault tried to forget them. He was now thirty-six and one of the leading French manufacturers. His Billancourt factory employed 5,200 workers; it covered 41,860 sq. yards and had over 3,000 machine plants. In that year, 1912, he sold over 10,000 vehicles (the total French output being 50,000). He was developing a network of agencies and his vehicles were selling in Japan, New Zealand, India, Russia. In America, he could still compete with Henry Ford whose factories were producing the T model. He had noticed, however—more perhaps than his fellow industrialists had—that European sales to America had declined in the last three years. The Americans had cut the prices of their cars to a very low figure, and they talked of a new system of production in mass known as Taylorism. He decided in 1912 to visit America and examine these methods.

8 | **Henry Ford**

'Every time I reduce the price of my car by a dollar, I get a thousand new buyers.'

Henry Ford

In the first decade of the century motor-car production had presented the Americans with a special problem. Machines could be produced in Europe only if there was a large force of skilled and relatively cheap labour. But the American manufacturers had less skilled labour, and costs were higher because they paid their workmen better. They therefore had to dispense with European methods and devise their own. Out of necessity, they evolved a method of mass or cheap production, which was later to replace every other form the world over. Louis Renault was one of the first Frenchmen to sense that America would soon be 'the land of the automobile'. By the First World War, the U.S.A. was turning out as many vehicles a year as all the other car manufacturers put together.

What we call 'mass production', and regard as a modern phenomenon, is by no means new. As early as 1804, the British naval arsenal at Deptford constructed a large biscuit factory to supply Nelson's fleet, using what would now be called an 'assembly-line' of skilled workers and kneading-machines; with clockwork accuracy it turned out seventy ship's biscuits a minute. Later, just before the American Civil War, the meat-packers of Cincinnati devised an assembly-line, or rather a de-assembly-line, for slaughtering, dressing and packing pigs. In 1896, the French sporting journalist, Paul Meyan, suggested bicycle mass-production; this was depicted in *L'Illustration*, but, as so often happens in France, it was never put into practice. It was not until the first decade of the twentieth century that the American Frederick Winslow Taylor expressed these ideas clearly in his *The Principles of Scientific Management*[1].

---

[1] Harper, 1947. Originally published in 1911.

His method consisted essentially of making a precise and detailed study of the work, and of the workman's movements and gestures to accomplish it, in order to eliminate those that were unnecessary. For example, if a workman has to fetch spares and pieces from a pile not at hand he is wasting time and effort. The pile must be so arranged that his effort is minimized. Both the position of the machine and the method of distribution of the pieces are therefore important. The time which should be taken for any given task was calculated from the performance of an average qualified worker (if he were exceptional, like a Stakanovite, it could not be attained by the others). Any worker who did not come up to this 'norm' was described in workshop parlance as having 'lost' so many minutes.

Taylor advocated simplicity of design, speed and continuity of production, large sales and falling prices, with small unit profits. Whereas before Taylor a stationary group of men would assemble an automobile, the work was now divided into a number of separate operations, each of which was carried out by the same man, thereby increasing the speed of production. Taylor called this 'phasing'—every man doing a job at which he became so skilled that it was uneconomical to transfer him elsewhere. For instance, in order to assemble an axle fifteen different operations were involved. One man joined the parts together and inserted a bolt; another put a nut on the bolt; another tightened the nut and inserted coffer-pins; another used the hand-lever arbor press to impose the inside ball-bearing cone upon the stub-axle; another brought the steering-arm and stub-axle into co-ordination. Meanwhile the stub-axle connecting-rod had undergone eleven different operations, drilling, filing, reaming, milling and counter-sinking in eight different machines before it reached the assembly-lines.

In the past, a skilled worker dipped into a small pile of parts to assemble a fly-wheel magneto, producing on an average thirty-five to forty magnetos in a nine-hour day, taking twenty minutes for each. Taylor divided magneto assembly into twenty-nine operations, each performed by a different man, spaced with his fellows along a moving belt. Assembly time was immediately cut to thirteen minutes ten seconds. Later, when the height of the moving trolley had been raised to a more convenient level, the average time was reduced to seven minutes.

Further study of movements and speed brought it down to five minutes.

It was thanks to this system, which came to be known as 'Taylorism', that an American industrialist erected the greatest industrial empire of all time. Charlie Chaplin may have satirized Henry Ford's methods mercilessly in *Modern Times*; but he was really mocking something which made life more, not less, human for his workers.

Henry Ford's father had wanted his son to be a farmer. All his life Henry Ford was to show interest in agriculture; but he felt at the time that there were newer, more lucrative fields for his energy in the domain of mechanical invention. Even here, he thought at first in terms of agriculture, of a steam traction-engine to take the place of the horse in the laborious business of ploughing. He immediately saw that the chief problem was that of weight (the ability to divorce the concept of weight from that of strength was one of the most remarkable achievements of this extraordinary man). 'Weight may be desirable in a steam-roller,' he wrote later, after making his first vehicles, 'but nowhere else. Strength has nothing to do with it. . . . The most beautiful things in the world are those from which all excess weight has been eliminated. . . . The automobile that I designed was lighter than any other then made. And it would have been lighter if I had known how to make it so.'[1] Here we see how both Ford and Renault, working independently, had come to the same conclusion.

Until 1903 Ford bought the individual parts of his cars from a number of specialist companies. He found this wasteful, and was soon running his own foundries to make cylinders and other castings. He set up his own drop-forge plant for steel axles and crankshafts; his own pressed-steel plants for stamping and drawing other parts. By 1906, he had close links with the sources of raw material, steel, leather, rubber. Annually, he bought the hides of 400,000 cattle for the upholstery, 2,000,000 sq ft of glass for windscreens, and 90,000 tons of pig-iron. He made 1,300,000 electric-lamps and 100,000 tyres on his own. Exactly the right amounts of nickel, brass, leather, rubber, lubricants, and so on, had to be brought to the factory in hundreds of ever-flowing

---

[1] Quoted in *Ford: The Times, the Man, the Company.*

rivulets, and delivered at the moment when they were required. To market it all, he had—by the time Renault visited him in 1912—a sales organization with an army of seven thousand dealers supplied by forty-seven branch agencies and a corps of foreign representatives. 'We are as well represented in Bangkok, Siam, as in any American city of similar size,' he proudly told Renault.

Ford and Renault had much in common.[1] Ford regarded the Frenchman as one of the few foreign manufacturers up to his own level; and the two of them spent hours together at the drawing-boards examining blueprints and models, communicating largely by signs. So well did these master-mechanics understand one another, each talking simultaneously in his own language, that they even dispensed with the services of an interpreter. Apart from their passion for machines of all kinds, they had other things in common. Both had built up their firms from nothing. Both, in their respective countries, had been the first manufacturers to abandon the principle of constructing few vehicles and selling them expensively. On the contrary, both believed that a low-priced vehicle would open up large markets and bring general prosperity and a higher standard of living. Renault paid his workers well; Ford said, 'The ambition of the employer should be to pay better salaries than in any other industry.' Ford distrusted Wall Street and protective tariffs as much as Renault disliked borrowing from the French bankers. Conclusions about wealth which Renault had reached independently were expressed later by Ford in his autobiography[2]: 'The cult of which money is sometimes the object, as an equivalent of real riches, completely destroys its value . . . exaggerated profits are bad for business.' Both men worked in offices which were unpretentious and bare. When Henry Ford welcomed Renault, the Frenchman was ushered in through a small door in the corner of the second floor of the factory. Inside, the only furniture was a 4 ft × 6 ft flat-topped

---

[1] René Gimpel, in his *Diary of an Art Dealer* (Farrar, Straus, 1966), says of Henry Ford: 'He has a great admiration for France, and especially for French engineers. "It's with French skill," he said, "that the Ford was constructed." He recounted how one day he and his engineers found themselves faced with an old French car which didn't look solid; but when they dismantled it they were astonished at its resistance as they tried vainly to smash the steel to learn its composition.'

[2] *My Life and Work*. Doubleday, 1922–26.

desk, and there were no armchairs. A mammoth blackboard, a drafting-table, a turning-lathe and several hundred patterns, castings and samples completed the interior of a workshop rather than an office.

The private lives of the two men were similar. Both preferred simple pleasures, with a dislike of purely social activities, receptions, banquets, parties of all kinds. Neither had worn tails or morning-dress more than half a dozen times in his life. Ford read little and only in the company of those who possessed his confidence would he let his ideas flow, for he disliked small talk and had no fund of anecdote or reminiscence. Like Renault, he regarded reading as a kind of dope habit. 'A man who cannot think is not an educated man,' he said, 'no matter how many college degrees he has.' One was a Catholic and the other a Nonconformist, but both took the same very unspiritual view of the Deity—'The Lord is working, and will clear the land of those who do not go ahead.' Both regarded work as the salvation of the world. 'I do not believe a man can ever leave his business,' said Ford. 'He ought to think of it by day, and dream of it by night.' And he announced a principle which Renault never forgot: 'The man who can produce a car which is entirely sufficient mechanically, and whose price is within the reach of millions who cannot afford one now, will not only grow rich but be considered a public benefactor.' And he added a maxim which to most businessmen at the time seemed madness: 'Increase the salaries of the workers and lower the price of the product.'

Where the two men differed was in national temperament. The French industrialist had a hard, professional manner and a dislike of publicity; whereas Ford's democratic folksiness endeared him to the public as much as to his own staff. The American was so well publicized that he appeared at once as business genius, economist, social scientist and great philanthropist all rolled into one. To the French public Renault was just another faceless businessman.

When Renault was taken round the great Highlands plant at Detroit, he seemed to be back in the old familiar Devil's Kitchen he had created at Billancourt, only much bigger. There were the same grimy workers in their caps and overalls; leather-gauntleted mechanics bending over dangerous-looking levers; jets of steam spurting on one side; men with oxygen torches brazing metal on the other; belts swirling, presses clanging, chutes rumbling, trains of low-wheeled trucks filled with metal parts shunting across the floor; great cranes swinging piles of iron chassis and stacks of castings; in one corner, men machining camshafts; further on, men working on universal joints and connecting-rods, the rear axle, the front axle, the transmission. . . .

Louis Renault returned to France convinced that at least a part of this system must be introduced at Billancourt.

In spite of all the two men had in common, Ford's view of mass production differed in certain respects from Renault's—as these words of the American manufacturer attest, 'I regard the problem fundamentally not as mechanical or technical, but one of social organization.' He was more of an idealist than Renault, and contended that from the new methods a new civilization was being born, which would solve the contradictions of capitalism, and bring peace and prosperity to the planet. Unlike Renault, he believed in 'paternalism', introducing all sorts of extra-mural amenities for his workers, instituting sports-fields, lecture-rooms, concert-halls, social security plans, hospital and hygienic installations. As Ford saw it, 'Taylorism' took into account the psychological factor in the workman. Social welfare did not therefore, as Renault contended it should, 'leave the worker in the evening at the factory gates'; it followed him into his home. In the Ford plant it was discovered, for instance, that an experienced drop-hammer operator was suddenly unable to meet even moderate production standards. His health was sound, and he had no grievance against the company. But careful inquiry showed that his wife was ill; as a result his children were being neglected and his debts mounting. As soon as the 'psychological branch' of the company removed these worries, his production returned to normal. Renault knew that the French workman would not stand this kind of interference in his private life, however much it improved it.

Nevertheless, there were certain elements of the Ford and Taylor systems which he knew he must introduce if his factory was to survive. If he and other French manufacturers did not modernize, the expanding world motor-car market would fall into American hands. Here he collided with the innate conservatism of the

French workman. When he attempted, on his return to Billancourt in 1912, to modernize, they objected strongly to the automatic tasks which the scientific method demanded; the notion of remaining a simple but essential cog in the production machine irked them. As an individualist, the French worker likes to think he understands something about all departments. His mind is occupied less with one aspect of the work than with its broad conception. This attitude dates no doubt from the crafts of the Middle Ages, when great pride was taken in individual skill acquired over many years. As early as the first decade of the century, the politician, Paul Boncour, had spoken of 'the hostility of the French worker towards modernization. Not to have adopted measures of standardization is here considered a virtue'. In many factories before the First World War some French workmen, the fitters for example, used their own tools, which they brought to work and departed with in the evening. Mass production clearly had no place in the conception of such men. It was not until the war, when there was a shortage of labour, as well as a demand for huge quantities of standardized material, that mass production made any headway in France.

All this may seem anomalous in the country which invented the metric system, and gave birth to the author of the *Discours de la Méthode*, who must certainly have been an ancestor of Taylor. It was not that the French were incapable of understanding mass production; rather they failed in its application. It is not enough to appreciate a method intellectually; plans must be laid and carried out, requiring endurance, conscientiousness, an ability to resist the boredom of the assembly-line, above all that quality which the French lack more than any other race—team-spirit. The American worker, on the other hand, has always been ready to accept anything new and inventive. His is a new land, whose development has been made possible by his ability to develop and adapt himself to new and better methods in all domains. Traditional methods which, even today, hamper the conservative European workman are easily rejected in America.

The workers in the Renault factories were in the habit of taking off three minutes an hour to roll and smoke a cigarette. This contravened every principle of Taylorism. 'You have ten thousand workers,' Taylor would have said to Renault, 'who work ten hours a day. This cigarette habit represents thirty minutes per man per day. That is five thousand man-hours a day! All lost! You should tell them to smoke their cigarettes at home, or going to and coming from work.' By attempting to curb this habit, Renault nearly caused a revolution at Billancourt. The workers formed a delegation under one of their most ferocious representatives, a huge, bearded proletarian popularly known as 'Ali Baba', who organized demonstrations and coined the punning soubriquet for Renault *le saigneur de Billancourt*. He pointed out that Taylorism enabled non-qualified men, simple 'machine-minders' who were regarded as inferior beings, to draw equal salaries with the craftsmen. To such men it seemed that a new element had been introduced to destroy the old master-employee relationship. Man had been master of his machine; now the machine was to be master of the man. 'We are not machines—we are men!' cried 'Ali Baba!' 'The modernization of the factories can only increase the riches of the rich and the poverty of the poor.'

In *Crowds: A Study of the Popular Mind*, the book by le Bon already referred to, which was Renault's bedside reading, is a passage he has underlined describing his attitude to the workers and their lack of comprehension:

The masses have a servile respect for tradition and an unconscious horror of all inventions and novelties capable of changing their existence. If the workers in the eighteenth and nineteenth centuries—when mechanical techniques, steam power and the railways were discovered —had possessed the democratic power they have today, these inventions would not have been applied, or applied only at the cost of massacre and revolution. It is indeed fortunate for the progress of civilization that the power of the masses was born only after the great discoveries in science and industry had been made.

Had it not been for the help of a Trade Union politician, Albert Thomas, whom friends had introduced to him, it is unlikely that Louis Renault could have done much with his workers. Thomas, although a socialist, was also a patriot who realized that to compete in the modern world French industry must be modernized. He addressed the workers with all the skill of the trained orator, telling them that if they thought they were opposing M. Renault, they were mistaken; they were opposing themselves. If they did not accept some of the new methods, they would soon be out of work—because there would be no work. America would have obtained all the markets. He explained that if the new methods increased production, they also increased salaries. Everyone knew that Renault paid his workers fairly; he would keep his promise and pay more if output increased. Instead of talking about 'socialist equality', Albert Thomas emhasized 'increased prosperity'. His arguments had their effect and the strike was at last called off.

Thanks to his American experience, Louis Renault was thus one of the first industrialists to introduce certain essential, if elementary, aspects of mass-production into his country. They were soon to change its economic life no less fundamentally than had the French revolution.

9 | The Great War

Louis Renault does not seem to have been aware, as were most French industrialists in 1914, that after the series of international crises in the first decade of the century, war with Germany could not be far off. Although he had been making aeroplane engines for the French army since 1910, his hatred of war made him ignore the implications. André Maurois quotes him as saying, 'War? In the modern world! The very idea is monstrous! I am a constructor and creator. I hate and abominate anything that destroys.' Yet his personal experience of Germany just before the war should have warned him. In early 1914 he went to Berlin for a business conference with Walther Rathenau, the head of the Allgemeine Elektrizitäts Gesellschaft, which was interested in the Renault 80 hp air-cooled aeroplane engine. Rathenau said the Germans wanted to buy a licence to construct it, and he offered 100,000 marks, which was a good sum in those days. Louis Renault's first reaction was less a patriot's than a businessman's. He said he knew his aeroplane engine was the finest in the world; the offer was too small. Whereupon Rathenau summoned an assistant with a set of blueprints. They were placed before Louis Renault who saw, to his amazement, that they were his own Billancourt designs for the 80-hp air-cooled aeroplane engine. Rathenau said that the Germans wanted to behave correctly about patents, in accordance with international rules; but of course, if M. Renault would not do business. . . . There was little Renault could do except remonstrate at this piece of effrontery and espionage, and refuse to have anything to do with it. The plans, it was afterwards learned, had been stolen by a German agent who had been engaged as a clerk in the Renault drawing-office. On 2 August 1914, this man suddenly disappeared and was never seen again in France. Such was the 'security' in those days before the First World War.

Renault's comment on all this when he returned to Paris was typical, revealing his attitude to international politics in general —'If the Kaiser and M. Poincaré [then French premier] wish to make bloody fools of themselves I intend to keep clear. I will do nothing to be ashamed of.' When the Sarajevo crisis occurred, he was on a holiday cruise in the Baltic. He could not believe that anyone would be stupid enough to go to war.

The French mobilization had been perfected over many years, and worked so smoothly that within three days the Billancourt factory had lost 90 per cent of its workers. For some inexplicable reason the firm had not been classified as producing 'war material' and Louis Renault found himself on the fourth day of mobilization in uniform as *soldat 2e classe*, bound for his unit at Toul. But on the eve of his departure he was visited by Captain Martinot-Legarde, the War Ministry official with whom he had been dealing about aeroplane engines. The Captain took it upon himself to countermand the mobilization order, telling him to remain at the factory and continue producing aeroplane engines as 'first priority' with what staff remained. Renault did his best. After a month he complained that the manufacture of cylinder-heads required malleable pig-iron, the source of which was in the Ardennes, now overrun by the Germans. A similar situation arose over aluminium, because the factories were near Creil, also in the *Zone des Armées*. He therefore suggested that a society be formed for controlling the remaining national sources of these essential raw materials; and that they should requisition the Paris branch of the German firm Bosch, which made magnetos.

In the months that followed, he was confronted with all the difficulties known by businessmen in wartime; administrative and technical services disrupted by mobilization; the design and project department deprived of its best brains; the workshop personnel recruited from old men and women, most of whom had no knowledge of metallurgy; raw materials in short supply; transport irregular; relations with foreign countries almost non-existent. Hardly had he begun to work on the big orders for aeroplane engines than he was ordered to transfer his manufacturing machinery to a safer place, farther from the front (now on the Marne). The authorities wanted it re-erected in the Rochet-Schneider factories at Lyons. At this time the Billancourt works were not served by a railway, so the heavy machinery had to be transported by lorry to the Moulineaux station, from where it left by train for Lyons. The organization at Rochet-Schneider was not as good as Billancourt's; and for the next four years Louis

Renault was continuously on the road, generally at night after a day's work, between Lyons and Billaneourt, where his other activities continued.

Meanwhile his first contribution to the country's war effort had been made. On 7 September 1914, with the German armies on the Marne, Gallieni, the military governor of Paris, gathered three thousand reservists around the capital and transported them to the front, with a speed which surprised the Germans. For this he commandeered one thousand Renault municipal taxis, each of which took five soldiers. The Germans were halted. However much the importance of this feat may have been exaggerated, the episode has gone down to history as 'The Taxis of the Marne'.[1]

At the outbreak of the war, military planning was based on the theories of Colonel de Grandmaison, chief of the Operational Section of the General Staff. His was the famous *attaque à l'outrance* which presupposed that the active army (as distinct from the reserves) would win the war outright in one devastating blow, hurling themselves at the throats of the enemy, the pantalooned Frenchmen charging with fixed bayonets against the solid ranks of grey-coated Germans—'when the time comes we shall charge the foe and let cold steel decide'. That hundreds of thousands, indeed millions, of reserves would really be required was not considered a serious possibility. All that mattered was that the spirit of the offensive should penetrate the Regular Army. But when the time came, officers and men who had been given inadequate training and equipment for defence found themselves in full retreat before a German army that had disobeyed the rules by using reserves as front-line troops. Because the French High Command counted army corps only in terms of 'active' or Regular troops, it at first refused to believe reports that German units were sweeping through Belgium in the main attack (German Regular troops had been identified at Malmédy and Sedan).

When the war of manœuvre turned into one of trenches and continuous fronts, the French found themselves short of artillery. In the mobile warfare originally envisaged the artillery had been given a relatively minor role. The representative of the General

---

[1] They were 1,100 c.c. 2-cylinder engines, the company's pre-1914 best-sellers.

Staff in the Chamber of Deputies had said in 1909, 'You talk of heavy artillery. Thank God we have none! The strength of the French army lies in the lightness of its guns.' He was right about their artillery strength, or lack of it; when the French went to war they had only three hundred heavy guns while the Germans had three and a half thousand. Yet warfare was to consist almost exclusively for the next four years of immense artillery barrages blasting entrenched positions, so that the infantry might creep a few yards forward. Already by October 1914, shells for this were being used at such an alarming rate that the output of the state arsenals, a hundred and fifty a day, was totally inadequate. Some more modern means of production had to be devised. Fortunately a civilian industry was at hand which already had some experience of mass production. M. Messimy, the War Minister, summoned the automobile constructor, Louis Renault, and asked him if he would turn over a part of his factory to shell production.

Renault was ignorant of ballistics, and he replied that he must first study the question. Whereupon he was told to consult Colonel Remo of the artillery, who showed him the famous one-piece French 75 shell, which could be used for either high explosive or shrapnel. Renault said that owing to certain technicalities connected with his machinery being intended for motor-car, not missile, manufacture, he could only produce such a shell in two pieces, not in *one*. After some argument, in which his technical objections could not be refuted, he was told to get to work—although the artillery colonel was shocked at the idea of a two-piece shell. For as long as anyone could remember, the army had been using one-piece shells. 'Anyway, what does it matter?' said the Minister of War, a civilian, 'provided Renault's shell kills Boches.'

Tests on the Renault shells were satisfactory, and he was put in charge of manufacturing them for the Paris area, instructing other automobile manufacturers on how to adapt their machinery. Forty-five days after his first meeting with the War Minister a large part of the automobile industry of northern France had been converted to shell production on the Renault two-piece missile principle. By the end of November, his team was producing ten thousand shells a day, of which six thousand came from the Renault factories at Billancourt. By March 1915, the net production was twenty thousand shells a day. In handling the other automobile constructors, many of whom had been his rivals in peacetime, tact was required, and Renault suggested that they should form part of a Chambre Syndicale. In this way, he centralized the work of eighteen firms. It was during this period that he found himself working with a young man called André Citroën who had also realized the importance of shells in modern warfare, and had obtained a large Government contract for them. Louis Renault did not pay much attention to him at the time, except to note that Citroën produced his shells on the Taylor method (by 1917, Citroën was producing fifty thousand a day).

In these early days, when the French military leaders were still trying to adapt themselves to a kind of warfare they had not envisaged, the work of Renault and his collaborators was made much more difficult than it need have been. Orders and counter-orders followed at regular intervals. One day, he would be asked to produce a hundred mobile machine-gun carriers, a problem complicated by the shortage of armour-plating. After much effort, they would be produced on time—whereupon fresh instructions would be received to transform them overnight into ambulances. He adapted himself as best he could, often working at Lyons or Billancourt, then driving himself down by night to Bordeaux to confer the following morning with the Ministry.

The Government soon came to regard him as a kind of mechanical Jack-of-all-trades. One request, for example, was for aeroplanes that were faster than the Germans'. The first aerial dog-fights had shown that, all others things being equal, victory went to the swiftest. Louis Renault had started the war with his 80-hp aeroplane engine which, as the incident with Rathenau in Berlin had shown, was one of the finest on either side. But the Germans were improving their Fokkers, and soon Renault was having to employ all his inventive powers to keep ahead. By February 1915, he was producing a 200-hp water-cooled engine for the Maurice Farman fuselage, which temporarily held the advantage. When in turn it was surpassed by a German aeroplane, he produced a 300-hp machine, with aluminium pistons, for the Bréguet fuselage, and turned it out at the rate of seven hundred and sixty a month. This last engine remained, with modifications, the French contender for aerial supremacy until the end of the war.

We have seen that Renault's only contribution during his

military service in 1899 had been a vehicle for transporting general officers to visit one another behind the lines. The military authorities had then thought little of mechanical transport. But nearly two decades had passed, and the automobile firms were now called on to produce a whole range of vehicles—machine-gun carriers, ambulances, wireless-cars, and above all, lorries and trucks in tens of thousands.

The Germans had realized the importance of mechanical transport much earlier than the French had, and were already towing their heavy artillery by lorry. The maximum weight a horse could draw was half a ton, and the greatest number of horses that could be harnessed to a heavy gun was twelve, a cavalcade that moved at $2\frac{1}{2}$ miles an hour and occupied 26 yards on the road. A motor-vehicle, drawing the same gun, could cover five times the distance in a day, while occupying a fifth of the space on the road. It also weighed about a quarter of the horse cavalcade, and its petrol consumption weighed a tenth of the horse fodder.

Louis Renault was soon at work on tracked lorries to draw these artillery pieces, the heaviest of which, the long-range 220 C, weighed eight tons. Thanks largely to the efforts of two manu-facturers, Renault and Berliet, the French were able at Verdun in 1917 to concentrate 1,318 heavy guns at the strategical point and hold off the desperate attacks of the Crown Prince's armies. On the Voie Sacrée near Bar-le-Duc French lorries passed at the rate of six thousand in twenty-four hours, or one every fourteen seconds. They made a 'one-way' circuit, never stopping night and day, their driving teams being changed every eight hours. Ver-dun was sustained largely by this mechanical transport which brought up rations, munitions and hospital equipment in a kind of Taylor chain of delivery, or perpetual motion, flinging their contents into the furnace and returning for more. So successful were the French after this with their mechanical transport that they even surpassed the Germans in the new domain. Ludendorff said after the war, 'the French victory was in part that of the French automobile over the German railway' (for the Germans had developed to an even greater degree the use of railways for concentrating troops, as in the opening moves of 1914).[1]

---

[1] F.-J. Deygas, *Les Chars d'assaut*. Paris, C. Lavauzelle, 1937.

In the first days of August 1914, when warfare had been for a short time mobile, offensive methods had been so much more effective than defensive that the 'untakable' fortress of Liège had fallen within forty-eight hours. The aim of all general staffs in the years that followed was to return to this desirable state of affairs, to the warfare which professional soldiers had known from Marathon to Waterloo. On the long nights, as Louis Renault drove between his factories in Lyons and Billancourt he, too, thought about the problem of making warfare mobile again. He was being approached almost daily by inventors with plans and gadgets for ending the deadlock on the Western front. The problem was, essentially, to obliterate the barbed wire; to enable men to move forward in the face of machine-guns protected by this wire. One inventor suggested enlisting all the country's steamrollers to roll down the enemy wire. He had evidently not thought about the mud of Flanders. Among the many plans which Renault conceived was one for a mobile gun, light enough not to get bogged in the mud yet capable of crushing barbed-wire fences, and impregnable owing to its armour. It would move with the speed of cavalry over broken ground, across trenches and up earth slopes, firing as it went.

10 | The Renault Light Tanks

'The appearance of tanks on the field of battle was an event as important as the invention of gunpowder.'

General Estienne, in a speech, 7 May 1921

The use of some sort of armoured vehicle in warfare can be traced back to the Egyptians and the chariot of Boadicea. Leonardo thought about it; in more modern times Voltaire, of all people, during one of the Prussian campaigns presented the French War Minister with his plan of an armoured protection for horses, a kind of metal housing with a gun on top. He added characteristically that he felt 'ridiculous' at having invented a machine for killing human beings; but anyway, 'if a monk with the help of some charcoal, sulphur and saltpetre could change the face of warfare on this sorry globe, why should not a poor scribbler like myself add his little bit to the killing of those damned Prussians, incognito . . .?' The French military authorities were sceptical about Voltaire's project; and he later tried to sell it to Catherine of Russia. She showed more interest; but again the idea was opposed by the military men. That was the end of *Voltaire miles*.

Until the 1914–18 war, the idea lay dormant. From Voltaire's day down to modern times, all mobile warfare, including Napoleon's exemplary campaigns, had been conducted satisfactorily without the use of bizarre weapons. Before 1914, the tank had reappeared only in the fantastic imagination of H. G. Wells. It now required trench warfare to turn fantasy into reality. It also required the unremitting efforts of one man, Colonel (later General) Estienne, to persuade his superiors of its value. Estienne was a regular soldier and had been through the Polytechnique and had studied the problem of tracked vehicles for use in the overseas territories. He had written a monograph, *Les Cuirassés terrestres*, but little notice had been taken of it. Nevertheless, he continued to press for an armoured vehicle right up to the outbreak of war.

By the middle of 1916 the French General Staff, desperate to extricate entire armies from living in trenches, was ready to try almost anything. It was owing to a chance meeting after a military conference in July 1916 between Colonel Estienne and Louis Renault—perhaps one of the most fateful meetings of the war—that the armoured vehicle became a practical proposition. Earlier, when Renault had been approached about an armoured vehicle, he had pointed out that he had so much to do, from making aeroplanes and artillery tractors to shells and lorries, that he could undertake no new commitments. But Colonel Estienne's enthusiasm fired his own. The machine they discussed would have as crew a driver and a gunner; it must be transportable by lorry to the front, so as not to be worn out on the long approach journeys. This would limit its weight. Renault offered to draw up designs.

What he produced was different from anything conceived before in France or England. Other projects had envisaged tanks[1] of over thirty tons, but his was to weigh only six, and the side armour was to be only 18 mm thick. When Colonel Estienne presented the project to the General Staff, they at first opposed it on account of the lightness and inadequate armour-plating. The artillery men, who now dominated the battlefields, also objected that the construction of their tractors at the Renault works would be curtailed in favour of chimerical projects and unfruitful experiments. In spite of this, permission to construct a trial tank was finally obtained, largely because Estienne obtained approval from Joffre himself.

The first Renault light tank was ready for trials on 22 February 1917, with the constructor himself at the controls. It did everything that was required of it; it climbed earth slopes, tramped down barbed wire, crushed trench revetments, scrambled out of them, all the while firing a small gun. The only objection was that the ventilation in the turret was inadequate, and the gunner might be asphyxiated by the fumes. Louis Renault was given an order for a thousand.

Armour-plate was one of the main problems, for most of it had

---

[1] When the British were constructing their thirty-ton tank, they gave the secret project the misleading name of 'water-carrier'. The mania for initials in all armies converted this to 'W.C.' which had other connotations. So 'water carrier' was changed, logically enough, to 'tank'. Related by F.-J. Deygas in *Les Chars d'assaut*.

to come from England. The quality was poor and the delivery dates were uncertain. Bullets penetrated its plate, and Renault had to send 40 per cent back. Then there was the turret which he ingeniously designed as hemi-spherical so that bullets fired at it from any angle would ricochet off. The steel for this was not available, and a polygonal turret composed of laminated plates had to be constructed instead. The supply of equipment was delayed because tanks did not have 'first priority'. Even at the end of 1917, the Ministry of Armaments, which disposed of material, was unenthusiastic. Moreover, the troops who were to man these vehicles, who ought to have been fit and full of *élan*, were mostly rejects from other units, the inefficient, the wounded and other misfits.

One morning in April 1917, Louis Renault came to Estienne in a state of despair. He had just received a letter from the War Minister cancelling tank production. The reason given was that the modification for the turret ventilation was unsatisfactory. At a secret test of the Renault tanks the gunner had been half asphyxiated. Estienne immediately rushed round to the Ministry, where he discovered that the test had been carried out with a *tall* soldier in the turret; the man had succumbed less to asphyxiation than to cramp. Estienne insisted that the tank personnel must be under 5 ft 8 in. With the greatest difficulty he persuaded the Ministry to make another test.

It was typical of the atmosphere of almost continuous crisis at the time that after the new test (which was satisfactory) had been carried out, the Ministry not only renewed their order, but increased it from one thousand to three and a half thousand tanks. Their requirements were always urgent and always varying: today, priority for machine-gun carriers, tomorrow for ambulances and wireless cars. This sudden increase of 250 per cent was quite beyond the resources of Billancourt, and Louis Renault suggested that the balance should be obtained from the United States who were now in the war; the Americans had his designs and were beginning their own tank production. But the nationalism which had dogged the Allies from the beginning prevented this. The Ministry insisted that the work should be given to *French* firms. Louis Renault accordingly suggested the firms of Schneider, Berliet and Delaunay; with the following division of work:

Renault	....	1,850 tanks
Berliet	....	800 ,,
Schneider	....	600 ,,
Delaunay	....	250 ,,

These rival firms were to construct tanks from his designs, and, in the national interest, Renault waived his licence rights. Being French, however, each firm wanted to construct its Renault tank in its own way; uniformity was not achieved, and the spare parts were often not interchangeable.

An even worse blunder due to lack of Allied liaison was caused by the premature use of British tanks. The British had also been working independently on the project which they had kept a carefully guarded secret, from their allies as well as their enemies. They suddenly decided to test their tanks on the field of battle. On the morning of 15 September 1916 on the Somme, thirty-six huge British tanks, each weighing thirty tons, with a crew of one officer and six men, lumbered out of an early morning mist in front of the German lines. They achieved some success, but there were too few to take advantage of the German disarray.

The French plan had been to use a large number of light Renault tanks, six or seven hundred (a weapon which, to achieve secrecy, would not have been previously tested on the field of battle); these would tear a hole in the enemy front. Two entire Army corps could then be passed through to open up mobile warfare in the rear. But the surprise element was now lost, and the Germans began preparing counter-measures, armour-piercing bullets, anti-tank ditches, and so on. The French cursed their British allies, none more vehemently than Estienne and Renault.

Liddell Hart, the British military historian, has some damning things to say about the first use of British tanks[1]:

The early employment of tanks on the Somme in 1916 before large numbers were ready was a mistake; losing the chance of great strategic surprise, and owing to tactical mishandling, and minor technical faults, they had only a limited success . . . only forty-nine were employed, to work in tiny detachments of two or three machines—another break in the instructions of Colonel Swinton [the principal British advocate], who had pointed out to the Cabinet that their production should be secret until masses could be launched in a great

---

[1] In his *A History of the World War, 1914–18*. Little, Brown, 1935.

surprise stroke; and that on no account should they be used in driblets as they were manufactured. . . . Field-Marshal Haig expressed his full agreement with this memorandum in the spring; yet on the Somme he suddenly decided to use the mere forty-nine then available. . . . The scant and hasty preparation combined with the mechanical defects of the early model to reduce the total, so that only thirty-two reached the starting-point. Of these, nine pushed ahead with the infantry, nine failed to catch the infantry but helped in clearing captured ground, nine broke down, and five were 'ditched' in the battlefield craters. . . . Later, the British used them more successfully at Cambrai; but even here with surprise the success would have been greater.

Of the French, Liddell Hart has this to say; 'The French had independently begun similar experiments [in tank production] through the initiative of Colonel Estienne . . . although both idea and machine were later in making than the British, it is a significant contrast that the French first order was for four hundred; and that order was soon doubled.'[1]

Meanwhile the war had gone badly on the Eastern Front, where the Russians had collapsed and the new régime had asked for an armistice. It now seemed certain that the Germans would make a supreme bid for victory in the West, using the additional resources released from Russia. Clemenceau was now Président du Conseil. He had appreciated the importance of the tank, and had also hoped to use it offensively, as a surprise weapon; but when in March 1918 the British front broke and the Germans reached the Chemin-des-Dames in large numbers, he ordered the French tanks to be thrown in defensively. At Chaudon, on the morning of 31 May, the new Renault light tanks were employed. Although forewarned by the earlier British attack, the Germans had not expected anything so mobile and fast. The tanks penetrated deeply, and again only the relatively small numbers employed saved the Germans from a rout.

But in the great series of Allied offensives between June and November 1918, the Renault tanks were used in hundreds (and had the war continued into 1919, they would have been used in thousands, for by 1 October 1918, France was producing twelve hundred a month). They were completely successful, trampling down the barbed wire, crumbling the trenches of the Hindenburg

---

[1] Ibid.

line, squashing the machine-gun nests. They brought warfare into the open again.

According to the French military historian, Commandant F.-J. Deygas in his *Les Chars d'assaut*, when the war finished the Renault tanks had been involved in 4,356 engagements; the British heavy tanks in 3,000. That the light tank was the more effective was proved, he claims, by the losses. The Renaults lost 746, or 17 per cent of those engaged. Of the 3,000 British engagements, 733 were lost, or 26 per cent. The tank had also proved relatively cheap to make. Artillery preparation for the unsuccessful battle of Arras in April 1917 cost £10 million; the tanks used in the successful battles of July–November 1918 cost £2 million. Deygas points out that the only successful offensive battles of the entire war on the Western Front were those in which tanks were employed.

Renault had deserved well of his country. Just before the end of the war, he received this letter from the Minister of Armaments[1] referring to Clemenceau's satisfaction:

Paris, 13th July, 1918.

Dear Sir,

I am pleased to send this extract from the President of the Council's letter to the General commanding the Assault Artillery:

'The effect of the light tanks in the recent battles has been highly successful; they have enabled us not only to face a numerically superior enemy, but to evict him from his positions and cause him heavy losses. Our troops on all fronts have welcomed the appearance of this powerful weapon which, while contributing so much to victory, has economized in lives. Everywhere, the enemy has retreated and is in disarray before the tank.

'This should be made known to your factory workers. I am sure it will stimulate them to redouble their efforts, to increase their work both in quantity and quality. They will realize when at work that a screw which is loose, a bolt left carelessly in a gearbox, can cause a breakdown to the tank when in the heat of battle, compromising our Victory and causing the death of brothers-in-arms. They will realize that every extra tank makes victory more certain, and saves the lives of brave men. With this knowledge, they will work harder and better.'

In communicating this letter to me, the President of the Council

---

[1] The letter survives in the Renault Archives.

tells me to regard it as a homage to the Ministry of Armaments, the firm of Renault and all those responsible for constructing the light tank.

I am pleased to see that the combatant troops confirm the congratulations which I have recently addressed to all those whose efforts have been responsible for these new engines of war.

I remain, Sir,
Yours etc.
(Sgd) Loucheur

In the Armed Forces Victory Parade down the Champs Elysées, the Renault tanks took a prominent place. Louis Renault was created *Officier de la Légion d'Honneur*, an unusual distinction for a civilian. His citation reads: '*Renault, Louis*. Industrialist. Greatly contributed from the beginning of hostilities to our troops' armament: shells, guns, engines, aeroplane engines. He conceived and executed the design of the light tank whose arrival on the battlefield greatly supported the valour of our soldiers.'

To put Louis Renault as a tank constructor in his place internationally, the performance of the other warring powers in tank production and use may be briefly mentioned.

Once American production was under way, that country surpassed all others in war production.[1]

Ford built a small tank on the lines of the Renault (three tons, speed $10\frac{1}{2}$ mph) armed with a Browning machine-gun. But America did not come into the war until 1917, and Ford was thus a late starter. His tanks were not ready for action until the beginning of 1919. The American Tank Corps commanded by General Rochenbach distinguished itself signally in the last battles of the war, but using Renault tanks (incorrectly described in the Press as 'the marvellous little American tanks'). In fact General Pétain had handed two hundred and sixteen Renault tanks over to General Pershing; and Pershing writes in his memoirs that for the Saint-Mihiel attack he had 'only 267 tanks, all of French manufacture'.

---

[1] Military vehicles of all kinds, guns, rifles, even helmets poured out of the Ford works at Detroit. As a result of his patriotism one of the slogans after the war was 'Ford for President!'

In England, the chief advocate of tanks was Winston Churchill. He had drawn up a project for it as early as September 1914, but this had to be abandoned when he resigned after the Dardanelles failure. The War Office and Lord Kitchener were sceptical about tanks. And Liddell Hart writes[1], 'It is a sobering reflection that the price in lives might have been cheaper if tanks had been available in thousands instead of hundreds. The numbers manufactured under the reduced programme of 1917 sufficed to bring victory; but they could not bring back the dead.'

Of the other Entente nations, the Russians were negotiating for French tanks when the revolution overtook them. The Renault tanks they bought were later used in Siberia in 1920 against the Bolsheviks.

The Italian Fiat works made a heavy tank of their own (thirty-eight tons), but it was a fiasco. They then bought a licence from Renault for 500,000 Frs. By October 1918, they were turning out their first Renault tanks, but none had appeared by November, and on the eleventh of that month hostilities on the Western Front had ceased.

Why were the Germans, a scientifically gifted race, so overwhelmed by the new weapon? Why did they not develop more themselves? In the words of Ludendorff after the 'Black Day of the German Army', 8 August 1918, 'the mass employment of tanks was our most redoubtable enemy'. Why was it not until the day after that the German General Staff belatedly ordered tanks in any numbers? The only occasion when they had used them before, and then in only very limited numbers, was at Villers-Brettoneux in April 1918—of which General Sir J. E. Edmunds wrote in the official history of the war, 'whenever they were used the British line broke'.

One reason was, paradoxically, the performance of the heavy tanks when the British High Command tested them on the Somme and later at Cambrai. Although they had had a certain tactical success, the Germans regarded them as clumsy and ineffective. The German press and propaganda mocked them as 'inhuman and barbarous monsters' presenting a large slow-moving target to the artillery, and which anyway would be 'swallowed up in

---

[1] *A History of the World War, 1914–18.*

the mud'. Well-disciplined infantry, said the German High Command, had nothing to fear. Yet when in 1918 the French threw in their hundreds of Renault tanks, the effect on the German troops as the tanks emerged out of the mist was demoralizing, and many fled.

11 | Family Affairs

'If industry is hostile to Love, because it takes up too much
of an industrialist's time, it is favourable to that activity
on account of the money it can offer.'

Propos de O. L. Barenton, Auguste Detoeuf

Until now, for over twenty years, Louis Renault had led a life
of unremitting toil. He had built up one of the largest concerns in
France from nothing. To make it known in the early days he had
often risked his life in the inter-city races. He had lost a brother
in one of them. Latterly, to help his country, he had transformed
every department of the firm into a mart of war, driving it and
himself for four years with irrepressible energy. In two decades—
one of unlimited construction, the other of almost unparalleled
destruction—he had hardly relaxed. He was now over forty, and
he stopped for a moment to take stock of his personal situation.
In the early days, when his brother Marcel had joked about his
marrying, he had laughed, 'Marriage! I shall not marry until the
factory has five thousand workers.' It now had twenty thousand.

He had had mistresses of course, and he had even proposed to
Jeanne Hatto; but that was long ago, and he no longer found
her attractive. It was only now that he felt the need for the
stability of a home life, for an heir who would one day succeed
him at Billancourt. He had been heard to say, 'Every man wants
to leave four things behind when he is gone: a house he has
built; a tree he has planted; a book he has written; and a son he
has produced.' He was to achieve all these except the third. Even
if he had a son now, he would be over sixty before he could take
him into the firm.

Towards the end of the war he had proposed to several
women. But the approach of this man, accustomed to unques-
tioning obedience, was often too brusque. Moreover, outside the
factory he was still extremely uncommunicative and taciturn;
and most French women like talking and being talked to. In
character unscrupulous yet conscientious, by turns gloomy and

cheerful, affectionate and irritable, trusting and suspicious, he was far from irresistible to women. One woman from a very different stratum of society to his own who attracted him was a certain Mlle de L. Here he might have found the ideal wife, whose restraint and innate good manners would have saved him from the mistakes he was to make later in life. But although she found his male force attractive she decided—curiously for someone in her position—that he was 'too rich'; it was no doubt her way of saying that Caliban could not be tamed.

However, when Louis Renault had set his mind on something he usually got it; if he could not get one wife, he would get another. He was after all an excellent match, a millionaire with a town house in the Avenue du Bois (the Avenue Foch today) and an estate at Herqueville. At a tennis party in the summer of 1918, he met Christiane Boullaire, the daughter of a Parisian notary. She was twenty-one and he was forty; but he pressed his suit and she accepted. She was beautiful, intelligent and ambitious, and with his fortune behind them, even if he was a trifle Boetian, they could go far. The marriage took place at Herqueville on 26 September 1918, in the presence of a small group of friends, including the ubiquitous Serre and Hugé; for Renault still knew knew no one in 'society'. His wife was soon to correct this deficiency.

In the changed world after 1918, many of the old taboos had gone. What mattered primarily in an easier, less restrained society was money; with this you could do anything, go anywhere, meet almost anyone. Even the *faubourg* opened its doors to the rich, particularly to one who had been officially recognized as a war hero; or to opulent foreigners of doubtful origin, as well as to *avant-garde* artists and writers. The cynosures of the *salons* were no longer dukes of ancient lineage, but American and Canadian millionaires, Austrian psychiatrists, surrealist poets. Cocktails and whisky had replaced Madeira and champagne. *Le monde* rubbed shoulders with people whose existence its parents had systematically ignored; while its younger members drove their Hispano–Suizas and Bugattis themselves, at dangerously high speeds. The most audacious bought or borrowed a small Renault aeroplane and piloted it to London, Algiers or Rabat. Women in society were prepared to advertise wares for money.

Christiane Renault liked the best—in jewellery, flowers, pedigree dogs, antique furniture, oil-paintings, horses, yachts—all tastes Louis could satisfy. She was intellectually nimble, and could address herself to almost any subject and readily acquire enough knowledge for dinner-table talk; she was quick to absorb what clever people said on artistic subjects. She introduced her husband to good music, and this took the place of the ballads and sentimental songs he had learnt with Jeanne Hatto at the Opéra Comique.

Before the marriage, when Renault came back from work to Herqueville, he used to change from his 'town suit' into a pair of overalls and start tinkering in his private workshop. His valet had had to organize two costumes for him daily; one, the city suit, its pockets full of what he might need at Billancourt, keys, wallet, business papers, gold watch, fountain-pen and so on; the other, the overalls, which contained the keys of the property, a notebook to write down any ideas as he walked in the grounds, a pencil, a tin watch, a penknife, an adjustable spanner. This little eccentricity his wife discouraged. She also persuaded him that when guests arrived for lunch, and he happened to be in his overalls at the lathe, or under the car, or tinkering with his boat, he must not tell his guests to 'get on with it. I'll be along.' Soon the weekends at Herqueville were graced by greater social and intellectual luminaries than Serre and Hugé with their interminable talk of nuts and bolts and universal joints.

M. Jean Seruys, the industrialist, relates that once in 1920s he was invited to lunch at the Renault house in Avenue Foch. Louis Renault arrived rather late at the table with his arm in a sling. His son, Jean-Louis, had just been born, and there was good-natured banter about the father clasping the infant so joyously that he had strained his arm. In fact, Seruys afterwards discovered, he had returned from the factory where, just before lunch, some-one had produced an American car with a new type of clutch. Renault could not wait to have it dismantled, to learn its secrets. The mechanic entrusted with this failed to detach some essential part, so Renault took off his coat, got under the engine and set to work. But the device had a powerful spring which 'kicked', and sprained his arm.

Christiane Renault belonged to that class of woman from the French bourgeoisie who, perhaps on account of that origin, wish to shock it. She despised some of their traditional qualities, indeed those of the *faubourg* itself, as 'stuffy', and 'out of date'. She wished to be *avant-garde* and 'emancipated', as was the fashion in the twenties. Among other eccentricities a rich woman could allow herself was the cultivation of unusual pets. She kept a number of snakes which would be crawling about the room on the arrival of guests (some looked like vipers, but the guests could not know they were non-poisonous), some entwined around her neck or in her bracelets. It amused her to watch the reaction of the more conventional guests, particularly the women. She kept these reptiles in the bath; and on one occasion, when she and Louis Renault had been away for the weekend, they returned to find that all the servants had left and were living in a near-by hotel. Somehow the snakes had got out of the bathroom and were at large all over the house.

Some of her women acquaintances called her 'The Tigress', which no doubt pleased her. In the years to come the wives of some of their important friends, the de Vogués, the Flandins, came less seldom for weekends at Herqueville; and often the company was largely masculine. This only pleased Christiane Renault more, for she had a poor opinion of her own sex, and she excelled in all the masculine sports, particularly riding, swimming and skiing. She was an excellent shot, and even on her wedding-day went off immediately after the ceremony, throwing off her veils, to a shooting-party. Under her guidance, Louis Renault himself became quite a passable shot. But her attempts to turn him into a horseman failed. He gave it up when, while he was out riding with her one day, his horse bolted and did not draw breath until it reached the stable door, depositing him when his head hit the lintel.

No self-made man may be said to have arrived socially until he has a shoot; and Renault's shoot at Herqueville was considered one of the finest in France. When he was developing it, he found that a small plot belonging to a peasant was in the centre of the area, adjacent to and masking one of his best stands. Renault used all his bargaining powers to persuade the owner to sell, offering sums far beyond its market value, employing local farmers to argue for him, as well as lawyers and notaries—to no purpose. The pig-headed peasant refused to sell. Renault then offered to buy at least the shooting rights over his land. Again in vain. So he took his revenge on this peasant who was as stubborn as himself. He surrounded the small area with a palisade of corrugated iron 14 ft high; this at least would prevent the man from having the pleasure of shooting at his partridges.

Even here his mechanical bent was in evidence. He designed special fences along the edges of the woods with mechanical shutters for allowing ground game to leave the woods for pasturing in the fields, but which shut when they tried to return to cover, so that the rabbit or hare remained outside, staring and bemused, a target for the guns of his guests. It is hardly surprising that the guests of such a sporting host did not always follow all the rules of shooting etiquette. Often they did not bring their own cartridges, confidently expecting to use those of the millionaire. Many of them were, in the truly Latin sense of the word, his 'clients'. Those whom he particularly liked were allowed to inhabit properties on his estate, farmhouses, windmills, and so on, without paying rent; and he installed a system of electric bells for summoning them at short notice, should he want them for a shoot, a game of tennis or a trip in his boat on the Seine.

His wife's social aspirations reached their zenith when the King of Spain, Alfonso XIII, came to shoot at Herqueville. But at this Louis Renault jibbed; all his peasant modesty came to the fore. 'No, no! We're not in *that* class surely! It's quite ridiculous for *me* to entertain a King.' But the shoot was good and the King of Spain enjoyed it.

The impression Christiane Renault gave was later well summed up by the journalist René Miguel in *L'Aurore* (August 1936): 'Christiane Renault is now one of the most distinguished hostesses of France. Presidents of the Council and foreign ambassadors dine at her table. In the house at Avenue Foch, at Herqueville, one meets kings and princesses. On less auspicious occasions the guests are academicians and artists, renowned tennis-players and aviators.' (He does add that her husband had 'a hatred of social activities'.) 'Madame Renault,' he said, 'takes out a list of names from her bag before a weekend party and says to her husband, "Now in which room shall we put the Flandins?"'

On the whole, social life still embarrassed Renault. He despised small talk with smart women who made conventional remarks about the latest art galleries, theatres or books; and he would generally choose one of the male guests who interested him and say, 'Let's go for a walk in the garden after lunch and get away from all these people.' Although he did not make friends with politicians, there was one exception to this rule, Aristide Briand, with whom he would talk for hours, reforming the world. If Briand were present at lunch, Renault would turn his back on the other guests and plunge into lively discussion with him.

A man is set in his ways at forty, but Louis Renault was in love; he followed his wife's advice and did all he could to make her happy. The early birth of his son, Jean-Louis, cemented the marriage and developed his strong family sense. During the twenties Renault satisfied his wife's, and his own, acquisitive sense by the purchase of more property—an island off Brittany, Chausey, with its ancient castle, and another in the south, Gien, in the Hyères peninsula.

He came upon Chausey in a typical way. Every summer after their marriage, his wife used to like spending a part of the summer by the sea at Dinard, which was then fashionable; and Louis would go down at weekends to visit her. After a while he found the maritime social life, the tennis and tea parties, too much for him, and he would find some pretext for escaping for a few hours. One Sunday, while his wife was playing tennis, he went off on a sea excursion to admire the rocky islands of blue granite in the bay of St Michel, which is part of an archipelago detached from the mainland by a gale in A.D. 709. On the biggest, Chausey, with its long seashore strewn with rocks and reefs, he came upon a gloomy, dilapidated castle built in the fourteenth century as a defence against pirates and other marauders. He inquired about it and learnt that it had belonged to two pious old sisters called Hedouin, who had left it in their will to a Versailles priest who could not afford to keep it up. It had fallen into decay, abandoned to the storms and gales, and was now for sale at a very low price. He bought it on the spot. Reconstructing it with materials brought from the mainland was the type of work he loved. He engaged neither architect nor builder but a Piedmontese master-mason called Cargelli, whose work he much admired. He gave him orders every Sunday night, telling him to, 'Build that wall like *that*! Build the other like *that*!' If the work did not satisfy him, he had it pulled down and gave fresh orders to Cargelli the following Sunday. The exterior of the castle looked like a prison, but he is said to have spent between five and six million francs on renovating and decorating the interior.

Those who visited the castle when the Renaults were in residence talked of its 'bad taste', for it appears that Louis Renault indulged his liking for false antiques and he filled it with sham Gothic furniture, with expensive paintings and bound editions. One large room was reproduced like the famous *Salle des Chevaliers* of Mont St Michel. Georges de Braux, a visitor at the time, talks of Renault flying 'large Japanese paper fishes from his flagpole'. There is undoubtedly something Wagnerian about the place, in its savage setting off the Cotentin peninsula, which was in keeping with Renault's rugged character. At the foot of the castle the swirling waters of the Atlantic are subject to the greatest tidal changes in Europe; so that as the tide rushes out 'at a speed faster than galloping horses' a whole mass of islands in the bay, hitherto invisible beneath the sea, gradually appear to arise out of the water. Here Renault was as happy as he ever could be with his motor-yacht, *La Bécasse*. It was the best that the shipyards of Amsterdam could produce: it had a steel hull, was powered by two Renault Diesel 70-hp engines, was large enough to weather any storm and commanded by his own private captain, the ex-naval officer and hydrographer, Gaston-Rivier.

Louis Renault developed a strong family sense, which was soon extended to members of his wife's family, for whose unemployed or unemployable members he found jobs in the firm. One of those was a certain artist, a youth of considerable personal charm, but not a worker. Louis Renault found him a job on the 'public relations' side, where he had to interview clients and calm the refractory. This young man was once listening sympathetically to a client's tale of woe, when he suddenly said he must write it all down. The client went on expatiating, thinking this a tribute to his own importance. But he saw as he rose to go that the representative of Renault had been drawing a caricature of him.

Although, as we have seen, Renault had treated his dying brother Fernand harshly when acquiring his shares in the firm, he was good to his children, two girls and a boy, after their father's death. He took the son, Jean, into the business and sent him for a year to Russia and a year to America, to obtain experience. The young man never showed much talent for business as he was more interested in the arts. When the 1914–18 war came, Renault found him a job in the Transport Corps, driving Generals about behind the lines. Jean was then the only Renault of the next generation, and Louis considered that he ought to be 'preserved'. But Jean did not want to be preserved, and insisted on taking an active part in the war. He was killed flying over Verdun. Louis Renault's only comment was: 'Silly boy! And I'd got him a job that would have kept him out of trouble!'

One of Fernand's daughters (the other married François Lehideux, who was to play a large part in the Renault firm) married a certain Lefèvre-Pontalis, with a most distinguished war record, but who was not a great worker. Renault gave him, too, a post on the commercial side of the firm. This new nephew always arrived late to work, and Renault took to checking his office every morning to see if he was there. If he wasn't Renault would wait until he made his appearance and give him a good ticking off. However, Lefèvre-Pontalis had no intention of changing his habits, and he therefore tipped one of the *huissiers* every night to hang up a hat and coat, left in the office especially for the purpose, on the umbrella-stand behind the glass façade of the office—so that when Renault came along on his rounds of inspection he would suppose his nephew had arrived.

In all these matters of relatives working in the firm Renault, who was notorious for being 'hard' with his workers, was surprisingly indulgent. He preferred to allow them to continue their idle existence rather than dismiss them. It was only when they were clever and hard-working, and wanted to take an active part in the firm—as we shall see in the case of the other nephew by marriage, François Lehideux—that he became difficult.

Renault's loyalty to anyone who had been a trusted servant of the family, or of the firm, became legendary. Although he could be difficult and irritable, and in spite of his many changes of temper and plan, his domestic servants, too, were faithful to him. The fact that they remained with him so long is a proof. Joseph Hartmann, his chauffeur, stayed with him for over twenty years. His cabinet-maker, Boulangeau, at Herqueville, a brilliant copier of French classical furniture, was with him for forty years. He spent many hours with Boulangeau, for there was nothing Renault liked better than watching another skilled craftsman at work. After the death of his mother, Renault took into his service her old cook, Clementine, and her 'butler', Désiré, installing them both comfortably at Herqueville. Even when they were well past working-age he retained them until they died in 1937. In their last years he liked sitting reminiscing with them about the 'good old times'. His head-gardener, Perreault, who on four separate occasions gave notice owing to his master's temperamental behaviour—only to withdraw it each time—had entered his service in 1922.

The extreme case of Renault's curious loyalty concerned Verdure, an old associate at the factory who had been with him almost since the beginning. He was in charge of a department from which he once dismissed two female workers because they refused to sleep with him. This naturally caused a tremendous upheaval with the Trade Unions, who came to Renault with angry representations. But nothing would make him dismiss Verdure or take the girls back; for him they were 'bad workers'. If Verdure did not forget this loyalty, neither did the Trade Unions when the time came to settle accounts.

12 | **The Summit of Power**

'The factory has changed everything. A steel ingot, a motor-car, a fabric, have become today abstractions, a synthesis representing the labour of a multitude. Their product is anonymous, as is the corporate body which sells it.'

Propos de O. L. Barenton, Auguste Detoeuf

If the war had done nothing else, it had shown that the machine and its makers were the masters of contemporary society. The internal combustion engine dominated the planet. The 'Machine Age' had, of course, been ushered in some decades before: but its champions had stood modestly in the wings, as it were, of modern society. The war had now given them a vulgar shove into the middle of the stage. Without Ford and Renault and their fellow constructors that stage would not have resounded to the names of Foch, Haig and Pershing. The military men were in fact relatively expendable; most replacements could have done their work.[1] This could not be said of the Fords and Renaults. In twentieth-century warfare, the importance of mere material, as distinct from soldiers, was proved by the figures. Before 1914, the French Army had 6,000 vehicles; in November 1918, it had 92,000. In 1914 the impedimenta of that army, fully mobilized, weighed 27,000 tons; in 1918, it weighed 1,040,000 tons. The years 1914–18 had created their own mechanical world; such hideous words as 'Technocracy' and 'Belinogram' pointed to the future.

Due largely to the wartime development, two attitudes towards machines appeared in France after 1918. The first was a desire to forget them and their cacophony, to return to a world in which they did not exist, and in which it would have been physically impossible to exterminate so many men in so short a time. This form of nostalgia was expressed by the writer, Georges Duhamel. Not only did he deplore the human butchery made

---

[1] See *The Donkeys* by A. Clark, published by Arrow Books 1963, a bitter attack on their incompetence.

possible by the machine, but he envisaged its future tyranny, in peace as well as war. 'Our modern philosophers,' he wrote[1], 'see little prospect of an agreeable existence ahead. They tell us, the victors as well as the vanquished, that all we have before us in the technical age is greater effort, harder and more dehumanized work.' He foresaw an endless round of striving, to construct ever more efficient machines which would, in turn, destroy their creators more efficiently, in a kind of Devil's Dance of Death. Against this soulless civilization he contrasted, 'the love of nature, a taste for the simple but real things of life which the ancients enjoined.' To him, places like Billancourt were the fount of all evil, veritable Gehennas of iron and steel, where any individual worker must inevitably be damned.

The second attitude was diametrically opposed to this. It regarded the new methods and materials as a benefit to society, and it wanted more, not less, machines. Louis Renault naturally subscribed to this point of view. He knew that revolutionary methods were required to cater for a completely new type of demand. As early as August 1919, in an interview with the magazine *Je sais tout*, he said, 'Billancourt must be modernized, or it will disappear.' Parts of his factory had become top-heavy as a result of the wartime production of shells and lorries. It now had, in addition to the normal plant, a steel-foundry occupying three hangars which furnished 500 tons of molten steel a month for war production; three iron-foundries; an aluminium-foundry; a brass-foundry (using the turnings from the lathes); a rolling-mill; a drawing-(or metal-stretching-) mill; and a stamping-mill. Two hangars of 75,000 sq ft in area housed several iron-forges, 23 drop-hammers from 225 lb. to 7 tons, and a press shop in which twenty-three hydraulic presses of from 60–800 tons were in action. There was a general workshop with a floor-space of 110,000 sq ft, in which any new piece of war machinery could be assembled in a day. Finally, there were a number of hangars for the assembly of aeroplane and lorry engines.

Although the plant had greatly increased since the war, Renault knew that most of it was worn and out of date. About this time he made one of his rare speeches to his staff, in which he pointed out that the clock could not be put back; man had

---

[1] *Scènes de la vie future*. Paris, Mercure de France, 1951.

created contemporary society and must adapt himself to it. The new world across the Atlantic had surpassed Europe in production and was now setting the pace. What Frenchmen refused to do would be done by others. If France turned her back on the technical struggle, she would become simply a poor client of America. The speech showed what lay ahead for Billancourt.

'We must,' he said, 'change the attitude of the workers before applying the new methods. If the worker is not in favour of change, our efforts are wasted. In all work any bad method, any waste, is a crime against the community. A worker who is paid for doing something badly puts up the price of the product—and in the last resort he, as consumer, has to pay for it. Although, at first sight, this attitude may seem severe, demanding a certain abnegation, it brings with it very tangible advantages—more leisure, more well-being, more security, less effort. . . . We should attempt to convince our men of the need for working in the minimum of time, with the minimum of effort. I know that the French worker is full of goodwill and intelligence, and as hard-working as any in the world. What we lack perhaps is a sense of discipline, and a knowledge of the principle of production. We have too great a tendency in France to consider that because we have solved a problem, our work is over. To build a machine and put it in working order is not enough. It must be produced cheaply, with the minimum of labour and material. And here I must say that much of our education is still inadequate. The teachers in the primary and secondary schools should be concerned with the great problems of scientific production, and convinced of their importance. . . . If we could achieve this, France would be unbeatable. . . .'[1]

About this time he jotted down, as he often did in the middle of the night, some notes on the problems ahead (one of his habits according to his nephew, Lehideux): 'Iron, cement, bricks, quicklime, minerals, there they are! . . . we have discovered them and learnt how to use them . . . we cannot go back . . .' When he had said, 'Billancourt must be modernized, or it will disappear,' he had said all. He was right, at least commercially; for the other firms like Panhard and Mors, which did not change their methods, had all disappeared within the next decade. None of them could

---

[1] Quoted in *La Vie de Louis Renault* by J. Boulogne.

face the depression of the thirties. Thanks to his experience in America, Renault was also one of the first French industrialists to appreciate the need for a new approach to markets. If before 1914 French firms did not go out to find new markets, this did not matter greatly; rather, the French businessman waited for the markets to come to him. The situation was now reversed.

The Renault engines in production just before the war were the 2-cylinder 9 hp, the 4-cylinder 10/12 hp, the 4-cylinder 18 hp, the 5-cylinder 22 hp, and the 6-cylinder 40 hp. The Renault cars' distinctive mark was the celebrated 'Alligator' bonnet, and the naked chassis were then, according to usage, equipped by the coach-makers according to the wishes of the clients, as limousines, tourers, trucks, brakes, and so on. Only the 9 hp (the taxis of the Marne) were issued fully equipped from his factory. In 1919, Louis decided to retain these essential models, but turn them out with their body-work complete and ready for immediate use. After the war, the 'Alligator' bonnet gave way to a more modern shape which permitted better cooling, and the well-known Renault 'Losange' (trade-mark) was used for the first time. The principal qualities of his engines were their robustness and ability to stand up to punishment. The war had revealed two general faults in the cars. The brakes were by modern standards poor (in those days they operated only on the rear wheels); and the cooling system by thermo-syphon required an exceptionally large radiator, ten litres, which was placed behind the engine. After the war he dispensed with the quadrant change and his entire range of cars all had electrical equipment. In 1921 he produced the 9.1-litre 90-mph monster, which continued until 1928. In 1926 his light-weight stream-lined version of the 'monster' was the first car to average over 100 mph for twenty-four hours.

As all firms which had made large war profits were taxed 90 per cent, legislation was passed allowing them to raise the money by amortization or sinking-funds; otherwise they would have gone bankrupt. No one imagined that one of the industrialists would be able to pay off the entire sum on the nail; but Louis Renault did. Even in the early 1920s, when other businesses could not work without credit, he remained true to his principles; or rather, he *could* remain true to his principles. Yet at one point, when things were difficult, he was persuaded by two of his directors (M. Fuchs and M. Rochefort) to associate himself with a bank. For a short time the Banque Mirabeau became a shareholder in the Renault firm, and one of its technical counsellors, M. Marcel Champin, an administrator. From the outset, Renault felt uncomfortable; his authoritarian decisions had never been questioned as they were now. When financial difficulties arose in 1926, just before Poincaré's return to power, Louis Renault, to test the reaction of his new partners, proposed to the Administrative Council that the firm's capital should be increased to pay off debts. The bankers equivocated and asked for time to reflect, to examine accounts; they referred to difficulties here, limitations there, and so on. Such indecision was foreign to Renault's nature. He immediately terminated the relationship with the bank and produced the extra forty million francs himself. This was his sole experience of working with bankers, and it confirmed all his suspicions. Henceforth he would work only with men who could 'understand my mentality and methods'.

Apart from his hatred of war itself as destructive and futile, Renault now experienced its economic aftermath. Such a man naturally has a rooted objection to any form of State interference in business; and during the war the State had exercised an economic dictatorship. With the return of peace, most people (the Communists and Socialists excluded) hoped this was over. But the removal of controls proved far more difficult than had been imagined. For economic reasons, some of them remained for years—control of exported capital, rent control, special social legislation, imposed prices in agriculture, social insurance, and so on. All this was in direct contrast to the easy *laissez-faire* conditions in which Renault had founded his firm.

During the war he had learnt, too, what it is to be dependent on other firms, in particular those controlling raw materials, like the powerful steel monopoly the Comité des Forges. He had always objected to monopolies and pressure groups, and was as much against the C.G.P.F. (Comité Général du Patronat Français, or Employers' Association), as against the Trade Unions. He remembered that Henry Ford had never allowed other firms to dictate to him. If the price of steel was too high, Ford bought a steel-works. If the price of coal rose, Ford bought a coal-mine. He did the same for glass, wood and other raw materials. If labour became too expensive, Ford imported workers and built a town for them. This system, known as 'vertical concentration of industry', Renault decided to imitate as far as possible in France. He would not be dependent on other firms who were only interested in high prices, quick profits, and short-sighted, immediate advantages involving economies in tools and plant. By producing the primary materials himself, he would employ the most efficient methods, with the highest quality, the least delay, the lowest prices, and the greatest output.

In a sense the war had prepared Billancourt for this extension. Because the sources of aluminium had been overrun by the armies, an aluminium department had been opened in 1915. Renault had also built his own steel-foundry, a smelting-plant and a plate-cutting department. During the war Billancourt had been forced to make many of its own tools, and other primary materials such as bricks, crucibles, moulds and coal briquettes. Wooden shavings had been dried and pulverized for oil.

Renault first considered obtaining his own steel-works in 1919. Among the plants acquired as German reparations, and which the French Government was putting out to tender, was the steel-works at Hagondange in Alsace, built by Thyssen in 1912, and one of the most modern in Europe. Renault knew little about steel production, but he studied the technique and spent a week at Hagondange before making a bid. With a group of associates headed by Baron Petiet, he managed to influence the Commissaire de la République, Millerand, in his favour, and the bid was accepted. Hagondange was later known as La Société des Aciers de l'Etat, and its chief shareholder was Louis Renault. He installed a steel-research bureau, employing some of the finest technicians in France, including the Sorbonne professors, Trillat and Pomey.

A further advantage in making his own steel was that the problem of varying qualities could be overcome. Most European steel industries at this time had the unfortunate habit of 'declassing' their products when the quality deteriorated, so that they could be sold at a cheaper price for subsidiary uses—unfortunate at least for the mass production of motor-cars, where steel of constant quality is essential. When subordinated to the Comité des Forges, Billancourt had been using as many as seventy-four different types of steel, which was uneconomical and a source of endless technical difficulties. On acquiring

105

Hagondange, Louis Renault ordered that these seventy-four varieties should be reduced to twelve.

Secure in the primary material, he now began to organize what was to become a commercial empire around Billancourt with a number of satellite companies: La Société Nouvelle de Pontlieu at Saint-Etienne; La Compagnie d'Exploitation Automobile; La Société Algerienne et Marocaine des Automobiles Renault. He erected a 2,000-hp hydro-electric plant at Annecy, and a tool factory at Saint-Michel-de-Maurienne in Savoy. He set up saw-mills and sand-quarries at Gudmont and Salbris. He built a cotton-wool factory to deal with the interior coach-work. He even made his own bricks for these buildings. Glass had until now been a monopoly of the firm Boussios. It was of poor quality and expensive; so Renault bought a glass factory and made his own. Each of these concerns was independent and had to support itself financially, without help from the parent company. He even deliberately introduced a note of insecurity in these companies, hinting at times that he would curtail, or even close, those that did not show the requisite profit.

During this expansion period, he kept a close watch on the U.S.A., sending his representatives there regularly, with a view to copying or developing their technical and commercial methods. One of these was hire-purchase. This was a sales method which, theoretically at least, must have outraged all his principles. But he realized its importance in the creditless post-war world, and set up a special sales department, Société pour la Diffusion Industrielle des Automobiles à Credit, with branches all over France. By the end of the twenties, he had ninety-two sales centres with Renault repair garages attached. In their selection he revealed his old flair for choosing sites. He preferred them away from the centre of the town, at the entry, or even a little outside, on the roads into the main cities. These sites were cheap, but people thought he was taking a risk, because motorists would always go to garages in the centre. Here, however, he had foreseen the big development of French highways in the twenties when, he rightly assumed, motorists would be quite prepared to drive outside a little for repairs rather than pay higher prices in town.

His frequent and unexpected visits to these provincial garages caused much apprehension among the local staff. The most vulnerable were those on the sixty-three-mile stretch between Paris and Herqueville, the route which he took himself at least twice a week. Each time he passed, his penetrating eye examined every detail, the smartness, cleanliness and efficiency of the establishment. Should one not be properly illuminated after dusk, the manager had to produce an explanation or face dismissal. This route, which is today a large arterial highway, was then known among the factory personnel as La Route Impériale, ironically recalling the road taken by another, more famous, French dictator over a century before.

By this time, largely as a result of the war, 20 per cent of production was non-automobile. Renault supplied Diesel engines and machinery for the new battleships of the French Navy the *Turenne,* the *Sufren* and the *Dunquerque.* Perhaps the most important development was in aviation. Here again Renault was dealing with something he did not like personally (he was frightened of aeroplanes and never went in one); but he could not contradict his own principles about the future. During the war he had produced fifteen thousand engines for the Air Force, and he now began to adapt them to peacetime uses. The machine-gun turrets of the Bréguet 14 with its 300-hp engine were filled with mail-bags. The hull of the Goliath-Farman, also equipped with the 300-hp engine, was adapted for passengers. On 8 February 1919 a Renault-powered Goliath made the first regular Paris-London trip with eight passengers; and on 12 February, another Renault-powered Goliath made the first regular Brussels-Paris trip with thirteen passengers.

As before, when he produced his light cars and tanks, he was interested in light aircraft for 'tourism', and planned a cheap model for customers who were not millionaires. He considered that the separate construction of engine and fuselage by different firms was inefficient. For this reason, in the early thirties, he acquired the firm of Caudron, which had delivered fuselages to the French Army, and, before the war, won races in competition with the better-known firm of Farman. In this way, the group Caudron-Renault came into being, in which Renault engaged the well-known aviation engineer Riffard to design for him. Their light aeroplanes won the Coup Deutsch de la Meurthe three years running; and in 1936 one of them, piloted by Michel Detroyat, won the international Thompson Trophy at Los

Angeles before one hundred thousand spectators. The light aeroplane, equipped with the small 500-hp engine, became the fastest in the world when a woman, Hélène Boucher, broke the speed record in one; and Maryse Bastie crossed the south Atlantic with a Renault-powered aeroplane. He was soon producing engines for Air Union, later to become Air France. But, as in the early automobile days, records and races meant little to him unless they contributed to one thing—the production of a cheap tourist aeroplane. He announced that he would produce such a machine for the price of a good car; and had the Second World War not broken out he would probably have done so.

In the domestic and agricultural field Renault dominated France even more completely in these post-war years. His trade vehicles included a full range from half-ton camionettes to seven-ton lorries, in a Swiss Family Robinson complex of milk-vans, petrol-carriers, municipal dust-carts, ambulances, fire-engines, Black-Marias and cattle-transporters. Because he disapproved of Government ministers driving about Paris in foreign cars he formed a park of twenty chauffeur-driven limousines which they could rent at a nominal sum. In the class of big limousines he now had no rivals, with the exception of Hotchkiss. His new methods had driven them all out of business. The year 1935 saw him at the summit of his power, symbolized by his elevation to *Membre du Conseil de la Légion d'Honneur*—the greatest honour for a Frenchman, for the Conseil has only fifteen members; until now none of them had ever been a businessman.

Agriculture was another interest he shared with Ford. To both men it was really a hobby, and in their spare time they thought about the soil rather as they did about their factories—how could it produce more? Motor-culture for agriculture had existed in America for over a decade; and Ford had said, 'In twenty years' time, thanks to mechanization, agricultural progress will be comparable with the industrial progress of the last twenty years.' The French peasantry had been decimated by the war, and in 1919 there was a shortage of agricultural labour. Here was an opportunity for Renault to modernize agriculture in peacetime, as he had modernized industry in war, for a tractor could do the work of six men and horses together. He converted the engines of his light tanks for use in tractors, and financed an agricultural journal for demonstrating the advantages of mechanization to the conservative French peasantry.

In the immediate post-war years, the essential difference between the French and American markets became more apparent. Whereas Ford could concentrate on one model, Renault knew his countrymen demanded variety. The models he designed and put on the market in the twenties were so good that they remained the same with only a few alterations for the next ten years: the 2-cylinder, descendant of Gallieni's 'Taxis of the Marne'; the 4-cylinder, on Ford lines and equipped with a 10-hp engine which did not disappear until 1952; another 4-cylinder, the pre-war 12-hp type; an 18-hp, also dating from 1914; and the 40 hp, the 9-litre with huge cylinders, which was the luxury vehicle used by the President of the Republic and the Ministers (listed at £1,550 for a chassis). His smallest and cheapest model was the Monasix at £199. He was still inventing, too; the engine suspended on india-rubber shock-absorbers which diminished vibration and its destructive effect on the chassis is still in use today.

A feature of modern industry which he disliked, but to which he had to subscribe, was the limited liability company. Henry Ford had made his firm into a public company in 1927, although much against his will. Neither he nor Renault had any use for ignorant shareholders interfering in the running of their concerns, arguing with the directors at board meetings. But in the modern business world they had no alternative. Renault had to do so too, but he only paid lip-service to the transformation. He put his shares on the market, but immediately acquired 98 per cent of them himself. Later, he was much criticized for this, and it was used as evidence against him at the end of his life.

Like all industrialists who had built up their businesses before the war, he was a free-trader, disapproving of tariffs of all kinds. But in the post-war world tariffs were necessary, and here again he adapted himself to the new conditions so that they worked to his advantage. M. René Girard, who was in charge of the firm's publicity from 1930 to 1940, explains how, at the end of the twenties, Renault exerted all his influence on the French Government to keep out American automobile competition by means of tariffs. M. Girard was affected by this personally because he was, at the time, in charge of the publicity for General Motors in France. When the high tariff was imposed, General Motors closed down much of their French establishment and his services were no longer required. Whereupon Renault asked him to join Usines Renault[1]. In this way Renault achieved two things: he kept General Motors out of France, and acquired one of their best men.

He was now so powerful that everyone wanted to do business with him, even if it was only for a small item such as the sale of registration plates; he ordered ten thousand where other firms bought five hundred. He kept strictly to his rule of paying on the last day of every month; but such large sums were involved that the interest, if he bought early in the month, was considerable. Later his enemies claimed that he had unfairly increased his fortune in this way. For he had enemies; in spite of this extraordinary success, or because of it, he was not admired by his peers.

Because most French enterprises suffer from management understaffing their employers tend to supervise personally more activities than their American counterparts do. Although they often complain about this, many do not really want first-class associates, nor do they try to attract them with high salaries. And the distrust which many of them feel for talented collaborators extends easily to members of their family in responsible positions. They feel they are never so well served as by themselves, and they believe that a division of responsibility may lead to a reduction of power.

Having no academic qualifications or training, Louis Renault was suspicious of mechanical engineers with university degrees. He suspected that, because they had a broad theoretical education, they would be unable to specialize in one limited field and would take a general view while remaining too self-confident about the particular. They would consider it beneath themselves to concentrate on details. It is understandable therefore why, for decades, he preferred men like Serre and Hugé as his principal lieutenants.

But these men were growing old, and because Louis Renault was nearing fifty he now felt the need for managerial support. He

---

[1] In 1922 the name of the firm was changed yet again, this time to Société Anonyme des Usines Renault. Since 1945, after Renault's death, the firm has been known as Régie Renault.

wished to retire more often to his relaxations, the boat at Chausey, the agricultural tractors at Herqueville. His son, Jean-Louis, would not be old enough to replace him for at least ten years, so he began to look for another member of the family. Most of them were, as we have seen, incapable of occupying anything other than sinecures, and he had let them sleep. But his late brother Fernand had another daughter who had just become engaged to an intelligent young man, François Lehideux, a member of the well-known banking family. Louis Renault disliked bankers on principle; but Lehideux, it appeared, had no intention of becoming one. He had completed his studies brilliantly in political sciences and was about to go to America to take a job in industry. Apart from being impressed by such initiative, unusual in his insular countrymen, Louis Renault was quick to appreciate the young man's brains. Although Lehideux was not mechanically qualified—perhaps because he was not—Renault felt he could train him to take a leading part in the administrative side of the firm. Here was the man for the transition period, while awaiting the arrival of Renault's son, Jean-Louis, who would be twenty-one in 1940. Here was the Régent to prepare the way for the Dauphin.

After a year of reflection and pressure Lehideux accepted this proposal. He soon revealed his exceptional talents. In many ways the two men complemented each other, for Lehideux possessed something which Louis Renault lacked—personal charm and cordiality in dealing with people. He also had a first-class brain, and it was clear that he would soon occupy one of the leading positions in the firm. Fresh blood and new ideas had arrived just in time, for Renault, who had until now triumphed over, or obliterated, his rivals, was suddenly faced by a new and formidable competitor who had appeared on the French automobile stage—André Citroën.

13 | André Citroën

André Citroën had learned the technique of mass production with his shells during the war. He was younger than Renault, and had also been to America, had become 'Fordized', and was overflowing with ideas. Yet the motor-car was only one of the interests of this irrepressible man. A Polytechnician, he would have been equally at home selling sewing-machines, metal furniture, window-frames, anything for which there was a market, or for which he could create one. Apart from the front-wheel drive, he developed no technical device for the motor-car; nor was he in any sense of the term an inventor, as Renault was. He was a remarkable example of the post-war French business-man. Money meant nothing to him; the banks were there to provide it. He had ideas and conceptions to give to the world, and he did not worry about the material means of doing so. From America he brought back the notion of *one model*, a light popular car produced in such quantities as to be the cheapest for its value in Europe. Moreover, he intended to produce it as the Americans did, ready to drive away, its coach-work finished, fully equipped with spare wheel, electric self-starter, lights, and so on. The war was barely over before he was putting these ideas into operation. They conflicted with those of Renault, who deliberately constructed many models, believing that this very variety was an insurance against failure. To offer each member of the public a vehicle according to his means was better than Citroën's 'putting all his eggs in one basket'.

In character the two men could hardly have been more different. Renault was essentially a mechanic who had become, by force of circumstances, a businessman; Citroën was essentially a businessman who had taken up motor-cars because there was an expanding market for them. Renault objected to personal advertisement; Citroën was a showman, who hired the Eiffel Tower and lit it up at night with his name visible in thousands of electric-light bulbs. He provided villages with name signs and other traffic indications on plaques, *gratis*, but each prominently bearing his name. All over France were signposts to well-known landmarks, churches, châteaux, museums with the slogan 'Gift of Citroën'. He even had one on the Cotentin peninsula with the indication 'to the Château of Chausey. Gift of Citroën'. Renault was at first furious, although he later laughed about it.

Another of Citroën's stunts was an endurance test – running one of his family cars without stopping for a year round the Autodrome de Montlhéry. To sell some of his caterpillar tractors in England, he managed to procure a photograph for the Press of Queen Mary sitting in one at military manœuvres on Salisbury Plain—an extraordinary spectacle, the familiar, well-corseted figure, bolt upright, in a picture-hat, with her parasol, in an AFV. Renault had no interest in 'high life', the casinos, fashionable beaches, theatres, cabarets, expensive restaurants; Citroën was a social man who spent all his spare time at the gaming-tables. Renault was silent, saturnine, shy even, in the company of those he did not know; Citroën's personal charm and easy manner endeared him to everyone. Renault never borrowed a sou from the banks and paid cash within a month; Citroën took advantage of every modern credit facility—to the extent that Renault once said of him scornfully: 'Citroën builds with the money of others. I build with my own.' Citroën wanted money for itself, he needed money, not only for his ambitious commercial projects, but for private purposes, for his apartment in the Rue Octave-Feuillet, and the parties he gave. 'As soon as an idea is good,' he said, 'money is of no importance.' He could buy the American Chrysler's 'floating power' patent, which prevented engine oscillation being transferred to the body, for 25,000,000 frs. and yet own nothing himself, not even his apartment or the villa at Deauville. Renault was, fundamentally, a French peasant; Citroën was an ebullient Dutch trader whose grandfather was an Amsterdam diamond merchant (his father had settled in France in the mid-nineteenth century). Yet Citroën possessed something which Louis Renault did not enjoy, the good will, even affection, of his workers. Renault never fully understood that his workers did not, as he (Renault) did, live *for* the factory, but *from* the factory. Nor did he understand Citroën's ready handshake and cordial smile for his employees.

During the war Citroën had introduced into business the one idea of Ford which was repugnant to Renault—social services for his workers, the system known as paternalism. He had inaugurated it because many of the factory workers then were women, who brought their babies with them. Citroën provided them with *crèches*, or nurseries, in which the children could be placed during the day. With this went canteens and other social amenities. After the war—and the fillip it gave to female emancipation—many of the women remained in the factories; and so did the Citroën innovations, from which the male workers also profited. Other industrialists soon found they were forced to imitate Citroën, at least partly, or he would attract all the labour. (Not that French 'labour' and the Trade Unions appreciated this particularly; for bestowed benefits were not obtained 'as a right'.)

To this Louis Renault replied, 'A chief of industry must not interfere in the private affairs of his personnel. The moment the worker passes out beyond the factory gates, he regains complete liberty of movement and is no longer subject to discipline. The management of a firm should have nothing to do with social organizations. In the same way politics, of whatever shade, have no place in a factory.' Renault no longer enjoyed the convivial relationship of the early days with his workers. Men like M. Griffon (at present Head Librarian at the Renault firm) refer to him as having become harsh with his men; although Griffon admits that he was still scrupulously fair. On one occasion, he says, Renault noticed a dirty wastepaper-basket with refuse littered all around it, and asked a man working at a near-by lathe why it had not been cleared.

'It's not mine, sir,' said the man, not intending to be impertinent, but telling the truth. Louis Renault dismissed him on the spot. Later, when he was told that the man was a turner, not a workshop-cleaner, Renault said, 'It's not him I'm dismissing. It's anarchy. I won't have anarchy in my factory.'

M. Griffon also tells of how Renault, coming upon a man nibbling a sandwich while working at the lathe, sacked him on the spot. The difference between the firms of Renault and Citroën is summed up by another worker who left Billancourt for Javel: 'I found I had left an Empire for a Republic'. To Renault the idea of talking to his workers about their grievances, as Citroën did regularly during the economic crisis of the thirties, was distasteful. Yet failure to do so was one of the reasons why many of them thought he was responsible for their hardships.

The struggle between the two men began in 1919, when Citroën announced that he was putting on the market a popular model which would do for France what the T-Ford had done for America. Although Renault was sceptical, Citroën took his time, using modern advertising methods, building up the public 'image' of the car. His name was well enough known due to his shell production during the war, and he published his ideas in an album dealing with his wartime achievements; then in the last pages, he referred to the coming popular car, a vehicle produced with the 'same process as the one employed for making shells'. He would turn out a hundred vehicles a day as Ford did. Choosing the right moment, he brought on to the French market his new tool-steels, which he claimed could cut more quickly, and which he had used in his wartime shell programme. These would revolutionize the car industry too. In the spring of 1920, on a date carefully imprinted on the Parisian mind, he unveiled his Perseus in the Alda showrooms in the Champs Elysées.

The crowds waiting for it were impressed by the lightness, the apparent fragility, of a vehicle which resembled the T-Ford or the Chevrolet 490. Even more impressive was the price, 7,950 Frs, half the cost of any other car. Like Ford, Citroën was attempting to reach wider layers of society; and price reduction, he knew from America, meant a bigger market, mass production and greater profits. He had originally wanted to sell it for 7,250 Frs, but his colleagues, who had put money into the project, were against such a low figure.

Here at last was the cheap French car, which could be compared with America's best, a 4-cylinder, 10 hp four-seater with a maximum speed of 50 mph. When one of the first Citroëns sold to the public covered 180,000 miles before returning for servicing, its name was made: twenty-five thousand Frenchmen were prepared to buy it immediately. But unfortunately Citroën had overplayed his hand; he could not produce his cars quickly enough. Also, with the rising cost of living and devaluation, the price was too low. It soon had to be increased by nearly 50 per cent; but even at 12,500 Frs people bought it.

An ingenious sales device invented by Citroën was the individual letter to the client, known in France as the *de prospection* or 'forward-looking' letter. A filing system was formed containing the names of two categories of clients; those who might shortly change their car; and those who might buy a new one (an intention they had indicated by a visit to the local showroom). Each agent would draw up a list of these potential clients and send it to the Citroën firm at Javel. Here each name was filed, with details about the owner's present vehicle, if exchange was contemplated. Three letters were then sent out. The first, which thanked the potential client for visiting the local showroom, contained a description of the model considered suitable for him. Two weeks later, a second letter, emphasizing the exclusive qualities of the car, was dispatched. Finally, a week after this, the client received the third letter, informing him of the advantages and facilities for repair, exchange, and so on. The text of the letters was uniform and duplicated, but the ink and lettering were such that the client had the impression they were specially addressed to him. The agents were reminded not to forget any titles or letters after the name of the client, who was sent an illustration of the car showing a radiantly healthy family in it, with whom even the ugliest owner could identify himself. Everything was done to flatter the vanity of the French petit-bourgeois. If the sale was then made, the agent sent an 'erasure' letter to the factory, and the relevant card in the filing index was removed and destroyed. So successful was this method that all French manufacturers were soon following suit and sending out 1,500,000 of these letters annually. They were responsible, it was claimed, for 15 per cent of the sales.

Another publicity device employed by Citroën was the use of his scrap sheet-metal for small toy models of his cars. This too was so successful, particularly with children, that the manufacture of these toys was entrusted to a specialist firm. Other constructors again had to follow his lead, and by 1930 the sale of these models by one firm alone was eighty-five thousand. There was no question of profit here, only of publicity; models costing 25 Frs to make were sold to the public for 20 Frs. In every family, said Citroën, the first three words a child must learn were 'Papa, Maman and Citroën'.

All this may give the impression that the propaganda tussle between the two men was unequal. But this was not so. When Citroën was building a new workshop at Javel he found, to his annoyance, that all the bricks supplied to the builders had the

Renault 'Losange' imprinted on them. He did not know that Renault, in order to economize in the varied building projects of his expanding empire, had bought a brick factory that supplied the requirements of a large part of Paris. Citroën rang up the Renault works and requested that, if Renault had such a monopoly in the area, he should at least supply bricks without his trade-mark to another motor-car manufacturer. Renault replied that the trade-mark could not be obliterated without considerable expense; he would erase it if Citroën paid. He received no answer to this suggestion; and part of Javel is to this day built with Renault bricks.

Renault was delighted that Citroën overplayed his hand in the Champs Elysées showrooms. Renault's own showroom on the Champs Elysées was relatively modest; but Citroën, to make his appear more magnificent, filled the entire back wall with a mirror, so that his cars appeared multiplied as though in a huge hall. The glass for such a large space was defective, and it distorted the image of the vehicles ludicrously. Renault often wandered past this showroom and had a quiet chuckle to himself.

In 1924, Citroën introduced his all-steel body with soldered elements, which even the Americans had hesitated to employ. His methods were now being watched all over Europe. With the exception of Charles Weiffenbach and the Englishman W. R. Morris, no other constructor thought he could succeed. (Weiffenbach was a Frenchman who tried to form a syndicate of French constructors to emulate Citroën; but they were too individualistic and were unable to work together. Morris also saw the future in terms of mass-production. 'Produce in mass, by the masses, for the masses,' he said—a process he put into practice in, of all places, Oxford.)

Renault had been confident in 1918 that he had outdistanced all his competitors, the famous names, Panhard, Levassor, Mors, Peugeot. But that a man without any workshop experience, who had pushed himself into the limelight during the war by making shells, should oppose him in this way seemed an act of impertinence. What is more, in the space of one year Citroën's name had become better known in the world than his own—and he had been in the business since 1898! But Renault had always been a fighter, and he decided to meet Citroën on the newcomer's own ground. In the early thirties for example, Citroën became convinced that there was a big future in inter-city buses; the public would prefer comfortable cross-country buses to trains because they could see more of the countryside. He would select a good circuit, say Lyons-Marseilles, and announce that Citroën buses would run a regular service between the two cities. Renault was not slow to imitate. As soon as he saw a line was successful, he would open a similar service, generally in the same part of the country. If Citroën chose Lyons-Marseilles, Louis Renault would choose Marseilles-Toulouse; if Citroën chose Nantes-Rouen, Renault would select Rennes-Orléans.

Another propaganda field in which they clashed was exploration. Citroën organized great expeditions across equatorial Africa, Asia and as far as China, in teams of caterpillar-tracked vehicles. The ease of communications in the new age of the aeroplane had caused Europeans to look outside their continent. New sections of the population were becoming educated and they could read about the unknown countries being opened up by machines. One no longer had to be a Marco Polo to go to Cathay; Citroën's team of mechanics went there with motor-cars which one could buy oneself.

Louis Renault was forced to follow with similar expeditions—but wheeled, not tracked. He felt confident enough of his technical superiority to remain faithful to the wheel, which he contended would always be better for civilian purposes. His teams used six-wheelers to cross the sands of the desert; thus the struggle was not only between Renault and Citroën, but between caterpillar-tracks and wheels. Here Renault was right. In agriculture today a tractor with caterpillar tracks is seldom seen. Three Renault six-wheelers left Colomb-Béchar in Algeria on 24 January 1923 to link up its railway terminus with the Niger railway system, thus opening a regular route across the Sahara. Among the Renault team of six were the brothers René and Georges Estienne (sons of the Colonel Estienne of tank fame). It took them seven days to cover a distance of 1,500 miles. The speed of the crossing eliminated the water problem in places where no caravans had been able to travel before. This was followed by the lone crossing of a small 6-hp Renault—which provoked an immediate reply from Citroën with a 5-hp car. Renault then sent his cars to the Cape through the tropical forests of Central Africa. Citroën replied by sending cars through the South American jungle. In 1926 four Renaults left Beirut and crossed Persia for India. Later his vehicles crossed the Andes to Chile; while Citroën did his first trip through Alaska. Wherever there was a barren part of an unknown continent the issue was joined.

On one occasion the two men almost came to blows. Citroën had persuaded King Albert of the Belgians to accompany his expedition to Lake Chad—an astute move because the King was one of the most popular foreigners in France. Citroën had installed a series of staging-points, caravanserais, where the travellers could rest; and a number of journalists were accompanying the expedition. But shortly before its departure, when the King of the Belgians had already left Brussels, French consular officials in North Africa reported that there was a danger of native riots; the local authorities could not be responsible for the royal safety. In these circumstances, Citroën had to cancel the project and apologize to the King. Later, he learnt from travellers who had been there at the time that there had been no riots or disturbances of any kind. Someone had invented the scare to stop the expedition. The Citroën family today still contend that Louis Renault was behind this. If so, he revealed an unfamiliar crafty side to his character.

François Lehideux, who was by now his uncle's closest associate, tells of how Renault retaliated against Citroën's publicity. He bought a plot of land opposite Citroën's works at Javel, on which he built nothing, but around which he erected palisades bearing in large letters the word 'RENAULT', and beneath it an arrow pointing south along the river with the words 'RENAULT—2 km TO BILLANCOURT'. Whenever Citroën looked out of his office window he saw this monstrosity; he wrote a sharp letter of complaint.

'You'd better go and calm him down,' said Renault to his nephew. 'It's a chance to get inside the place too, and see what he's up to.'

When François Lehideux called at Javel, Citroën took him to the window and pointed. 'It's a provocation! Here, on my doorstep!'

Whereupon Lehideux, a man of unruffled urbanity, drew Citroën's attention to another landmark they could see on the

Paris skyline, the Eiffel Tower which Citroën had recently hired and plastered with his name, illuminated in electric-light bulbs. 'Isn't that a provocation too?' asked Lehideux. Citroën was a man of some humour and his anger turned to laughter. Louis Renault later removed the 'provocation'.

On another occasion, when Lehideux was lunching with Citroën, he thought he would make a joke and said, 'As my uncle is a great constructor and you are a great salesman, wouldn't it be better if you joined forces instead of being rivals—Renault will make the vehicles, and Citroën will sell them.' Somewhat to his surprise, he says, Citroën did not appear at all amused by this. Nor did he dare make the joke to his uncle, who would certainly have found it in bad taste.

Even when the battle was at its height, Renault admitted that Citroën had been of benefit to the automobile industry. 'He never let us sleep,' he said. Later he said: 'The struggle between Citroën and myself caused an emulation, and therefore progress, in the industry which even, sometimes, outpaced production.' When in 1934 Citroën produced his front-wheel drive[1] which obviated the transmission-shaft, Renault admired his daring but he did not imitate it. Although Renault out-distanced all his competitors in truck and lorry construction, with 50 per cent of French production, he lagged behind Citroën in private cars; he produced forty-five thousand a year to Citroën's sixty-one thousand. Citroën stated blandly: 'In a few years people will no longer be saying "motor-car" but "Citroën".'

A kind of Gresham's Law comes into operation in competition of this kind, and the best elements, technical and administrative tend to gravitate to one or other of the big rivals. It gave Renault pleasure to realize that, thanks to his and Citroën's efforts and rivalry, the average price of the French automobile was now down to 400 Frs a pound—a price that compared favourably with similar essential commodities, such as butter, meat, coffee and clothing. Shoes, for instance, cost nearly 2,000 Frs a pound; carpet-sweepers, just over 1,000 Frs a pound; men's suits, nearly 4,000 Frs a pound. It pleased him to regard automobiles

---

[1] A front-wheel drive had been used by the American automobile constructor, Cord, at least a decade before; but it had proved mechanically and economically unsuccessful.

like food, as essentials, and to think that America—even though she had out-distanced them all—produced five million private family cars a year, enough if placed head to tail to stretch from Moscow to the Chinese frontier. He and a few men like him had done all this in their lifetime. Now, without the motor-car, modern society would come to a standstill.

Most Frenchmen thought that Citroën would win the struggle, between the two rivals, that he was the real French Ford. Every year at the Salon de l'Automobile they waited to see what new model or 'stunt' he would spring on the public. But they had reckoned without the pugnacity of the Saumurois peasant. Confronted with Citroën's talent for mass production of one model, Renault replied with a host of models. Here, he probably understood his countrymen's psychology better; for the French have always liked variety. They had grown accustomed to choosing between front and rear engines of between 2 to 26 hp, and a large selection of body styles. Just as ten years earlier the workers in the Renault factory had opposed standardization of production, so the French public opposed standardization of design. Renault's output of tourist models ranged from the famous 6-hp to the Reinastella 8-cylinder 40-hp with a maximum speed of 90 mph (the Presidential-Ambassadorial model). His cheap tourist models sold at about 20,000 Frs. The 6-hp model had been brought out by Renault to counter Citroën's 5 hp. It was a robust, economical tourer with a new technical device, a detachable cylinder-head which facilitated repairs. The final and decisive blow was given when Renault confronted his rival with the most modern assembly-line in Europe.

For this he acquired the Ile Séguin in the Seine opposite the Billancourt works, and built a bridge connecting it with the factory. Six hundred and fifty thousand cubic yards of embankment were erected to raise the level of the island sixteen feet, as protection against a repetition of the 1910 flooding. A 35,000-hp electrical works was built to run a new coach-work assembly-line in a hangar several hundred yards long and five floors high. This private source of power ran the ironworks, forging-press, smelting-works, the workshops for pressing, gearing, machine-finishing, the sawmills and paint-drying rooms. Billancourt with its thirty-two thousand workers operating fifteen thousand machines was now the greatest industrial concentration in France, covering an area of two hundred and fifty acres, as big as the town of Chartres.[1]

In the building of the huge bridge connecting the island with Billancourt, Renault took a commercial risk. Legally, the Seine was a 'public highway', and Government permission was required to build a private bridge across it. François Lehideux was sent to negotiate with the Minister of Works, who said that if Renault built the bridge, he did so at his own peril; six months later he might be told to dismantle it. Most industrialists would have been daunted by the millions involved in such a venture. But Renault gave orders for its construction. He considered that his firm would always be working in one way or another for the Government, and he could invoke 'reasons of state'. The assumption proved correct. When rearmament began shortly after this, he received large Government orders, most of which he handled on the new site. It had cost him very little to buy, on account of its lack of communication with the mainland, but it is today one of the most valuable sites in Paris.

In 1931, when the new factory on the island was nearly complete, Renault did the unheard-of thing of inviting André Citroën to inspect it; and Citroën did the unheard-of thing of accepting the invitation. M. Reiner, Citroën's biographer, says that when Citroën arrived that morning Louis Renault, wishing to show off the extent of his domains, said grandly, 'We shall have to use a car to see it all in a morning.' Irritated by the insinuations of this, Citroën proposed at first that they should go on foot. But this proved too much of an undertaking, and he finally consented to be driven around in one of Renault's 80-hp Reinastellas. He was evidently impressed, and afterwards accepted Louis Renault's invitation to lunch at Maxims (not the sort of place Renault usually frequented).

M. Reiner says that Louis Renault, who was tongue-tied at first, soon warmed up, twisting his napkin excitedly as he talked

---

[1] As usual, Renault had to buy out or evict the inhabitants. He had some trouble with an old widow called Gallise who at first refused to sell her plot of land on the island because her son had been killed in the war driving a Renault tank.

Just after he had acquired the island he was approached by an art dealer wishing to sell him a painting of it by a 'certain d'Aubigny'. Renault refused to buy it 'because the painter was unknown'.

and jabbing the tablecloth with his fork to make his points. He showed off all his practical, workshop knowledge, which he knew Citroën did not possess, saying to the Polytechnician, 'Of course, I know you've been to a good school and have all sorts of academic qualifications. . .'

Four years after, when Citroën went bankrupt, Renault was reputed to have said to a friend, 'The only dirty trick I ever did to André Citroën was to show him the Ile Séguin that morning. He ruined himself after, by trying to do in three months what had taken me thirty years.' Whether these figures are true or not, Citroën undoubtedly tried to expand his works at Javel in a very short time. Had there been no 1930 world crisis, he might have succeeded; but here the gambler over-reached himself. Always heavily in debt, he could not face his creditors' sudden demand for payment. The old saying still applied: 'Citroën never realizes that the debit side of a firm can be greater than the credit side.'

One of the reasons for his fall was his commercial self-confidence and the fact that, thanks to his ingenious propaganda, the public had become mesmerized by him. He was always ahead of his time. For example, he envisaged the front-wheel drive (which is only today being developed with such astonishing results). He 'leaked' the information that he had something extraordinary to offer before he had constructed more than a few experimental models. Meanwhile, the car which had made his name, the famous 7-hp, was piling up in the stock-rooms because the public naturally refused to buy whilst there was a possibility of getting something even better. Louis Renault would never have allowed such a situation to develop; he would have exhausted his old stock first.

Another, less comprehensible, reason for Citroën's collapse was connected with Michelin, the tyre manufacturers, a firm of shrewd Auvergnat peasants who lived in watertight seclusion and economy, putting aside every sou. Michelin suggested that Citroën should have a 10 per cent discount on all tyres bought from him, if Citroën sold over eighty thousand vehicles a year. Citroën, as usual optimistic, assured him that this could easily be achieved. In fact, he sold only seventy thousand. Adhering strictly to the letter of the law, Michelin sent in his bill without the 10 per cent discount. This process continued for several years,

Citroën ever confident that he would soon be able to pay the balance. He never reached the eighty thousand annual sale, thereby incurring large debts, so that when the economic crisis of the thirties struck him he became insolvent and Michelin, his chief creditor, bought his firm for very little. It is still run today by Michelin.

Completely bankrupt, Citroën first approached Flandin, the Finance Minister, for help. But the world economic crisis had struck France a little later than the other European countries, and there could be no question of a Government subsidy. Flandin suggested that he should approach one of the other big automobile firms, Renault, Peugeot, Berliet. Today, the Citroën family claim that Flandin deliberately refused governmental help because he was a friend of Renault. This seems unlikely because, when Renault was approached about taking over Citroën's bankrupt firm, he said, 'That I could never do to André Citroën. If I did, people would say that I wanted to destroy him.'

On the contrary, he gave instructions to his sales department that Citroën was not to be embarrassed by Renault salesmanship. 'This is not the moment to take advantage of him,' he told François Lehideux. 'Let him sell if he can.' The rival firms of Peugeot and Michelin were less squeamish. The former immediately took a page in the newspaper for an advertisement showing their firm in a flourishing state, with spick-and-span mechanics welcoming clients smilingly at the door. This was contrasted, also in the advertisement, with the illustration of a broken-down, dirty, dilapidated garage, dustbins bulging at the entry; beneath it the motto, 'Buy your car from a going concern—not a derelict one!' This incident annoyed Louis Renault, who took the unusual course of ringing up Peugeot and criticizing his 'bad taste'. André Citroën never recovered from his bankruptcy, and died prematurely on 30 July 1935.

Thus Renault's methods were again vindicated. The peasant mentality of this man who never borrowed a sou weathered the financial hurricanes that struck Europe as if they were squalls of rain. His greatest rival was gone, and he stood even firmer on the soil of France, towering over the others. This was something for which they never forgave him.

Part Two

THE FALL

1 | **Politics**

This study has been divided into two parts. In the first, Louis Renault's life may be regarded as a continuous ascent from relatively humble beginnings until, by the mid-thirties, he had reached a pinnacle unattained by any other French industrialist. He was then one of the most powerful men in France. In the second, during the gradual collapse of European civilization, and of French civilization in particular, which culminated in 1940, he declined. When the time came for the settling of accounts, he was the scapegoat. No one stood by him, because no one loved him. He had chosen to walk alone, and he had to face his end alone.

Until 1935, he had managed to steer clear of politics, a subject of which he was both suspicious and scornful. He had been born not long after the foundation of the Third Republic, and had passed his life under it. Interested in it or not, he had been forced to observe it; and what he had seen had not pleased him. In the Third Republic, the gift for intrigue seemed as important as statesmanship, and all the worst sides of petit-bourgeois democracy were emphasized. Its financial scandals, from the fraudulent Panama affair to Stavisky, had caused many Frenchmen to abandon public for private careers. The business community regarded the governments of the Third Republic since 1918 as having neglected the true interests of the country. A trade association said, 'They misjudged fundamental economic and financial laws and were guilty of demagoguery, incompetence and greed for power.' The lowest point was reached in 1933 when Stavisky was found to have been in contact with a number of Deputies, including Garat the Deputy for Bayonne, Bonnaure for Paris, and Dalimier for Seine-et-Oise. The Président du Conseil himself, Camille Chautemps, was accused of trying to hush up the affair, because Dalimier was his Minister for Colonies. The tradition of despising the Third Republic was old and fashionable, particularly among the upper classes. Before the 1914 war, that arbiter of Parisian taste, Boni de Castellane, said of it: '*Mais mon cher*, it lacks *style*! Félix Faure? Why, he looks like a provincial cattle-dealer!' (Félix Faure was then President of the Republic.)

Intrigue was foreign to the nature of Louis Renault, who disliked verbiage and rhetoric, and who had shown throughout his career that the qualities by which he set most store were rapid, clear, workable solutions, above all results. His attitude to politicians was roughly, 'You keep to your affairs, and I'll keep to mine. I'm a creator and producer.' If he had remained a *small* producer, this might have been possible—just as in the Middle Ages a small landowner might, by lying low, keep out of the turmoil. But if he were a territorial Baron he was, whether he liked it or not, pitchforked into politics; and if he played the game poorly, he often lost his head, literally. It was the tragedy of Louis Renault that he never realized this. By his very position at the head of a huge source of power, he was automatically 'political'. Poincaré himself said of the automobile industry in the thirties, 'It leads the industry of France, and its health and prosperity is an index of the financial state of our land.'

Renault was also important in military terms. It was useless to say he disliked war. In modern technical warfare, his position in France was roughly equivalent to that of a Field Marshal. General J. F. C. Fuller says at the end of his book:[1]

Weapons now form 99 per cent of the victory. Consequently the General Staff of every army should be composed of mechanical clairvoyants [*sic*], seers of the new fields of warfare, able to exploit the new tools . . . what is required is the understanding that progress in weapons of war is a similar problem to progress of tools in manufacturing . . . the history of the evolution of machine tools is that of the elimination of the workman and the replacement of muscular energy by steam, electrical or some other form of power . . . fewer men, more machines, higher output is the motto of every progressive workshop. A similar motto will have to be adopted in every progressive army. Nations which have proved their ability as leaders in mechanical engineering will be those that produce the most efficient armies. . . .

That France no longer satisfied these demands in engineering and machine production was proved by the export of French

---

[1] *Tanks in the Great War, 1914–18.* Dutton, 1920.

motor-cars, which dropped between 1925 and 1931 from 63,769 to 25,461. Whenever the French car competed on a basis of equality with the cars of other nations it proved incapable, in spite of all Renault's insistence on modernization, of fighting commercially. Due to the relatively few models in America, and the cheapness of the resulting mass-production, American cars cost 5 Frs a pound, whereas French cars cost 10 Frs a pound. It seems, too, that the French never fully appreciated, as did the Anglo-Saxons, that the twentieth century was an industrial age, of big business and assembly-line production, of governmental power and regimented peoples, of huge mechanized armies.

At the end of the twenties the situation had, for a moment, looked brighter. The material losses of the war had been replaced. The franc was at last stabilized. Neither social peace nor public order were troubled. The danger of war seemed to have receded, and the affair with Germany was being settled. The League of Nations was the organ of the future. Simone de Beauvoir has described this atmosphere of false optimism in *Prime of Life*.[1] In 1929, she writes, 'Peace seemed finally assured: the expansion of the German Nazi party was a mere fringe phenomenon, without any serious significance. It would not be long before colonialism folded up: Gandhi's campaign in India and the Communist agitation in French Indo-China were proof enough of that. The world economic crisis, when it came, indicated only that capitalist society could not last much longer. The "left" believed they were on the threshold of a Golden Age.'

Far from ushering in her socialist Golden Age, the world economic crisis, on whose threshold they stood, was to give birth to the most extreme form of nationalism. If France had remained prosperous after this crisis, politics might have mattered less. But when millions of men are out of work and their families starving, the subject obsesses them. Men can talk of little else, and they turn in their bitterness on those whom they think are leading, or misleading, the country. No such situation had arisen in Louis Renault's lifetime before. The strikes of 1912 had been local affairs compared with the events leading up to the Front Populaire of 1935. It seems ironical and unfair, that Louis

---

[1] World, 1962.

Renault, who was apolitical, and who had little contact or friendship with other capitalists,[1] was classed at the end as the arch-capitalist and 'bloody war merchant', the scapegoat for the entire 'Right'. In view of the part he is supposed to have played here, it is worth while examining for a moment the composition of this 'Right'.

The 'Right' between the wars was less a party than an attitude of mind, originally in protest against the revolutionary ideas of 1789. There were three 'Rights', identifiable according to their different traditions.

The oldest and, academically, the purest, was that of the original counter-revolutionaries, who were hostile to 1789, advocating a return to the monarchy and aristocratic rule. They were the *ultras*, or true reactionaries, who could be easily identified and were never very powerful. Apart from them, and less easy to define, was a second 'Right' to which, in so far as he had any politics at all, Louis Renault belonged. This 'Right' did not represent an aristocracy of birth, but of authority founded on experience and competence. Its followers were perfectly content with the Third Republic, provided it was stable. In this sense, associated with the material interests of the governing classes, they may be described as conservative rather than reactionary.

The third 'Right' concerns us less here (but it will later, in the events after 1940). It was both nationalist and anti-constitutional, that is anti-Parliamentarian, a combination of elements loyal to the First and Third Empires, and notable for its xenophobia. It advocated a strong central authority delegated by the sovereign people to a few chosen 'born leaders'. It is not difficult to understand why this 'Right' in the twenties and thirties, fearing revolution which now appeared in the form of communism, could look favourably on Mussolini's fascists, and be prepared in 1940, in spite of its nationalism, to incline towards Vichy and collaboration with Germans.

These distinctions are important because there are still people

---

[1] Once a letter from a prominent financier making some request was handed to him. 'M. X . . . . ?' he said, looking at it. 'I don't know him.' And he put it in the wastepaper basket.

in France who describe Louis Renault as a 'Vichy collaborator', a member of the third 'Right'. He was nothing of the kind.

Faced with the social unrest of the thirties, Renault's attitude was that, as the head of an enterprise bears the responsibility and takes the risks, he must administer it as he sees fit. He can engage and dismiss any member of the staff, determine salaries and working conditions. Any attempt from outside to interfere can only affect the business adversely, and therefore the prosperity of the nation. From this it follows that Renault opposed workers' collective agreements and the growing power of the Trade Unions. We have already seen that he objected to 'paternalism', by which the workers were provided with playgrounds, special hospitals, co-operatives and other devices of the 'welfare' state. He contended that this made them slaves of the donor, whether of the State or the factory, that the worker should be free to do what he liked after leaving work. He wanted a worker to be able to say, 'I hate your place, I'm leaving tomorrow.' It is only fair to emphasize that he was against *all* pressure groups, those of the right, such as the Confédération Générale du Patronat Français (the C.G.P.F.), as well as those of the left.

The 1930 slump he regarded not as one of over-production, as orthodox economists maintained, but as due to bad organization of production. To a man whose one aim in life had been to produce, there could be no such thing as *over-production*. He believed that after the war most industrialists had been short-sighted; instead of putting profits back into their businesses, they had thought of nothing but high prices and quick returns. He was partly to blame himself for not letting the public know these views or the way he administered his business. Yet here again he was typically French. French employers have always attached great importance to secrecy—the inheritance no doubt of a peasantry exploited for centuries by an insatiable exchequer. As soon as a Frenchman acquires any private property, he conceals how he acquired it. The passion for anonymity is deep in the French businessman, who tries to efface himself before his sceptical countrymen.

Contrast this with the American attitude. After the First World War, the American public learned that large profits had been made by many big corporations. Because high profits mean an efficient and healthy industrial system, this was considered a reason for congratulation. In France, on the other hand, instead of making people rejoice in the healthy state of the national economy, it would only arouse misgiving and jealousy. French industrialists were therefore very reluctant to communicate to trade associations (even to those which supported them, like the C.G.P.F.) information about their output, production methods and other business details. In the early twenties, an energetic civil servant from the Ministry of Commerce travelled round the country at his own expense, visiting factories for information about their output in the war and immediate post-war periods. He had the greatest difficulty in obtaining any. He found it almost impossible, for instance, to discover details about rubber tyres, although a number of the firms he visited manufactured nothing else. The figure for automobiles had finally to be estimated from the number of car licences delivered by the police. If Louis Renault had opened up his books, and given time at least to explain himself and his firm through 'public relations', the reputation he was gradually gaining as a 'bloated capitalist' might have been quite different.

At this time, too, monopolies were being much criticized. More than other countries, France concealed the degree of concentration in industry and banking. Partly responsible for this was the French law against restraint of trade (Article 419 of Napoleon's Code). In its original form, it penalized those who agreed, 'Not to sell, or to sell only at a fixed price.' In its revised form of 1926, it provided for the punishment of those who 'exercised any influence on the market for the purpose of acquiring profit other than that derived from the national operation of the law of supply and demand.' This law against restraint of trade was ill-adapted to solve the competitive problems of a modern society. Its principal result was to encourage evasion of the penalties by the concealment of cartel and other price-fixing arrangements; it was unable to control or bring to light the high degree of actual concentration and domination of the market.

All this was used between 1930 and 1936 by the Trade Unions and socialist parties to obtain the support of the middle-classes. The obscurity in which the leaders of industry directed the French economy made people inclined to believe that free competition had ceased; and whenever it seemed to exist, the parties concerned were merely staging a sham fight in order to conceal a general conspiracy. The scarcity of credit facilities for small and medium-sized enterprises was easily attributable to the strict conditions for discounting—conditions which could be met only by the bigger concerns. Here again an exception can be made of Louis Renault, who never went near the banks. Then why did he not let the public know?

If there were three 'Rights' in the French political arena at this time, there were a plethora of 'Lefts', Communist, Socialist, Independent, Independent Socialist, Radicals of all colours, endlessly merging and splitting like amoebae. Immediately after the armistice, these variegated left-wingers were convinced, like Simone de Beauvoir, that the capitalist system had been so weakened by the war and the destruction of the European economy that it would collapse of its own accord, without any outside assault. Like the Russian Bolsheviks, they believed that the proletarian revolution was at hand. In fact, through the centralized power obtained by industry during the war, and its need for 'vertical organization', capitalism emerged in 1918 if anything strengthened; and French management soon found it could retract most of the concessions made to labour during the war emergency. This was particularly easy because in 1920, in the true tradition of the French 'Left', the Trade Unions, instead of coalescing, split up into three mutually antagonistic groups: the Confédération Générale du Travail (the C.G.T., reformist in the constitutional sense); the Confédération Générale de Travail Unitaire (the C.G.T.U. the communist or revolutionary element); and the Confédération Française des Travailleurs Chrétiens (the C.F.T.C., whose title is self-explanatory). The French people after 1918 remained essentially what they had always been, industrious, thrifty, irreverent yet suspicious of innovation, verbally revolutionary but fundamentally conservative.

It is interesting to contrast the French type of labour organization and tactics with those in England and America. Whereas the methodical Anglo-Saxons constructed large centralized Labour organizations with relatively high individual dues, and substantial strike and other benefits, the French were content with loose, federalist organizations in which the individual retained full autonomy within the Union, the Union, in turn, full

autonomy within the Bourse du Travail, and the latter full autonomy within the C.G.T. The dues paid by the French worker have
always been a fraction of those paid by his English and American
counterparts, which means that his union cannot support a
strike for long. It is generally accepted in France that strikes are
spontaneous in origin and supported by voluntary subscriptions,
communal soup kitchens, and so on. The French worker has
always been irregular about paying even the low dues charged by
his unions; and any attempt to enforce discipline has generally
been followed by wholesale desertions. A British delegate to one
of the Congresses of the 1st International said that the French
delegates were always the first to raise their hands for some
revolutionary measure, but the last to put them in their pocket
when contributions were demanded.

After 1918, the 'Left' was distrustful of industry in general,
and of the capitalists of the *metallos* or metallurgical industries in
particular (among them automobile manufacturers). It contended
that during the war the special interests of these men had been
given precedence over efficient production and armaments at
low cost. They said that collusion between these capitalists and
the military leaders had prevented the bombing of the Briey
region in 1918, so as to preserve the French steelworks which had
fallen into German hands in the first weeks of the war. All these
words fell on fertile ground, for during the war and immediately
after it, a new type of non-specialist worker from the country or
small towns had been arriving in the big industrial centres. In
these people mass production had induced a kind of cynical
despair; and they offered a particularly fertile field for communist propaganda.

These sentiments lay dormant while France was relatively
prosperous throughout the twenties; but they exploded during
the economic crisis of the thirties, the Left denouncing what it
described as the 'economic oligarchies' and 'financial feudalism',
claiming that, through common stock-holding and other devices,
two hundred families held the key positions of French economy.
It provided details to reveal that fewer than one hundred and
fifty persons, most of them connected through birth or marriage,
held more than nineteen hundred seats in the primary industries,
coal, electricity, steel, oil, chemicals, railways, banking and
insurance. It alleged that the directors of the Banque de France

were all enlisted from the great banking and business families.[1]

Louis Renault, we have seen, would have nothing to do with anything of this sort. He disliked the Comité des Forges and his attitude towards the other big capitalists and bankers, his hatred of 'money made from money', should have endeared him to the communists. (For this perhaps they feared him even more; his novel methods might supplant their own.) The only blame that can be attached to him for the unhappy state of affairs is a negative one, in connection with a new organization called the Nouveaux Cahiers. This was a right-wing group prophetically aware of the dangers ahead, which attempted to awaken a civic sense in a business community that, confronted with the 'corrupt' Third Republic, had retreated into its shell; in short, to persuade businessmen to take an interest, if not a part, in politics, before it was too late. It included men like Dautry, later Minister of Armaments, and Detoeuf. The group was, however, actively and effectively opposed by a paradoxical alliance—certain stubbornly authoritarian big business leaders like Louis Renault, hostile to any voluntary reforms in industrial relations, and the socialists themselves, who characteristically saw in the Nouveaux Cahiers only a 'cunning tool of capitalism . . .'

This was short-sighted, for by 1933 the social and economic situation, not only in France but all over the world, was deteriorating rapidly. In Germany, England and the U.S.A. there were millions of unemployed. Bands of starving men marched on Washington, yet people were throwing cargoes of tea and coffee into the sea; in the U.S.A. deep south, they were burning cotton. The Dutch killed their cows and gave them to the pigs as fodder; while the Danes slaughtered one hundred thousand sucking pigs. Bankruptcies, economic scandals, suicides of businessmen and financiers filled the columns of the French newspapers.

After the Wall Street crash, the French were the last nation to be struck in Europe, but they hardly took advantage of the respite. The last affected, France was the last to come out of the 'great depression', in an atmosphere of violent social unrest and

---

[1] Just before the Second World War, as a sop to the Left, Léon Jouhaux, the Secretary-General of the Trade Unions, was made a member of the council of the Banque de France.

political dissension. The industrialists were soon dimissing workmen in thousands. There were two million unemployed. A wave of xenophobia, directed particularly against foreign workers, Poles and Italians, swept the country. Anti-democratic propaganda became more violent. The Croix de Feu movement gained ground daily with its mouthpiece the weekly paper *Candide*, from whose columns Colonel de la Roque noisily proclaimed his crypto-fascist programme. Carbuccia defended another form of fascism in *Gringoire* which, by the end of 1934, had a circulation of 650,000. Intellectuals like Drieu la Rochelle openly proclaimed their sympathy with Nazi Germany. As Léon Blum himself stated, everything in France suggested that the bourgeoisie 'was using up its sap'. The French bourgeois had once been upright and honest, patient and prudent, modest and decent, thrifty and reasonable. Now these upright and honest bourgeois were acquiring a reputation for tax evasion. He added that they carried their thrift and prudence to the point where they failed to keep French industry abreast of technological achievement. An exception to this was undoubtedly Louis Renault who never stopped urging modernization. But the remaining industries, textiles, metallurgy, paper, rubber, leather, lagged far behind their foreign equivalents.

2 | The Occupation of the Factories

'A new dawn arises. It shines with brilliancy which at last dispels our darkness. In its light we shall achieve our emancipation and liberate the world.'

Léon Jouhaux, Secretary-General of the French Trade Unions. May 1936

The Popular Front Government of 1936 was that unheard-of thing in modern France, left-wing unity—the communists, radicals and all shades of socialists coalescing. It did not last long, but while it did it struck terror into the industrialists, particularly because at one point the workers occupied all the factories, and locked up any of the owners who happened to be in them. Although it was headed by a most mild and intellectual man, M. Léon Blum, the factory owners saw behind him the shadow of the guillotine or the Soviet firing-squads. It came into being only two months after the outbreak of the Spanish Civil War, stories of whose communist atrocities were already arriving; and the French, as neighbours, felt that in some way the two events were connected.

There had been plenty of strikes since the war in France, but none on such a nation-wide scale. The two Trade Unions—the constitutional C.G.T., and the revolutionary or communist C.G.T.U.—had been continually at loggerheads. The latter had used any pretext for proclaiming a strike: insufficient wages, an eight-hour day, the abolition of night-work, a protest against a comrade being sacked (they had even at one point incited the waiters of Paris to strike for the right to wear moustaches). Their evident aim was to paralyse the economic life of the country and overthrow bourgeois rule. Their power had been limited, however, by the more numerous C.G.T., which deprecated violence. Now, however, these two Trade Unions came together.[1]

---

[1] See the pamphlet by J. Berlioz, *The Programme of the People's Front*. International Press correspondence, 18 January 1936.

Although in most countries the opinion of the intellectuals is pretty much ignored in politics, in France more weight is attached to it. Although French intellectuals may have little practical effect, they create a 'climate of opinion', and they are extremely noisy. So when the intellectuals also acclaimed this left-wing unity, the property-owning bourgeoisie had further cause for alarm. Simone de Beauvoir, a typical representative of the Left-wing intellectual circles, writes openly of her hope for a proletarian revolution She regarded the bourgeois as an enemy (she was one herself, of course), and she wanted their liquidation. She had great sympathy for the workers, because they had none of the bourgeois moral defects. There was something crudely fundamental about their physical contact with nature and its matter; they seemed to face the human condition in its true and naked form.

Only a short time before, left-wing unity had seemed as distant as ever, because the French communist party, faithful to Moscow, was still announcing that Léon Blum's programme was 'childish and Utopian' and that they would ignore him and fight on for their goal, 'a French Soviet Republic'. Naturally, when they suddenly joined Blum and his moderate socialists, the capitalists became alarmed.

The *volte face* as a feature of communist policy is familiar enough today; but before 1939 no one really understood it. For years, the French communist party had been instructed by Moscow that all social-democrats like Blum and the C.G.T. were traitors to the working-class, 'puppets of the bourgeoisie'. It had also assured them that the Nazi movement in Germany was a temporary phenomenon, from which there was little to fear. But now, in face of German rearmament, the leaders in Moscow suddenly changed their minds. They realized that the Nazis were not going to be overthrown by the expected German bourgeois governments, from which they had little to fear. In face of Hitler's threatening statements, they now wanted every ally they could lay hands on, and told the French comrades to form an anti-fascist front with the socialist parties. Stalin suddenly announced that he 'fully understood the French policy of national defence, to keep up its armed forces'. Before, every French soldier had been in his eyes an 'instrument of imperialist aggression'. The barrier which had separated the petit-bourgeois from the extreme socialist and communist parties suddenly fell. Newspapers of all shades published a profusion of benevolent reports about Stalin, Moscow and the powerful Red Army. The term 'Popular Front' was coined. But for all the employers knew it might simply have been a synonym for 'French Soviet Republic'.

The employers were partly to blame, it is true, for the present situation. Some of them had taken advantage of the unemployment after the 1931 crash to pay their workers low wages. They had often refused to discuss the situation with workers' delegations. Often too, they had refused quite unobjectionable demands, such as the installation of proper wash-rooms or blue-glass windows in the factories as protection against the sun. At the height of the mid-thirties' unemployment, when the workers were powerless, the Employers' Association, the C.G.P.F., blamed the situation on the social security system. Unemployment assistance, it said, abetted the idle; and it criticized the forty-eight-hour week as too short. Isolated in their offices, the employers appear to have been ignorant of the true state of affairs. In these depression years of monetary instability, they had their own problems, and were much concerned with credit difficulties and competition in a narrowing market; they had little time for worrying about the mentality or working conditions of the workers. Had they granted only a part of what was now asked, it is generally admitted that there would have been little bloodshed, no occupation of the factories, and they need have made no more than half the concessions finally granted.

In spite of this, the workers' bargaining position was still so weak that it required an outside event, the Stavisky affair, to set light to the tinder. When Stavisky was accused of embezzlement, he fled to Chamonix, where he committed suicide—or, as was alleged by the communists, he was murdered to prevent members of the Chautemps government, who had benefited with him, from being compromised. (Blum's government had not yet come to power.) This was the spark that converted the general discontent into a mass demonstration against the Government. Thousands of workers gathered in the Place de la Concorde and prepared to cross the bridge, announcing that they would occupy the Palais Bourbon and eject the corrupt Deputies. In the scuffles with the police, seventeen people were killed and 2,329 hurt. Then with tempers at their height came the communist-socialist coalition. Confident of their new-found unity, the workers now began a wave of strikes, the first being in the *metallos* or metallurgical industries.

It is ironical that the workers in the *metallos*, which included the motor-car industry, were the highest paid in France. At this time they earned 5 Frs an hour—whereas textile workers earned 2 Frs an hour. Yet they were always the most discontented and revolutionary. One explanation may be that the Trade Unions, anxious to ferment and prolong strikes, preferred working with richer groups because they could stand the strike longer. Another more logical explanation is that the motor-car industry, unlike most others, is seasonal. The big sales take place between February and June in preparation for the summer. So that generally, after September or October, some 20–30 per cent of the workers were 'laid off', and were on the streets for the winter. If this was on a human level reprehensible, it was also, on a purely profit level, of questionable value; because in the spring new teams had to be found and trained. But Louis Renault would not hear of a change in this practice. It had served him in the past, and it would continue to serve him in the future.

The strikes of 1936 incorporated a new and, to the employers, a sinister element—the occupation of the factories. This began in May, with the factories in Le Havre, Amiens and Toulouse being occupied by their personnel in a sit-down strike. Not much attention was paid by the Government or Press at the time. Then Hotchkiss went on strike in Paris; but it was not until the twenty-five thousand workers at Billancourt occupied the Renault works that the strike was taken seriously.[1] It soon spread all over France, embracing a wide variety of industries, from the big *metallos*, the textile and building trades, the stores and insurance companies, down to cafés and restaurants. Several million workmen were affected. At Billancourt, the Renault workers, after laying down their tools one evening, instead of

---

[1] These occupations were new at least in France. During the Russian revolution in 1918, the workers had occupied certain factories. The procedure was repeated later in Hungary, Bavaria, Poland and Italy, but on a very small scale. Its success in Poland even caused it to spread, in 1920, to England, to the miners at Nine Mile Point. The reason then given for the 'occupation' was that it prevented the 'blacklegs', or non-strikers, having access to the tools and machines.

going home, took up their quarters in the factory and announced that they would not leave until certain demands had been satisfied. As the days passed and no one evicted them (it was impossible for the police or the army to deal with all the factories of France), their demands increased. The days turned into weeks, and the good bourgeois of France were convinced that the 'Red Terror' had arrived, that soon the French Soviets would take over. In the first days they may have had some justification for thinking this, because the occupation, in Renault at least, took place in two parts. For the first three days, it was uncontrolled; the workers were disorganized, some got drunk, women were allowed in, and the atmosphere was generally riotous. Then suddenly the iron discipline of the communist party was imposed. An atmosphere of calm and quiet determination set in, accompanied by almost a feeling of *kermesse*, of a village fair. Normally, the word 'strike' implies, at least in France, barricades, arrests, bloodshed. But once these strikes were under way, they were in the words of M. Jean Coutrot, 'pacific and joyous'. The word 'occupation', he says, was incorrect. 'Installation' would have been better, because no factory was occupied from the outside; rather, the workers who remained when work was over 'installed' themselves—an action which was very different from that in Italy in 1920. There, the workmen were armed and tried to run the factories themselves. This showed that the French 'occupations' were not an attack on private property, for no attempt was made to take over the factories as a source of wealth or work them. All the strikers wanted were better conditions; and the newspapers' headlines, *'Graves incidents révolutionaires. Les usines sovietisées'* were unfounded. Hardly a disorderly act took place in the thousands of occupied plants; it was, as Herriot later remarked, a case of *'Restaurant ouvrier, cuisine bourgeoise'*.

The only condition the strike committees in each plant made was that all personnel had to stay in the factory, night and day; and guards were put at the gates to see that no blacklegs escaped. Some workers who managed to do so were followed in the street and forcibly escorted back. M. Griffon says that after a week he wished to see his family, and the only way he could escape was by climbing over the roofs and descending by a drain-pipe. When he found that all was well at home, he returned to the factory.

Any employer who happened to be in his office when the factory was occupied was politely but firmly told that he could not leave; he must sleep in the office, and food would be brought to him. It is not hard to imagine the frame of mind of these employers as the days passed, and they remained prisoners in their own factories. The thoughts of many must have gone back to 1789, when things had started in the same orderly manner. They remembered ruefully that Danton was replaced by Robespierre. Or perhaps they reflected on what had happened in Russia in 1918, after Kerensky had been deposed. If one of them wanted to leave the factory to visit his family on compassionate grounds, illness, and so on, he had to take his turn in the queue with his employees, explain his case, and obtain a pass from the strike committee.

Fortunately for Louis Renault, he was not in the factory when it was occupied. In any case, he had such a horror of the mob that he would have refused to discuss the slightest concession under duress. This was left to his nephew, François Lehideux who lived in the factory during the occupation and took part in all the subsequent negotiations. He and M. Griffon give a graphic picture of what it was like.

A notice was pinned on the main gate explaining the reasons for the strike, with beside it a box for contributions bearing the words, 'Today is the 12th day of the strike (or whatever day it was). Please help! Thank you!' Another notice announced the names of the members of the strike committee together with the various sub-committees for commissariat arrangements, dormitories, cleaning and upkeep, leisure, (to feed and sleep twenty-five thousand men required considerable organizational skill).[1] Leisure arrangements were important, because the strikers had nothing to do. Most of the time they played cards, *boules* or football in the courtyard, or chatted with their wives, who were allowed to visit them until 9 p.m. The women sat on the steps knitting and sewing, darning their husbands' socks. Music was provided by amateurs or gramophones, and sometimes in the evenings there was a dance. The popular song of the time, 'Madame la Marquise', was accompanied by accordions and some

---

[1] In the occupation of the big stores, e.g. Les Magasins du Louvre, the strikers slept on the counters.

horseplay. The only drink allowed was beer, and wine and spirits were forbidden. Sometimes a theatrical evening was improvised; and once they performed their own Grand Guignol, in which effigies of Louis Renault, François Lehideux and a hypothetical member of the Comité des Forges in a top-hat, were thrown into the Seine amid general hilarity. (It is significant that they readily identified Renault with the Comité des Forges, which he hated.) There were several political meetings and discussions, and once a Trade Union leader came down and addressed them, telling them what was happening in the other factories all over France. A feature which was later emphasized by the employers to explain their fears were the flags at the gate—the French tricolour intertwined with the hammer and sickle of the Soviets.

To feed this multitude, ex-army cooks among the staff were discovered, and food was brought in daily, much of it contributed free by well-wishers. Lunch cost 1 Fr; dinner was free. Vegetables were collected by a team in the neighbourhood, and the communist newspaper *L'Humanité* published a list of shopkeepers who refused to sell produce to the strikers. The image of the *Tricoteuses* in the shadow of the guillotine quickly caused these frightened bourgeois to sell their goods.

What surprised certain observers was the condition of the machine-shops themselves. Although the wheels were not turning, the plant was kept in perfect condition, oiled and polished daily. The floors were swept, improvised beds, mattresses and hammocks were rolled up during the day beside the work-benches. Precautions were taken against fire, and a man with a brassard on his arm was in charge of the petrol pumps, where he cried every five minutes, 'Comrades, smoking is strictly forbidden!' Whereupon a worker is said to have laughed, 'Why, he's as bad as the boss, that one! Talking about what is *strictly forbidden!*'

Each worker was on duty eight hours a day for three days, with the fourth day free. In this way, the factory was permanently under supervision by a quarter of the personnel. One of the most curious incidents concerned two devout Catholic workers who complained about being deprived of Communion. A priest was summoned to administer mass, which they and several others attended. This irritated some of the militant atheists, one of whom deliberately smashed a crucifix in the room where the service had been celebrated. His action was universally deplored, and a subscription list was opened for replacing the crucifix. The strike, incidentally, received support from an unexpected quarter, the Catholic Church. The Archbishop of Toulouse, Mgr. Saliège, congratulated the Jocistes (Jeunesse Ouvrière Chrétienne) on taking part. 'We believe that present social conditions cannot last,' he said. 'They are contaminated by the supremacy of money, which is devoid of all Christian spirit, and steeped in injustice and egoism.'

The strike at Renault was not entirely pacific, and there were one or two incidents in which the strikers showed their teeth. Some of them did not observe the safety rules on the Ile Séguin, and two were electrocuted. Naturally the administration was blamed, and the local communist Deputy, Coste, came over to remonstrate with Lehideux. The two men decided to address the strikers and recommend that the central electrical plant on the Ile Séguin should be put out of bounds. As they crossed the bridge to address the workers they were greeted with a hail of steel nuts and bolts. Lehideux went on to deliver his address, but when he looked round for Coste, the Deputy was nowhere to be seen. He had taken to his heels.

Louis Renault and other industrialists often referred afterwards to the 'illegality' of the occupations. Strictly, they were right, for Renault owned 98 per cent of the shares of the firm. Legally, the situation was no different from that of a private house invaded by strangers who lock up the owner in one room, and live for weeks in the others. To this legality Thorez, the communist leader, replied with his own. 'They call us illegal, do they? Well, we've created a new sort of legality. That's all there is to it.' This 'new legality' was also expressed by Alain Lambreaux in his *Georges Sorel à Mahatma Gandhi—Nouvelles réflexions sur la violence:* 'There is no more violence here than in the case of the Hindoo who lies in the road. An eye split open, a broken arm, a bloody wound, *this* is violence. But to take possession of what belongs to you by the sweat of your brow is not violence.' Renault had an undoubted right to bring an action for trespassing; but when the strike was settled by the Matignon Agreements, one of the conditions agreed to by the employers was that these legal rights would not be enforced.

A strike of this kind is particularly humiliating to the owner. A factory emptied by a strike is still under his control, but in a factory filled with idle workers he has lost his place. His very position seems questionable, which is perhaps worse than the temporary loss of profits. Some of the owners never overcame the shock of being humiliated by their workers. For nearly a month, Louis Renault could not set foot in his own factory. He later issued a proclamation to his workers condemning them for 'forsaking French methods and employing those of a foreign nation' (Russia presumably), and he had to be dissuaded from following the advice of one of his counsellors, Duvernoy, who wanted all the communists sacked on the spot. The test of a communist, Duvernoy suggested, would be to go through the pockets of workers for propaganda; anyone with a party card or copy of *L'Humanité* would be dismissed.

François Lehideux says that Renault was so depressed by the attitude of the workers, their misunderstanding, even hatred of the owners, that one night during the strike Renault telephoned him at the plant and asked him to come at once to see him. Lehideux obtained permission from the strike committee and went to the Avenue Foch, where he found Renault in a state of great excitement, brandishing a document which he handed Lehideux proclaiming his decision to retire and leave the running of the factory to Lehideux. Renault could not imagine—to quote Lehideux's own words—that he, 'a hard worker, a man devoted to his factory, and through it to the welfare of his workers, who had never taken a purely financial or selfish view of his activity, who never mixed in politics, who, unlike others, did not take money out of the plant, but invested and reinvested it in the firm—he could not imagine that he could be so misunderstood as to be treated like those who hid behind the screen of anonymous boards of directors.' Lehideux says he knew that this was done in the heat of the moment; he accepted the document, but handed it back to Renault when the strike was over. Louis Renault accepted it and never referred to the incident again.

The strike ended with the Matignon Agreements, when the representatives of the owners (Confédération Générale du Patronat) and those of the Trade Unions (Confédération Générale du Travail) met in the Rue de Varenne. There was little the owners could do and they had to accept every condition. The principal ones were: the forty-hour week; paid holidays; the recognition of collective agreements; full wages to the workers throughout the strike; no dismissals for striking. Left-wing intellectuals like Simone de Beauvoir were delighted. 'We welcomed the picketing of factories with great enthusiasm: workers and employees astonished us, not only by the courage and solid unanimity with which they acted, but also by their skilful tactics, discipline and cheerfulness. . . . The signing of the Matignon Agreement filled us with joy. . . . Stupidity, injustice, and exploitation were losing ground. . . .

'That summer the beaches and countryside had their first wave of vacations-with-pay visitors. Two weeks is not very long; but all the same, the workers of Saint-Ouen or Aubervilliers did get a change of air from their factories and suburbs.'[1]

Afterwards, Louis Renault discovered that his workers had 'behaved well', had cared for the machines and destroyed nothing. But he believed the restraint was only temporary, that after the Matignon Agreements worse was to come, another proletarian uprising which would destroy the rights of ownership altogether. To quote again from his bedside book, *Crowds: A Study of the Popular Mind*—he has underlined this passage, 'How many mobs have been led astray by beliefs, ideas and words they hardly understand. They go on strike less to obtain an increase in salary than to obey an order from some authority they admire. . . .'

It was only when, some months later, the victory of the Popular Front was seen to be temporary that the owners began to regain confidence, although some of them never overcame the shock of these events. On the whole, French management regarded Matignon as a capitulation. In the Chambre des Députés the right-wing Fernand-Laurent criticized the agreement as 'an inexcusable expression of imbecile cowardice by Management, which has capitulated to Labour in the face of threats'. Re-echoing Sorel, he said that if the bourgeoisie continued to show such weakness, they deserved to disappear. An ominous feature after the Matignon Agreements was the creation of a special group within the owners' organization, the Comité de Prévoyance et d'Action Sociale, which expressed admiration for foreign authoritarian and co-operative régimes. The fascist youth

---

[1] *Prime of Life.*

organizations were praised as setting a desirable example to France.[1]

To Anglo-Saxons, who have never really had to fear communism, it is perhaps difficult to understand how this occupation could have frightened the French middle-classes so greatly—particularly when the Red Terror turned out to be nothing more than, in the words of Alain Lambreaux, *la terreur rose*. But even balanced and sane journalists like Vladimir d'Ormesson, who had been repeating since Hitler came to power that Germany was the greatest danger to France, changed overnight after the occupation of the factories. In a pamphlet, *Le Communisme c'est la guerre*, he said that France should get rid of the Popular Front government and start a policy of 'an understanding with Germany which is both realistic and chivalrous'.

Statements like this naturally made people think the occupations were communist inspired; and Robert de Beauplan wrote in *L'Illustration* on 13 June 1935, 'Perhaps orders came from outside France. In many cases the workers laid down their tools without having made any previous demands for increased pay or other advantages. . . . The communist cells within the Trade Unions appear to have been very active and played a dominant part. . . . The way the strikes in various industries appear to have been carefully timed is also significant—methodically, as on a previously determined date for each of the industries. . . .'[2] François Lehideux, who was at the centre of the negotiations, says that the Minister of the Interior, Salangron, told him that the communists nearly attempted a *coup d'état* during the occupation; and they would have done so had not things been going so badly for their cause in Spain.

If the strikes were communist inspired, the communists were quick to call them off when their demands were met. Contrary to public belief, the communists generally know exactly how far they can go before taking the next step. When some of the Renault workers were disinclined to abandon their sit-down strike

---

[1] During the Munich crisis in 1938, the head of this group, M. Germain-Martin, was one of the most outspoken advocates of appeasement.

[2] Blum himself said during the Riom trial in 1942, 'We felt after some days that suspicious manoeuvring behind the scenes was attempting to change the character of the strike.'

after the Matignon Agreements, Thorez told them, 'The strike must stop because your demands have been met'.[1] To achieve this, he recommended them to show that they had called off the strike of their own accord, having yielded nothing to Louis Renault and the management, by massing behind the communist party vehicles and parading down the Champs Elysées.

So, in this eminently bourgeois part of Paris, the last act in one of the most unpleasant episodes of Renault's life consisted of thousands of his workers marching down the great Boulevard singing the 'International'. There was something equally sinister in the numerical membership of the communist party members in the Renault works before and after these 'occupations'. In 1936, of the 30,000 workers only 240 were party members; by 1938, the figure had grown to 3,200. These facts and figures can hardly have filled the owner with much confidence in the future.

---

[1] See the magazine *Etudes, Les Conflits de Juin,* 5 December 1936.

3 | Lost Opportunities

After the First World War France had thousands of small Renault tanks at her disposal, and she at first used them to good purpose. It was the tanks which kept the peace on the Rhine. When in January 1919 the Germans refused to sign the armistice, Foch simply ordered out the tanks; whereupon Germany signed in the Gallerie des Glaces. When later, over ratification, Germany jibbed at what she called a *Diktat*, Poincaré again called them out and occupied the Ruhr, the heart of industrial Germany. When trouble arose in the twenties in France's overseas territories, Tunisia, Morocco, Syria, Indochina, they were again used effectively. In view of their remarkable success, all nations, great and small, wanted the Renault light tanks. They were bought by Poland, Jugoslavia, Japan, Rumania, Czechoslovakia, Greece, Spain, Brazil, China, Manchuria. Using Renault tanks in 1927, the Japanese successfully attacked Shanghai.

All this took place in the twenties before the League of Nations made its fateful distinction between 'defensive' and 'aggressive' weapons. The former were considered to represent peace; the latter, including the tank, were regarded as bellicose. In accordance with international feelings, therefore, the victorious nations scrapped them. Renault saw the weapons he had forged, and which had kept France powerful, and Europe at peace, turned overnight into pig-iron. It is ironical that at the first Geneva conference on disarmament, it was the Germans who demanded the total suppression of tanks. In 1933, when Germany had her new master, she noisily left the League and within a few months was displaying the tanks she had been secretly constructing in monster parades and marchpasts.

Renault, the biggest tank constructor in Europe, had watched all this happening. Can he be blamed for the view he took of the politicians? Seldom in the history of Europe have political affairs been so disastrously conducted as in the thirties by, broadly speaking, two classes of men, fools and criminals, the first west, the second east, of the Rhine. On the western side were the Simons, Daladiers, Halifaxes, Chamberlains, Flandins; while on the other, were a band of gangsters who had mysteriously been allowed to enlist an entire nation to carry out their plans. International affairs now moved forward to their climax with sickening speed.

We have seen that in 1936 the Russian communists, faced by the growing German danger, did a swift turn-about, and instructed the French Communist Party to co-operate with the Social Democrats in a Popular Front. But although the Popular Front achieved some reforms, it did not help the cause of peace, because it frightened the employers into regarding the fascist powers more favourably, or at least as a lesser evil, than the 'Red Terror'.[1] During the Popular Front government, Hitler announced grandiloquently what he was doing for Europe against the Red Terror. His comment on the Popular Front was, 'I have warned Europe. I tremble for France.' This was seen by the French 'Right' as a sign of his goodwill towards France. Meanwhile true to the French 'Left' tradition, the Popular Front government had disintegrated, and the left parties were back again in the old antagonistic splinter groups.

It was now that Moscow, seeing no hope of an anti-German front in the West, began the secret negotiations with Germany which were to culminate in the German-Soviet pact of August 1939. The command went out from the Kremlin to the French Communist Party for another 'about turn', a return to the old tactics of undermining the French bourgeois governments. The best field for this sabotage was industry, particularly the *metallos* factories. So Louis Renault found himself once again, as during the occupation of the factories, unwillingly in the centre of the political stage.

---

[1] After the Popular Front came to power, some French conservatives who had criticized the Third Republic, looked back almost with nostalgia to its bourgeois governments, and to one of its last ministers who had seemed passable, Pierre Laval. In this way, he became one of the hopes of the ruling classes. Because this class hated Stalin's Russia and genuflected before Italian fascism, they approved of Laval's sentimental ideas about *la soeur latine*.

The Matignon Agreements, far from satisfying the demands of the workers, seemed only to have multiplied them. Between 1936 and 1938 strikes occurred almost weekly throughout the country, most of them communist inspired. Lehideux, who was one of the representatives dealing with the automobile industry, and to whom one might suppose the workers would have been grateful, was rewarded with hundreds of threatening anonymous letters. And for the next year and a half, Coste made dozens of inflammatory speeches against the Renault management, some at the very gates of the factory.

The occupation of the factories in 1936 had been carried out exclusively by Renault personnel. Now, a more sinister and extraneous element was introduced into the strikes. When a workman was killed in an industrial accident, the whole of Renault went on strike, as a protest 'against the negligence of the owners'; and all the workers attended the funeral. The factory was occupied and picketed during this time by men who came from as far away as Vincennes and other working-class districts of Paris. The atmosphere was quite different. If in 1936 it had exhaled something of a popular *kermesse*, it was now charged with hate. To demonstrate against the Munich agreement of 1938, the workers of Paris went on strike when the English statesmen Chamberlain and Halifax made an official visit in November and were entertained to a gala performance at the opera. The factories were occupied again—as before at Renault, partly by non-Renault workers—and a feeling bordering on civil war filled the air.

So serious was this, in view of the deteriorating international situation, that the Daladier Government decided to act. A force of six thousand police and gardes mobiles was sent down to the Renault plant, where the workers had barricaded themselves in. What was now virtually a battle, with revolver shots and tear gas, took place. From the windows the workers threw bottles of sulphuric acid at the forces of order, and one of the gardes mobiles lost an eye. (In the middle of this the Mayor of Billancourt, who had been at the Chamberlain-Halifax reception, arrived, still wearing his ceremonial dress.) The police used a battering ram on the back of a lorry to break down the wall of the building occupied by the workers, making a hole through which they pumped tear gas. This put an end to the resistance and by 10 p.m. the

151

strike was over. But the wave of arrests which followed did not augur well for the future.

Renault himself reacted most vigorously this time, sacking some two and a half thousand workers who were regarded as communists. Temporarily, the harsh measures seemed to have a beneficial effect and the situation improved. Whereupon Renault, who had spent as little time as possible at the factory during the strike, attempted to double the dismissals, and he even had to be restrained from breaking the Matignon Agreements. He was now receiving big government defence orders, to which the workers, following Moscow instructions, responded by calling him 'the bloody merchant of death', 'imperialist war-monger', and so on. From now until 1944, the communist party regularly issued clandestine tracts about the 'unjust Renault dismissals', repeating the old pun about *le saigneur de Billancourt.*

It seems that in the last years of the thirties, Louis Renault deliberately ignored the dangers ahead. Although physically in excellent health, he had recently begun to suffer from a speech impediment which gave, quite wrongly, the impression of a certain slowing of the mind. Together with this went the stubborn refusal to listen to advice, characteristic of a man who had always relied only on his own judgement. Here, in the domain of politics into which he was being drawn, and for which he was singularly ill-equipped, he needed the best advice. Yet when it was offered, he refused it. After Matignon his nephew, François Lehideux, who had negotiated with the workers and understood something of their mentality, suggested that the time was past for one man to have absolute control of so big a firm. Socially and politically, the reign of Louis XIV was over; the era of constitutional monarchy had arrived. He pointed out that should Renault's son, Jean-Louis, who was now reaching maturity, inherit the business, he could hardly run it on his own. The firm needed to reinforce its staff, especially with men having powerful and political contacts, who could help in solving the social and political problems ahead. What was needed, in his view, was a new way of handling employment problems, the administrative staff, the workers, their insurance, their participation through delegates in certain activities of the firm; at the same time, an image of M. Renault must be produced which showed him as fully aware that the welfare of thousands of workers and their families depended on him.[1]

Lehideux also believed that the structure of the company should be modified, by allowing loyal collaborators to become shareholders, and at the same time associating more closely, both financially and technically, with other powerful industrial concerns. He proposed therefore two things: firstly that Louis Renault should sell on favourable terms a proportion of Renault shares, about 10 to 15 per cent, to members of the company, workers as well as administrators who had been at least ten years on the pay-roll. If they later wished to sell their shares they must do so to other workers who would be eligible; and secondly, that Louis should negotiate with an American automobile company for an exchange of shares, the Americans to take a further 10 to 15 per cent of Renault shares, in return for which Louis would receive the corresponding value in the American company, the exchange being completed by agreements on exchange of techniques, and commercial undertakings for selling on each market the products of both companies. In fact, Lehideux, who had learnt a shar lesson from Matignon, had already sounded one of the big three American automobile manufacturers about this possibility.

To these suggestions Renault gave a point-blank refusal. He had never been, he said, at the beck and call of a flock of ignorant shareholders. Nor did he want to become involved in foreign entanglements. He reproached Lehideux with 'giving in to the workers' during the Matignon negotiations and even accused him of plotting behind his back to take over the firm. From this moment, relations between uncle and nephew began to deteriorate. Louis Renault assumed firmer control of a firm whose direction he had, at one point, appeared to be handing over, at least partially, to his eventual heirs. That he still lived, mentally, in the old days when he had founded the firm, was further illustrated by his

---

[1] Renault paid higher salaries than any other French industrialist; the latter obviously disapproved of this, because he attracted away their workers. It was the same in his private affairs; his valet, M. Clément Pouns, states that at Christmas he gave all the household staff, if he was satisfied with their work, presents which often represented two or three months of their annual salary.

attitude to the large debts incurred during the occupation of the factory by the workers. All the big French firms were in debt, because for weeks no goods had been produced and yet the workers had to be paid while on strike (one of the Matignon conditions). Other firms solved the problem in the modern way, using the credit facilities offered by the banks. But such was the healthy state of Renault's plant and economy, his ability to return immediately to full output, and the confidence his clients had in him, that he could still avoid the hateful step. He survived the strikes without having to borrow a sou. Once again the old system worked. But for how much longer?

Meanwhile, with the German danger increasing daily the problem was to turn a large part of the factory over to war economy. As early as 1927, a bill had been introduced in Parliament by the far-sighted Deputy Paul Boncour for organizing the nation and its industries in event of war, providing for broad powers of government requisition and direction. But the country was then in its most pacifist phase, and it was ignored. At Geneva, all the nations were arguing that if only armaments were destroyed there could never be another war. Moreover, neither employers nor workers approved of Paul Boncour's bill. The communists said it aimed at subjugating the workers; while the big industrialists like Renault disapproved of its governmental controls. It was finally dropped.[1] Now, in the present crucial situation, it had to be resurrected. Much against his will, Renault had to start making tanks again.

As early as 1934, Weygand, then chief of the General Staff, had consulted Renault about a *low* tank, easily concealable and manoeuvrable in close country. Here, the constructor of the light tank of 1918 had shown his old inventiveness. He had designed a low vehicle with caterpillar tracks for two men, who had to lie prone, one at the controls, the other with a machine-gun or light cannon. It could move and turn with the ease of an ordinary car, and had a maximum speed of 50 miles per hour. It could be produced like a tourist car on the Ile Séguin assembly-lines.

---

[1] Even when much later, Blum wanted to spend money on rearmament, certain right-wing political groups objected. They preferred the dictator across the Rhine to the defence of the republic under the Popular Front.

But the credits were not then available, and the programme of the military experts did not include this kind of weapon.[1]

Even in 1939, M. Raoul Dautry, the Minister of Armaments, found it difficult to turn the bigger industrialists to war production. He later attributed their apathy to 'excessive taxing of war profits', adding, 'Many industrialists who did a great deal for their country in the 1914–18 war appear prevented today for political reasons from showing the same enthusiasm.' These 'political reasons' were undoubtedly the result of Matignon; many industrialists, Renault among them, had little faith in a government which might at any moment 'produce another Matignon'. That Renault was no longer the man of 1918 might be read in his face. It was deeply lined, 'as with one of his own engraving tools,' said a contemporary, and a strange light burned in his eyes. It was the face of an utterly wearied man, confronted by a situation which he regarded as no more than a repetition of 1914–18. He had had enough of war.

He became further suspect among the communists and socialists by a visit to Berlin in 1938 to the automobile *salon*. He went purely on business but he spoke to Adolf Hitler. Contrary to later allegations, he did not admire the German dictator, but he wanted to see the new German Volkswagen, hoping to incorporate some of its features in his own new small car, the Juvastella. (He admitted later that had there been no war, he would have taken the best ideas from Germany and developed them, just as he had years before developed those from America.) He certainly admired German industrial efficiency, and wanted to see the *Autobahnen*, which did not exist in France. After Hitler had opened proceedings with his usual harangue, he visited the stands and spoke to Renault, through an interpreter. Renault made some remark about Franco-German friendship and his hope that there would not be a war between their two countries again. Whereupon Hitler is reported to have replied, 'If there's so much talk of war today, it's the fault of your French journalists. They always have that word at the end of their pens.'

Renault undoubtedly shared something of the general attitude

---

[1] It was not until June 1940, with the Germans pouring into France, that Weygand, again chief of the General Staff, asked Renault if he could produce it. But then it was too late.

of the French industrialists towards Hitler. They did not realize
that he was exploiting their anti-communism to conceal his
immediate goals, the British and French empires, which he
regarded as rich and vulnerable. Nor did most of them realize
that if he left a certain autonomy in Germany to the old governing classes, he would be unlikely to do so in any conquered
territories.

During these last years before the war, the horizon was further
darkened for Louis Renault by something over which he had no
control. His wife became a close friend of Drieu la Rochelle.

Drieu la Rochelle was much admired in France between the
two wars. Tall, good-looking, of great physical courage (he had
been wounded several times in the First World War), he had
something to offer which Louis Renault, who was always uncomfortable in the presence of intellectuals, did not possess. To a
beautiful, intelligent woman Renault could, in purely worldly
terms, offer only two things—money and the prestige of an industrialist. Christiane Renault was a restless woman, always in
search of something new, some imagined perfection, which she
was always on the point of obtaining. In Drieu la Rochelle she
found the 'spiritual' element which her husband lacked.

The plebeian name of Drieu had been gilded in Napoleonic
times by a great-grandfather who had done well under the
Empire; he had simply attached 'la Rochelle' to it. Drieu la
Rochelle had written some twenty books which were widely
acclaimed in intellectual circles (although Montherlant has
described him as 'too interested in politics and social life, instead
of getting on with writing'). Like so many disillusioned soldiers of
the First World War, he was easily attracted by fascism, announcing, perhaps partly in reaction to his own bourgeois back-
ground, grandiloquently in a speech he made in Germany, 'I long
for the triumph of the Totalitarian man. The days of the Divided
man [i.e. of the Third Republic and its political parties] is over;
the day of the Unified man approaches . . .' He wanted, he said,
'to ally elements of Left and Right, to create a revolutionary anti-
Parliamentary movement in France'. In 1934 he met Otto
Abetz (who became Hitler's ambassador to France during the
occupation), and Abetz persuaded him to go to Germany and
lecture on Franco-German friendship. 'In spite of her Latin

origins, France possesses many Germanic elements,' said Drieu in one of these speeches. There was nothing wrong in this, (de Gaulle has said the same thing in our own time) but he now became rabidly pro-Nazi. In September 1935, he was at the Nürnberg rally. 'It was marvellous and terrible,' he wrote. 'France cannot remain aloof beside this new Europe . . . the parade of the troops all in black was superb . . . I have never seen anything like it since the Ballets Russes; these people are drunk with music and movement.' In 1936 he joined Doriot's Parti Populaire Français, the anti-semitic fascist party, and he went to Spain to fight for Franco.

The war led him into active collaboration with the Germans and for a time he edited the pro-Axis *Nouvelle Revue Française* and *Les Dernières Nouvelles*. He could hardly expect much mercy from the victors in 1945, because he had written during the war about de Gaulle, 'even more than in 1919 and 1939, the France de Gaulle will give us, if the Western allies win, will be one of chefs, café-owners, hotel-keepers and prostitutes. It will be what Mussolini has refused to let Italy become—a seaside museum-cum-brothel for Anglo-Saxon tourists.' In early 1945 when the warrant went out for his arrest, he declared, 'I want to die at the front—either with a Scottish regiment or with the S.S.' After several attempts at suicide, he succeeded on 16 March 1945.

His admiration for Christiane Renault was sincere. 'This woman,' he wrote, 'is all the Grecian goddesses—unfailing as Venus, faithful and inaccessible as Diana, reasonable and war-like as Minerva.' He told her that her husband, Louis Renault, resembled the frog in the la Fontaine fable who wished to inflate himself to the size of the American cow.

It seems certain that his short novel *Bélouika* is about Christiane Renault; in it he describes the love of Hassib, poet of Baghdad, for Belouika, the wife of a rich and powerful prince. Friendship between his wife and such a man could hardly help Louis Renault if, at some future point in his career, he fell foul of the communists.

4 | **1939-40**

France entered the wars of 1914 and 1939 in two entirely different states of mind, as well as with different conceptions of what lay ahead. In 1914, the confident cry was, '*A Berlin!*'—an entry in the best Napoleonic style, with drums and trumpets, the dismantling of the statue of Bismark, and hoisting of the tricolour over the Brandenburg Gate. It was to be a short war, and preparations for industrial mobilization were almost entirely lacking. In 1939, on the other hand, there were no chauvinist cries about Berlin and the Brandenburg Gate; but long before orders had gone out to the manufacturers for shells, tanks and aeroplanes; and few politicians or soldiers thought the war would be short. On 3 September, the factories of the entire country emptied almost overnight; three million men were put on the frontier. Nevertheless, according to General de Gaulle, France was not fit for war. In his autobiography[1] he writes, 'The interval of twenty years between the end of the first and the start of the second war had not been long enough for us to recoup our lost wealth. In particular, the accumulated capital the French possessed in France and abroad before 1914 had evaporated, while the 500 million shells we fired from the Somme to the Vosges exploded over a period of fifty-one months. . . . In 1939, it was a poverty-stricken, outmoded France that entered the conflict. . . .'

The country was far from united as it had been in 1914. Many people said they refused 'to die for Danzig'. Others simply refused to recognize war as a possibility. Alain said in his *Propos*, 'to believe in the existence of war is to consent to it'. While Jean-Paul Sartre said on 2 November 1939 that there would be no fighting, that this would be a modern war, 'without massacre, just as modern painting is without subject, modern music without melody, and modern physics without matter'. (How pleased Hitler would have been if he could have read these remarks!) Giono, Déat and Alain signed a manifesto demanding 'immediate

---

[1] Vol. III of his Memoirs. Simon and Schuster, 1960.

peace' (27 October 1939), the last claiming later that he had not read it properly—'Having seen the word *peace*, I signed without reading the text.' Why worry? Mistinguett was still in full cry at the Casino de Paris; Charles Trenet was singing 'Y d'la joie' and everyone was dancing the Lambeth Walk.

As for the politicians, some believed in a defensive war based on the Maginot Line; others wanted an immediate war of movement through the Low Countries. There were arguments as to whether the infantry should go in front of the tank, or the tank in front of the infantry. The general policy appears to have been 'Defence will always beat attack', which was the exact reverse of the one adopted in 1914. There was to be no more blood-letting as in the insane, frontal attacks of the First World War. 'In the long run, we are the stronger,' was the maxim, 'once the British and French empires are properly organized. All we have to do is to sit tight while weakening Germany by sea and air blockade.' Then, and only then, would the Allied forces take the offensive, against an already beaten foe. Ignoring the advice of tacticians like de Gaulle and moralists like Jean Prévost (who said 'the old instinct of defensive arms will bring about the same disaster as at Crécy and Agincourt'), the governments of the Third Republic decided to rely on the Maginot Line.

There was equal confusion in the automobile field. We have seen that in the first war the French had developed a military vehicle for hauling heavy guns and supply purposes, even eliciting the praise of General Ludendorff for it. But the lesson had been forgotten in the inter-war period. Between 1934 and 1938 the Germans produced 264,000 military vehicles, to France's 110,000 (and the Germans in 1940 invaded northern France along the roads). Paul-Marie Pons in his article on the French automobile industry between the wars in *Cahiers Politiques* (1945) explained why French car production had fallen, compared with that in the U.S.A., Great Britain and Germany. France, he said, tried to produce too many models. In 1939, the French were producing 4·2 different types per manufacturer; the English 3·2, and the Americans 2·3; and yet France had the smallest population of these countries. 'Every manufacturer,' he said, 'had to follow the disastrous custom of producing a new model for each annual *salon*. This meant that the tools and machinery, which had to be changed at the same time to produce the new model, were hastily adapted and indifferent. France had still not realized that her automobile industry must concentrate on a limited number of models, or perish. Instead of quantity, which was essential for war, she preferred peace-time variety.'

Dautry, the Minister of Armaments at the beginning of the war, found the industrialists' patriotism much diminished. He admitted later that when he took office certain politicians were granting favours to their business friends engaged in war production, preferably to the most 'anti-Republican' among them (another way of saying to the 'least anti-German'). Louis Renault did not, of course, come into this category; he was scrupulously honest in such matters. His lack of enthusiasm for the war came from other motives, first of which was that he had already, between 1914 and 1918, given his best in a war against the Germans. Interested only in civilian vehicles, he believed that war production in the First World War had been the primary cause of the decay in the French car industry after 1918. If this was to be repeated in 1939, while America concentrated on civilian vehicles, the French motor-car industry would be forced out of the world's peacetime markets. He had seen the destruction of his country in the first war, and had fought the commercial battle after to rebuild and make her capable of competing in the world automobile market. Now, it appeared, the whole process was to be repeated.

Dautry and Renault had something in common in that both objected to State interference in private affairs. In 1936, when the French railways were nationalized, Dautry had resigned his post at the head of a railway company. He had joined a private electrical firm, through which he had business dealings with Renault whom he greatly admired. It was ironical, therefore, that in 1939 he should be in a position to bring governmental pressure to bear on Renault.

His position was not easy. In the months before the war, in spite of the Matignon Agreements, there had been further deterioration in the relations between Trade Unions and management. In October 1939, a month after the declaration of war, he brought the representatives of the two sides together again—this time at the Majestic Hotel—where he exhorted them on patriotic grounds to come to terms, if only for the duration of the war. The Trade Unions heeded his call and offered temporarily to forget the differences; but the management would not. Paul Ramadier, the Labour Minister, said bitterly of the employers, 'In the Majestic agreements, the employers saw Labour's offer to collaborate only as a confession of weakness.' The owners, in fact, hoped to take advantage of Labour's conciliatory attitude as a revenge for the indignities they had suffered at Matignon. Some of them (the men who in 1941 applauded Vichy's disbanding of the Unions) even hoped to dispense with traditional Trade Unions altogether. Management stood discredited, therefore, at the outbreak of the war. And here, the attitude of Louis Renault hardly differed from that of his peers.

Certain of his actions in the first months of the war have been attributed to the strain he was under while converting a great industrial concern to war production. In dealing with any purely technical problem, his mind appears to have been as clear as ever; but not when the reasons, political or military, for any change in production were explained to him. That he was unaware of the seriousness of the situation, or perhaps deliberately unmindful of it, is shown by his suggestion that his Le Mans factory should be turned over entirely to war production ('The military can do their tomfooleries there to their heart's content'), while Billancourt should continue civilian production, in particular with the new Juvastella 40 on which he had set his heart. When his nephew, François Lehideux, still a relatively young man, was called to the colours, he reproached him as if he were a deserter—'a traitor to the factory,' he said.

With this attitude in the management, it is hardly surprising that Renault's war production flagged. When Dautry criticized delays, Renault complained, 'The Government asks me for everything, but does nothing to give me what I need.' On 8 November 1939, he wrote to Daladier, the Prime Minister, 'In a matter of days, mobilization depleted my 32,500 workers by 50 per cent. What remain are the older and less productive, including 4,000 women. I explained this to you in my letter of 21 September, in which I asked for the return of some of my best technicians. Steps to this end have, I know, been taken, but we are still far from the desired state of affairs. I would like to discuss the matter with you personally. I can come any time that is convenient to you.'[1]

---

[1] Quoted in *La Vie de Louis Renault* by J. Boulogne.

He received no reply to this letter.

Meanwhile François Lehideux, who had spent a few months with his unit at the front, was suddenly summoned to Paris by Dautry. He arrived on a Sunday morning in December, to find the Minister for Armaments in his office alone (the country was at war, but the staff still kept a forty-eight-hour week). Dautry explained that the Government was not satisfied with Renault's production. Louis Renault, he said, appeared more interested in producing a small family car, for which he was diverting material allotted to war production. He therefore wanted Lehideux to return to the factory and help his uncle. Lehideux at first demurred; he pointed out the effect on factory and public opinion if a young and active man appeared to take advantage of family connections to avoid military service. But Dautry was adamant. He insisted, and added that Lehideux would be helped by a special representative of the Government, to whom a report of work daily completed would be rendered every morning. This man was no less a person than Rochette, ex-director of the Skoda works in Czechoslovakia, who had fled to France when Hitler occupied his country.

The next day Dautry and Lehideux went down to the factory for a general meeting, at which Louis Renault and the departmental heads were present. Dautry made a speech which began with a tribute to Louis Renault and what he had done for his country in the First World War, as well as during nearly forty years of peace. He spoke of the extraordinary achievement in building up the factory before the First World War, of the famous light tanks, followed by Renault's well-merited *Légion d'Honneur*, the struggle for markets after the war, and so on. Then his tone changed. The same could not be said of the present circumstances. Billancourt was not producing enough for the war effort; deliveries were late; there was no feeling of urgency. As a member of the Government, he was well informed about the enemy, and he described Hitler's 'total war' in Poland. He spoke of the lightning campaign which had been won by tanks, and said it would not be long before France faced the same onslaught. He did not spare Renault's feelings, and spoke of 'inadequate management'.

Louis Renault sat listening to all this, in his own boardroom, surrounded by his staff who had never in their lives heard anyone criticize him to his face. In peacetime, he would have sent the impudent minister back where he came from. Today, things were evidently different. He was informed that Lehideux was returning and then—greatest blow of all to his pride—that Rochette, famous in his own line of business, would supervise, as 'the Government's special representative'. The errant French schoolboy was to be put in the charge of a Czech prefect!

When Rochette arrived a few days later at the factory, he brought with him his credentials from the Minister of Armaments: 'You are hereby empowered to give in my name all orders concerning priorities and the way in which production is to be organized. You will see that all the resources of the factory are fully exploited. You will keep me informed of everything under discussion. You will be assisted in this task by Lieut. François Lehideux, whose special function will be to maintain a permanent liaison between you and M. Renault.'

Louis Renault reacted to this characteristically: 'Ah, so they couldn't nationalize me with the Popular Front! Now they're trying to do it with State dictatorship.' What particularly offended him was that, whereas in 1914 he had been *asked* to produce for the State, now he was *ordered* to do so. His attitude towards Lehideux also became peculiarly ambivalent. When Lehideux requested again to return to his mobilized cavalry unit Renault asked him to stay 'because he knew the plant, and was a member of the family'. On the other hand, he became obsessed with the notion that his nephew was trying to supplant him and take over the firm. 'François Lehideux,' he wrote to a friend, 'is one of those technocrats who want to run the war by purchasing civilian vehicles in the United States, and turning Renault over entirely to war production. When peace returns, the U.S.A. will be ten times more powerful than today, and will inundate France with her products. France will be incapable of competing owing to her factories having been worn out by war production. M. Lehideux supports the cause of international finance. M. Renault supports the cause of France.'[1] Here again his mind was still thinking primarily in terms of peace production. It was clear to him that François Lehideux, having failed to bring in 'international finance' in the shape of an American association, was

---

[1] Quoted in *La Vie de Louis Renault* by J. Boulogne.

now trying to gain possession of the factory through 'State dictatorship'.[1]

In face of Dautry's attack, Renault defended himself valiantly; all the old fire returned. He wrote another letter to Daladier in which he said that in the 1914–18 war the Government had at least left private enterprise quite free to produce what was required. How was it possible to work when the Government interfered at every turn, when a bureaucrat was placed above the head of the firm? The letter ended pathetically 'Surely the best proof of my public spirit is my work for the country between 1914 and 1918.'

The Government's reply to this was to tell him that he had been selected to represent his country on a purchasing mission in the United States; he was to see President Roosevelt himself and explain the urgent need for war material. This may have been Dautry's way of removing him, while Rochette and Lehideux put the factory into full war production. Louis Renault again suspected that François Lehideux was behind this move, an attempt to get him out of the country and eliminate him. He replied that he would go to America only if his wife and son were allowed to accompany him; this was an unwise stipulation, because his son, aged twenty, had just been called up for military service, and this savoured of nepotism. He also insisted that during his absence he must have a man in the firm whom he trusted implicitly. This was M. Jean Louis, who had worked with him for many years in the Renault firm (now director of the French branch of Babcock and Wilcox).

In spite of these antagonisms, during the first months of 1940, the three of them, Renault, Lehideux and Rochette increased production. By March 1940, the mass production of the huge 150 hp B. I tanks was under way. They were turning out one a day, together with dozens of armoured cars, some thirty tracked vehicles a day, hundreds of trucks and lorries, and thousands of mines. Billancourt was at last in full production. In early May 1940, Pétain, who had just become a minister in the Reynaud

---

[1] François Lehideux was later informed by General Weygand that Louis Renault had told him of this incident. 'My nephew is trying to sell me to the bankers,' he had said.

Government, visited the factory and congratulated it on behalf of the Government, and it was *citée a l'ordre de la nation.*

That the industrialists of France, who were later blamed for the lack of material in the battles of 1940, were not alone responsible is revealed by the inept behaviour of the military authorities at this point. The Renault mounted machine-gun carrier was now being turned out in hundreds weekly; but because it lacked a small aerial at the rear the army refused to accept it. These vehicles therefore piled up on the quays and roads around Billancourt in thousands. When the Germans bombed Paris on 10 May, these vehicles had still not been accepted by the army, and it was decided hastily to use factory personnel to drive them to Cercotte near Orléans for safety. It was too late. Before these belated plans could be carried out the German Army had arrived and took possession of the lot, some six and a half thousand excellent machine-gun carriers which later saw action on the plains of Russia.

Renault's American trip was doomed from the start. It was unfortunate that it took place after the German attack, because the rumour quickly went round the factory and Paris that Renault was fleeing in face of the enemy, with his family and fortune. Travelling by clipper from Portugal with M. Guillelmon, one of his closest associates, he did not arrive in America until 2 June, when the Germans were already on the Marne. He saw Morgenthau and Roosevelt, but any talk of American tanks arriving by the end of the year was now hypothetical. There was to be no second Marne, no defence in depth in the 'Brittany redoubt', no retreat to North Africa. France had collapsed almost before the discussions began. M. Guillelmon says that apart from much sympathy and understanding for the French plight, the only remark of any interest that Roosevelt made to Renault was 'We [the U.S.A.] are slowly drifting into war.' This was small consolation to a Frenchman who wanted them to drift *quickly* into war.

Renault returned three weeks later, not empty-handed—America had promised much—but too late. When he arrived in Lisbon, the armistice had been signed and France was divided into two zones. He had to wait nearly a month for permission to enter the occupied part and visit his own factory.

5 | Collaboration

'I am much disquieted by news that France is putting all her resources at the disposition of Germany, to a degree not demanded by the Armistice.'

Letter from President Roosevelt to Admiral Leahy, appointing him ambassador to Vichy, 20 December 1940

'With one or two notable exceptions, the aristocracy and *haute bourgeoisie* gave full support to the régime installed after the defeat. They thereby abdicated from the social direction of the country, for which they had always considered themselves particularly qualified—giving the lie to their claim that their patriotism was more enlightened than that of others.'

From Pétain et le Pétainisme, The Marquis d'Argenson

Partly as a result of the return of Alsace-Lorraine in 1919, partly because of the development of new industries based on its iron ore and aluminium, France had grown into a big industrial country in the twenty years between the wars; its potash, bauxite and textile manufactures had greatly developed. But the French domestic market was still relatively small. In order, therefore, to dispose of their surplus, French industrialists entered international combines and became partners in almost every European cartel. The contrast between the natural wealth of the country and its demographic weakness affected the thinking of the businessmen. These very men, in fact, whom the communists called 'warmongers' became the staunchest supporters of European collaboration, of a 'continental order' for trade. Before the Second World War, daily contact with their German colleagues and admiration for German output and efficiency persuaded them to regard a Europe unified under German economic leadership favourably, and to look forward to the resulting opportunities for developing backward countries, particularly the Balkans and western Russia.

After the defeat of 1940, the motto of these industrialists was therefore 'business as usual'; to preserve the economic wealth of the country seemed the justification for collaborating with the victor. If France was to play any part after the war, so they argued, she must maintain her production, and this required German permission (the assumption being of course that Germany would soon defeat Britain). There were, as the Marquis d'Argenson, who castigates his own class so thoroughly, admits, exceptions among the businessmen, particularly in the O.C.M. (Organisation Civile et Militaire) resistance group, the underground movement which contained members of the management class.[1] But generally, in all the main fields of industry there was frank and fruitful collaboration. A typical example was that of M. Cognac-Jay, head of the Magasin de la Samaritaine who collaborated only because he considered he had been harshly treated by the workers during the wave of strikes just before the war. His business had been seriously affected, and he believed the only way to avoid a communist *coup d'état* was through some form of fascism. Already in the 1920s industrialists like François Coty had led a campaign in his paper *L'ami du peuple* against parliamentary methods, and supported those which were more or less inspired by fascism. When Mussolini, who had shown that he could suppress such disorders, roundly abused France and 'the turpitude of the Third Republic', such men could only agree. There were cases during the German occupation in which these employers got rid of possible communists or difficult Trade-Unionists by facilitating their deportation to forced labour camps in Germany. Moreover, these business groups were, broadly speaking, supported by the bureaucratic class, the famous French civil service with its *Inspecteurs des Finances* and *Ingénieurs d'Etat*. Because of the continual state of financial crisis after 1934, and the ever-changing French Governments, these bureaucrats had considerable power. Prime Ministers might come and go, but they remained; and they came to scorn their political chiefs at the mercy of shifting majorities. In the thirties, these high civil servants had become a kind of caste, rather like the Prussian Junkers; and they naturally disliked the public

---

[1] Notable exceptions were: M. Poniatowski, head of the Hispano-Suiza automobile firm who refused to make vehicles for the Wehrmacht and was deported to Germany; also P. Lefaucheux, the engineer and industrialist, and Hachette, the publisher.

debates of the Third Republic which unveiled the mysteries of their bureaux.

The Germans themselves also confirm this economic collaboration. Dr Michel, chief of the *Militärverwaltung*, which dealt with economic matters in France, states in his final report on Franco-German relations 1940–44,[1] 'We can conclude therefore that collaboration in the economic field during the four years of occupation led to a more or less complete integration of the French economy into that of Europe directed by Germany. . . . . French industry was in general disposed to produce and deliver. In the cases of certain industries which were behind-hand, the *Militärverwaltung* intervened with commissions and plenipotentiaries. This, however, was rarely necessary. The number of these commissions did not, in four years, exceed fifty.'

The French collaborators were not pro-Nazi, but they felt an admiration for a Government which could 'stand up to the Trade Unions'. Hence the attraction of Vichy, which announced it would not only do business with the New Order, but would enforce economic discipline in a country disrupted by the dishonest governments of the Third Republic. When Pétain announced that he had come to deliver them from lies, they applauded. The more sanctimonious could also regard the defeat as he did, as condign punishment for the country's frivolous and dissolute behaviour between the two wars. The Vichy régime made a number of attempts to explain why the defeat of 1940 was merited, the oddest of which claimed that its authors were Marcel Proust and André Gide, whose immoral writings had depraved and debased the country. Pétain's call to *'Travail! Famille! Patrie!'* seemed to strike a new and healthier note; and when he disbanded the Trade Unions in order to 'construct a fair society in which social conflicts will be abolished', the business community heaved a sigh of relief.[2]

---

[1] Quoted in *La France intérieure*, Nos. 50 & 51. Nov./Dec. 1946.

[2] Later, Vichy was to set up its own Trade Unions. But they were strictly controlled, and not allowed 'free association', as under the Third Republic. Their activity was purely professional, and non-political. The representatives of the various unions could not, for instance, meet to discuss foreign policy. Most important emasculation of all—strikes were forbidden. The Vichy Unions were constructed on the usual fascist lines, 'vertical' as distinct from 'horizontal' Trade Unions.

In the first months after the armistice, Pétain's policy depended on the assumption, to which most of the industrialists subscribed, that England would be rapidly defeated, and *Pax Hitleriana* imposed throughout Europe. The sooner, therefore, that France adapted her system of government to that of the victor, and the climate of a totalitarian state, the better. Pétain's régime has been described as a form of state paternalism, in which the Marshal was the father figure, ensuring that everyone had a fair deal. In return, the people were expected to get on with their work and not bother their heads about social and economic matters. Pétain expressed this in one of his early speeches: 'The aim which I pursue is the suppression of the class struggle. Experience has shown that whenever men of good will get together for a loyal and frank explanation, opposition dissolves into mutual esteem, even into friendship. . . .'

The essential feature of his economic system was, in theory, that any specific domain was to be organized by representatives of the interested parties themselves, the employer and the employed working in harness. The void created by the disbanding of the Trade Unions and the C.G.P.F., or employers' organization (regarded as not helping one another in the comradely Pétain way) was to be filled by 'corporativist' institutions. Class cooperation would be achieved by entrusting the administration of Industry and Labour to the same Minister (as distinct from the deliberate separation of such departments in democratic countries). With all this the employers were prepared to agree. If Vichy could protect them from the Trade Unions, they were willing to submit to a certain amount of governmental control themselves.

Indeed, the suppression of both employer and labour organizations worked in favour of the former. Through the Comités d'Organisation the employers had access to the bureaucrats. And they knew that social peace was not likely to be disturbed as long as the workers realized that insubordination might result in deportation to Germany. The Pétain Government, in theory fair to both owners and workers, soon contained a number of businessmen. When Darlan came to power, he was even accused of bringing 'the entire Worms Bank' into his cabinet; to which he contemptuously replied, 'Anyway, that's better than the choirboys who have been around here lately [he was referring to the

Third Republic professional politicians]. We want people who will get along with Fritz and cook you a good soup.'

A trenchant, if somewhat savage, comment on the attitude of the employers towards Pétain is given by Henriette Psichari in her novel *Usines '42*[1]: 'It was perfectly natural that if they didn't work, the Germans would requisition their factories. In any case, was it possible to imagine a torpid, half-Communist France defeating an efficient warrior-state like Germany? Impossible anyway to win without a leader . . . a leader, that was what every employer was looking for . . . a well-turned-out leader, preferably in uniform, with no special affection for the British or the Germans, but who would restore and maintain political order . . .' Such a man was Philippe Pétain. Who could be more patriotic than the 1917 saviour of the country, 'the most humane of Marshals?'

Unlike military and political collaboration, the economic and industrial brand is not easy to estimate. A good deal of German spoliation took the form of direct purchase, which cannot be calculated. Occupation costs of four hundred million francs a day paid by the French Government at a rate of exchange particularly favourable to the Germans enabled them to place large orders in what appeared the normal business way.

When they arrived in Paris on 16 June 1940, all business and production in the factories had come to a standstill. One or two workers were wandering aimlessly about in the deserted yards but most of them, together with the owners, administrators and bureaucrats, had gone south in the exodus. The Germans immediately set industry to work again, announcing that if the French did not operate their own concerns, they would take them over and run them themselves, if necessary transport them to Germany. In the departments of Le Nord and Pas de Calais, they had already begun Nazification of the working-classes, with propaganda against absentee French owners. In Lille, a 'Brown House' had been opened granting French workers the card of the National Socialist party, social assurance for themselves and their families on German lines. Certain factories in the north were already being dismantled and shipped to Germany. It was clear

---

[1] Paris, A. Michel, 1946.

in Paris that if the owners did not quickly reoccupy their places, the process would be repeated there. Apart from losing valuable plant and machinery, this would mean that many French workmen would be thrown out of work. In the second volume of his autobiography, General de Gaulle confirms this, referring to the 'huge quantity of plant transferred to Germany'. On 16 August 1940, the Vichy Government hastily passed a law instructing employers and workers to return to their own firms. The Prefect of Paris, M. Villey-Desmerets, made this despairing appeal to the absentee owners, 'All commercial and industrial establishments must reopen as soon as practicably possible. The Government requires that directors and heads of firms should return immediately to their posts. Return to work in all factories closed during the evacuation of Paris is now a national duty.'

Three weeks before this, on the day that Louis Renault arrived back in Portugal from the U.S.A., Maître Coulet, a lawyer employed by the firm, visited Billancourt to see what was happening. He found notices from the German military command on all the entrances, announcing the provisional seizure of the empty factory, its workshops, plant and stock.

'I had just finished reading this,' he says (related by M. Saint Loup in his book on Louis Renault), 'when a Wehrmacht vehicle drew up and three German civilians got out. One of them asked me if I represented the Société des Usines Renault. I replied that I represented them legally, but this did not mean that I had mandatory powers.' The man he spoke to was Herr Schippert, one of the directors of Daimler-Benz A. G. Stuttgart. Schippert said his orders were to initiate full production immediately, with or without the co-operation of the French owners.

The personnel of the Usines Renault who had been ordered by the General Officer Commanding, Paris, to leave Billancourt on 11 June 1940 were by now scattered all over France. The evacuation had been orderly, under the direction of the departmental heads and their shop stewards. The huge exodus of nearly thirty thousand people, to which was added those of the Renault factories in Le Mans and Orléans, had proved that, in spite of the earlier strikes and class antipathy, in a moment of national crisis the French workmen acted patriotically. Lehideux had left Billancourt last, on the evening of 13 June, and he returned on 26 June after the signature of the armistice. He was instructed by the representative of the Government, the Prefect Villey, the President of the Paris municipal council, André Chiappe, and the representative of the Government for Occupied France, Ambassador Noel, to reopen the factory and make contact with the Germans, who had taken possession of it on the ground that the owners and workers had fled.

Lehideux immediately gave orders for the construction of vehicles and trucks required for French domestic use. An order for two and a half thousand vehicles was passed to the factory by the Prefect, after pressure had been brought to bear by the municipal council of Paris, led by M. Chiappe. The principal aim of these orders was to provide the factory with a good reason for not accepting German work. This showed foresight, because the German commission now instructed the firm to repair French armoured cars and tanks captured by the German army during their advance. The firm of Hotchkiss at Saint Denis was already doing this. Moreover, according to the rules of war, the occupying power becomes automatically owner of any war material belonging to the defeated adversary. The only solution to how to refuse German work was to prevent the Germans finding any more war material—by ruse, dissimulation or destruction. The Departmental director-general, M. Grillot, who had been recalled to Billancourt by Lehideux, began destroying tools and parts necessary for the construction of war material, principally by throwing them in the Seine.

If captured material belonged legally to the Germans, nothing in International Law empowered them to force French citizens to repair it; and this was the basis on which Lehideux refused their requests. It may seem strange that the Germans did not react savagely to his disobedience; but they were still hoping that if they handled France carefully, they might persuade her to declare war on England. All the same, they continued their demands, even threatening to take over the factory and run it themselves. Lehideux therefore decided to visit Louis Renault who had by now left Portugal, and was living with friends near Périgeux, while awaiting permission to enter occupied France. Lehideux explained the difficult situation and Renault approved his action. They agreed that Lehideux should return to Billancourt and Louis Renault would not follow him while these problems were pending; in this way, Lehideux could always argue that he could not carry out German orders because he had been unable to obtain his chief's permission.

Unfortunately three days later, when Lehideux had repeated his refusal to the Germans, Louis Renault changed his mind and suddenly appeared in Billancourt. It seems that he could not imagine the factory wheels turning again without his presence. This suited the Germans, who now attempted to influence him directly; and he evidently made certain concessions of whose full import he was unaware. M. Léon Noel, who was a member of the armistice commission at the time, wrote later (after the war), 'When I was at Vichy, I was informed that M. Renault had offered the Germans his factories for the construction of war material. I immediately summoned him and warned him that this would be a criminal offence. . . . M. Renault said that what he had done was aimed solely at giving employment to his workers, but that he would not carry out the promises he had made (to the Germans). I then summoned M. Lehideux in front of whom M. Renault confirmed this. . . .'

Meanwhile the Germans acted. One Sunday in early August 1940, they sent a posse to fetch Lehideux from his house in Paris and bring him to their HQ in the Majestic Hotel. Simultaneously, a vehicle was sent to Herqueville to fetch Louis Renault for the same purpose. Renault refused to accompany them, but instead handed over to the German officer a signed letter in which he stated that 'M. Lehideux, the Delegate Administrator of the Usines Renault, has full authority for taking decisions relative to all questions.'

Lehideux accordingly found himself alone that morning in the presence of twelve high-ranking German officers who let him understand that the passive resistance methods practised by the Germans themselves in the Ruhr during the twenties would not be tolerated. Renault's letter was read out, and Lehideux was asked to give a definite reply. After much argument and listening to further threats about transferring the factory to Germany, Lehideux arranged that the Germans should have one of the workshops near the Pont de Sèvres, but that they should employ their own labour in it. It was a considerable concession. The following day Lehideux informed his uncle of this arrangement, which was to remain in force for four years.

During Renault's first meeting with the Germans, he had

probably underestimated the nature and political importance of their demands. Aware only of one thing, to preserve his factories, workers and machines at all costs, he had made concessions which, in other circumstances, he would certainly have refused. But by the time the Germans came to Herqueville to bring him to Paris, he had changed his mind. This is confirmed by M. Parodi, who was Director-General of Labour at the time (1940), and who stated after the war to the High Court of Justice in Paris (2 February 1946), which was examining the case and attempting to assign responsibility, 'When the Germans threatened to take over the running of the factory, Lehideux maintained his position, so that finally only certain subsidiary and unimportant workshops were occupied. . . . Louis Renault, however, temporarily gave the Germans permission to take over the running of the Le Mans factory.' Renault's reason for this was made quite clear later on when he said, 'It is better to give them the butter, or they'll take the cows.' But the general impression made in France at the time was unfavourable to Renault.

Renault still saw Billancourt as he had at the beginning of the war, in terms of civilian vehicles. He was already looking ahead to peace and saw his new Juvastella on the roads, whether of a German or an Allied Europe he did not much care. Whether he was making a vehicle for Hitler, Pétain, the English or the Pope did not concern him; if it was a Renault vehicle, that was what mattered.[1] The cunning French peasant in him also knew that to achieve his aim he must not be intransigent. When he arrived back at Billancourt that morning, he had had to pass through the gates of his own factory between German sentries and pickets. His aim now was to rid Billancourt of the Germans entirely and run the factory on his own. If he made no concessions, he realized that Billancourt would become simply an annexe of the German Daimler-Benz firm. How then to retain the maximum while offering the minimum? How to prevent his machines and personnel from being transferred to Germany? This was his problem for the next four years. His patriotism saw no further than that.

---

[1] In 1943 he said to M. Pommier (now one of the Renault directors), 'The war will soon be over. We must now—you in particular—draw up plans for our first post-war model.'

Confronted with continual German demands for trucks and lorries, Louis Renault behaved throughout the occupation with the tenacity of a French peasant. Just as the French peasant often concealed his cattle, pigs and chickens from the Germans who wished to requisition them, so Louis Renault managed to protect his machinery and the workers' interests. Confronted with a requisition order for food, the French peasant said to the Germans, 'Shall I let you into a secret? Old Lefèbvre with his farm on the other side of the stream has just got in thirty new laying-fowls. Get at him quick, while you can!' To protect his beloved Billancourt, Renault was quite prepared to send the Germans to his old rivals, Michelin, Berliet, Peugeot. . . . In all these tussles Renault tried to assess how far he could go, giving a little in one direction, to save more in another. The affair of the French tanks was finally forgotten, and the Germans repaired them on their own. It was a small enough incident compared with what was to come, and its importance has been much exaggerated since the Liberation.

By the end of 1940, it was clear that the Germans were not going to conquer England, and they had failed to persuade Vichy to declare war on her. Their methods with the French now began to change. They began to look east to the plains of Russia, where they would soon require a large supply of vehicles. The French automobile industry became of particular interest, and they eliminated the small manufacturers, leaving only the seven big ones, Renault, Peugeot, Citroën (under Michelin), Ford, Berliet, Sauer and Rochet-Schneider, all nominally under a special German department, the *Generalbevollmächtige für die Kraftführwesen*, who granted them priority in raw materials. This suited Louis Renault admirably, and many thousands of tons of German steel and equipment were surreptitiously diverted for the great day when the Juvastella family car would be on the roads again.

How the Germans attempted to interfere in the running of French automobile firms is revealed in the French Government report published after the war, '*Ingérances allemandes dans l'automobile industrie française*' (1948): 'On numerous occasions, and particularly in 1942, German technical missions visited our automobile factories where they recommended the use of certain German patents which, they claimed, would benefit and accelerate production. The French motor-car manufacturers did not follow these prescriptions. They objected either that they were using their own methods, which were quite satisfactory, or that they had already used the German techniques with disastrous results.' Most of these 'disastrous results' had been deliberately engineered.

Every French factory was given a German 'Special Delegate', an expert on the industry in question, with an office on the premises from which he issued instructions. His powers were defined in an order by the *Militärbefehlshaber* of Paris: 'By virtue of the full powers accorded me by the Führer and Supreme Head of the Wehrmacht, I am authorized to introduce delegates of the Wehrmacht and plenipotentiaries for the automobile industry in the factories. The proprietor of the factory will remain fully responsible for its running. Nevertheless, he will constantly inform the special delegate of all installation alterations and production figures. The special delegate is authorized to attend all managerial conferences, as well as to examine the accounts and any other relevant documents and transactions. The special delegate will deal with all visits by foreign or outside persons to the factory. His fees will be fixed by the service [German] which nominated him, and he will be paid by the factory in question. All infractions of this order are punishable by a fine, or imprisonment, or both, depending on the gravity of the offence.'

The German delegate dealt only with the head of the firm, quite inconspicuously, so that the workers and rest of the personnel were barely aware of his presence. The French workman still worked with his old mates, under the same shop steward, at the same wage as before the war; the shop steward was under the same departmental head. Together they produced the same automobiles, textiles, machinery or whatever it was, exactly as before. The only difference was that, although they might be unaware of it, they were producing it for the Germans.[1] H. Psichari has this to say[2]:

---

[1] M. Griffon states that on his return to Billancourt from German captivity in 1942, he was hardly aware of the German presence, which was always 'correct'.

[2] In her novel *Usines '42*.

Jeanne Hatto
*(Archives
Photographiques)*

**Sir Winston Churchill
driving to Buckingham
Palace in a Renault
taxi, 1911** *(Radio Times
Hulton Picture Library)*

Renault's
house in the
Avenue Foch
(*Sylvaine
Vaucher, Paris*)

Herqueville,
Renault's
country house
near Rouen
(*François
Bibal, Paris*)

Renault's light tanks in the victory parade, 14 July 1919 (*Régie Renault*)

François Lehideux
(Photo Harcourt, Paris)

Henry Ford I *(René Dazy, Paris)*

André Citroën *(René Dazy, Paris)*

1920s—A Farman Goliath ready at Toussus-le-Noble for an attempt on the 48-hour Endurance Record *(Radio Times Hulton Picture Library)*

1927—4-cylinder Torpedo-de-Luxe, 6-hp *(Renault Ltd)*

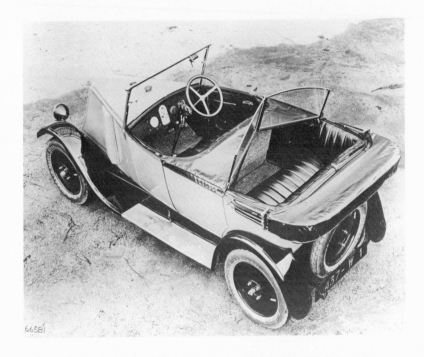

1930—Straight 8 Reinastella Cabriolet, coachwork by Million Guiet, 32-hp, radiator shutters controlled by thermostat *(Renault Ltd)*

1939—4-cylinder Invaquatre Cabriolet, 5-hp *(Renault Ltd)*

1942—Fifty per cent of the Renault workshop area at Billancourt destroyed by bombing (*Renault Ltd*)

Christiane Renault
(René Dazy, Paris)

Louis Renault talking
to President Lebrun at
the Motor Show held at
the Grand Palais in
1935 *(Keystone Press)*

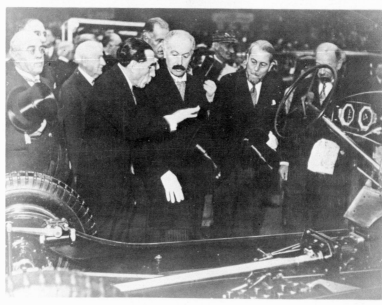

And so work went on for the profit of the enemy, but in a sporadic way, without the workers being aware of any constraint. The directors of the firm still had plenty of raw material and they used up their stocks with no evident worry that it might run out. Most of the returning workmen had picked up the same tools at the same bench; they still drew the same wage. Yes—had anything really changed? Thanks to the division of labour, few of them thought about the uses to which the piece of metal they were filing or soldering was to be put. After all, a lynch-pin is not an aeroplane, nor is a cylinder-head an armoured-car. On the contrary, they pitied the unemployed workers in the firms whose factory doors were still closed.

For Usines Renault, the largest automobile plant in France, the special delegate was carefully selected, a man of tact and urbanity unusual in a German, Prinz von Urach, tall and good-looking, with a perfect command of French. For nearly four years, he came daily to Billancourt, transmitting his instructions almost as if he were asking a favour. Louis Renault had no liking for the Germans, whom he referred to on all occasions contemptuously as 'Boches'[1]; but he could not object to this tall and punctilious German who occasionally sat in on his business conferences. By now the impediment in his speech was so bad that he had difficulty in pronouncing certain French words, let alone foreign names such as 'von Urach'. He always referred to Prinz von Urach as *le grand*. 'Don't tell *le grand*,' he would say about some project they were trying to conceal from the Germans. Once, during a conference at which von Urach was present, when something was suggested, he said involuntarily, 'Quite right. I agree! But what's the big Boche going to say?' An eye-witness, M. Debos, who was his personal assistant, says that not by a flicker of an eyelid did von Urach betray that he had heard this derogatory reference to himself and his countrymen.

On another occasion, the important question of the transfer of a Renault ball-bearing plant to a safer area came up with von Urach. The site finally selected was some two hundred miles west

---

[1] M. Clément Pouns, Louis Renault's valet, says that such was Renault's detestation of the Germans that on innumerable occasions when German troops marched down the Avenue Foch, his employer would go to the window and shake his fist at them, repeating '*Ces salauds de Boches!*'
When Saukel, the German 'Slave Labour' chief came to Billancourt to enlist workers for Germany, Louis Renault refused to see '*le sale Boche*'.

of Paris, in a place well camouflaged from the air. It was then discovered that a Luftwaffe airfield had just been sited near by, which would jeopardize the safety of the factory. Renault summoned von Urach and said that if his ball-bearing plant was to be transferred there, the Luftwaffe airfield must go. Von Urach said this would not be easy as the decision about the Luftwaffe base had been taken by Göring himself. Renault insisted, and finally von Urach said he would do what he could; if necessary he would see Göring about it. After a week of effort and difficult negotiations, he returned jubilantly to Billancourt with the news that the Luftwaffe would move.

Renault behaved very oddly. '*Ne veux pas!*' he mumbled, '*ne veux pas!*' (This conversation is related by M. Debos, who was present.)

'But it was the place you wanted, M. Renault,' remonstrated von Urach. 'Surely. . . !'

'*Ne veux pas!*'

'But if I have to go and tell the Luftwaffe we don't want it now, they'll think I'm an awful ass.'

Renault thought for a moment. 'No, they won't,' he said. 'I shall write a statement that it is not you, but Louis Renault, who is an awful ass.'

He had his way. Neither ball-bearing plant nor Luftwaffe units arrived in an area well suited to conceal both.

Some observers say that his mind was as clear as ever, and that he only pretended it was not to confuse the Germans. Once he said to von Urach (again according to Debos), 'Go and get those tyres from Citroën. He must have more than I have. I know. I saw him last night.'

'What did Citroën say to you?' said the German, to humour him.

'Don't be silly, how could he *say* anything to me?' said Renault. 'Don't you know the man's dead?'

Owing to the defect in his speech, people assumed he was incapable of managing his affairs. Once, on a tour of the factory with M. Debos, he suddenly pointed to the little shack in the grounds where he had started his career; it still contained his original lathe and tools (as it does today). 'Ah!' he said nostalgically. 'Good tools, good machinery we had in those days! Today—*pas d'orphelinat!*' Debos was mystified. *Orphelinat* means 'orphanage'. To what 'orphanage' was the boss referring? A little later, he realized that Louis Renault was trying to say '*artinisat*' which means 'craftsmanship'; his tongue had confused the two words.

As a result of this speech defect many people in authority felt by 1942 that he should retire. The Ministry at Vichy dealing with vehicle production suggested that he should withdraw to his property in the south, at Gien, and the direction be put in surer hands. He was also criticized for too much direct dealing with the Germans. Other employers preferred to approach the Germans through some French organization, such as the 'Automobile Manufacturers'; it gave them a feeling of support. But as usual Louis Renault was suspicious of all such organizations, which he was sure would represent him badly, and he decided to represent himself. He stubbornly fought the suggestion about retiring, finally demanding, and receiving, an audience with Marshal Pétain at Vichy.

The ministers had warned Pétain that Louis Renault was failing, and the Marshal had asked his age. On being told that Renault was 63, the old man laughed grimly, 'If everyone retired at 63! . . . Let me see him.' (Pétain was 83.) At the interview, the Marshal seems to have been sufficiently impressed to leave Renault in charge of the production side of the firm. But he was removed from *relations extérieures* (negotiations with the Germans); and also, as a result of Renault's repudiation in 1940 of the Matignon Agreements, from anything bearing on social questions. He was relegated to the domain for which he was best qualified, the design and drawing shop. This seemed like paternalism or state interference in its extreme form. It is hardly surprising, therefore, that Louis Renault began to revise any favourable views he may have originally had of the Vichy régime.

The question of repairing the French tanks was unfortunate because, although Renault did not repair them, his enemies were quick to claim that he had. Renault did not understand the power of the well-circulated lie. In a situation calling for careful counter-propaganda, he did nothing. Nor, as the fortunes of war began to change, did he, like some industrialists who were having to produce goods for the Germans, reinsure against an Allied victory by making clandestine contributions to the Maquis, or by transferring funds to the Free French forces overseas. Michelin, when he saw the way the wind was blowing in 1943, even sent a representative to London.

Louis Renault was approached at one point about contributing to the Maquis, whose operations, after 1943 and the German failure at Stalingrad, had greatly increased. He replied that he had never heard of them. This was probably true, because he paid little attention to the course of the war and the bulletins. If he had been asked where Dnepropetrovsk was, or what was happening at Guadalcanal, he would probably have nodded his head, mystified, and changed the conversation. When he was informed who the Maquis were, he said, 'No! Not a sou! Nor to those Doriot swine either!'[1] Anyone taking part in the war, on either side, was a 'swine' to him. This was far from wise because the war was now approaching France. The British had at first devoted their limited bombing capacity to plants in Germany itself, but by 1942 they had enough air power to bomb targets outside the Reich that were contributing to the German war effort.

Renault had many enemies, not only among the workers, but also in his own class, industrialists and bankers whom he had ignored or scorned. This was now to weigh against him. The unholy combination of big business and the communists put it about that he was making tanks for the Wehrmacht (which was not true—he was making only trucks and lorries, as were all the other big automobile firms, to save his factories and staff from being taken to Germany). But he took no steps to contradict this fiction, perhaps because he thought in his naïve way that the truth will always prevail, that his own workmen, who knew what they were making, would tell the truth. Lies can triumph in peacetime; but how much more easily in war when it is patriotic to use every form of publicity, press, rumour, radio to distort the truth! Once, when accused of *selling* vehicles to the Wehrmacht, he replied, 'Yes, I am—do you expect me to *give* them to the Boche as a present?'

---

[1] The 'Doriot swine' were the extreme pro-German movement, who tracked down the Maquis, executed their countrymen, fought in Russia wearing S.S. uniform.

Some time in early 1942, a highly placed technician from the Billancourt works named Restany, who had been there for years and knew the topography of the factory, joined the Free French. He escaped into Spain, thence to London. In the first weeks, he spoke several times on the B.B.C. French service about the iniquitous collaboration of the Usines Renault with the Germans. On 3 March 1942, the R.A.F. struck.

Beginning just after 10 p.m., in a low level raid, they dropped about three hundred tons of high explosive and incendiaries on the factory and commune of Billancourt. The raid lasted an hour, and it appeared at first that they had destroyed the Renault works. Some four hundred people were killed and twelve hundred seriously hurt, most of them having nothing to do with the factory. Louis Renault was at Herqueville at the time. But his wife was dining in Paris, and when she heard what was happening, she courageously drove down with her son, realizing that at such a moment a member of the family must be present. Unfortunately in the dark, not far from the factory, she failed to see a bomb crater, which she ran into and overturned. She was found to have fractured her skull, from which, she states, she has never fully recovered.[1]

The R.A.F. explained the reasons for the raid in tracts which were later dropped over Billancourt. 'The annual production of vehicles in France today is between 40,000 and 50,000,' they announced, 'that is, double the number in the year before the war. This production is directed almost entirely to Germany. The Usines Renault produces 25 per cent of it.' The British contention was that Renault was producing ten thousand vehicles a year for the Wehrmacht. The figure is fairly accurate.[2] The mistake was to imply that in the years before the war Renault produced only half this number for his own country. The figures are: in 1939, 17,802 vehicles; in 1940, 2,545; in 1941, 11,456; in 1942, 12,070; in 1943, 5,041; in 1944, 2,438. (What the British chose to ignore is that other firms, such as Michelin and Berliet, were doing exactly the same. Post-war inquiries show that their production for the Germans was, proportionate to their size, roughly the same as Renault's.)

---

[1] Stated to the author in an interview in 1967.
[2] Later statistics show 34,222 for four years of occupation.

Further, the British contended in their tracts that Renault was producing armoured cars and tanks for the Germans, an accusation they substantiated with aerial photographs of tanks lined up outside the Billancourt workshops. In fact, these were German tanks being repaired by German workmen in the department at Billancourt which Daimler-Benz had taken over, and with which Renault would have nothing to do. This is confirmed by the United States Bombing Survey Report (Munitions Division) which states that the allied raids on Renault denied in all to the enemy 7,221 trucks from the planned production. It adds, 'Renault produced medium and light vehicles—the highest rate being 1,600 per month.'

On 10 March 1942, Admiral Leahy, the American ambassador to Vichy, wrote to President Roosevelt, 'The bombardment of the Renault factories which are working for the Germans has caused varying reactions among the public. It has put the factory out of operation for several months. The Renault bombardment caused 397 deaths among the local inhabitants. . . . Admiral Darlan happened to be in Paris at the time. On his return to Vichy, his hatred of the English has much increased. In his fury he wrote me, "The English have piled error on error since the 25th June 1940 [Mers-el-Kébir]. They have just committed an even graver one. To murder for political reasons women, children and old men savours of the Soviets. . . ."'

The only inaccuracy in Admiral Leahy's report was that the factory would be out of operation for several months. Although his first impression was of great damage, this proved exaggerated. Walls and roofs were down all over Billancourt, but most of the machinery was intact; only about 10 per cent of the factory had been really hit. On the Ile Séguin, for instance,, the coachwork department for civilian models and their production lines had been destroyed; but this had nothing to do with the war effort, and had in any case been almost idle since the fall of France. On the other hand, the truck production-lines, the most important from the German point of view, had not been touched. The same could be said for most of the other departments working for German orders. Nevertheless, the Germans' first reaction was that, rather than rebuild, it would be better to take all the machinery to a safer place east of the Rhine. Louis Renault was on the spot early the next morning, closely examining the damage (it has been said, perhaps rightly, 'he thought more about his machines than his men'). On hearing what the Germans proposed to do, he called his workers together and put it to them that if they did not immediately repair the damage, and return to full production, they might find themselves in Germany. His words had an immediate effect. So hard did they work that within two months the factory was producing again. Here he enlisted the support of his 'gaoler', Prinz von Urach. The two of them had argued with the German authorities to such effect that not only was permission granted to rebuild, but Renault managed in the subsequent repairs to improve and modernize his factory at German expense. The electrical repair shop dating from early days was a relatively dilapidated construction; it was now rebuilt in reinforced concrete. The drying-room for the metal foundry had not been touched in the raid; it too was old, so he pulled it down and re-erected a more modern building. Within nine months the factory was in better shape than it had been in 1940.[1]

Not long after the repairs had been completed, in April 1943, the factory was bombed again by the R.A.F. The damage, however, was less, only about 8 per cent of the plant and buildings being hit, but the same heavy losses were sustained among the civilian population. For the second time there was the question of taking plant and workers east. Moreover on this occasion, the Paris municipal authorities were in favour of such a dangerous target in the metropolitan area being transferred. Renault fought tenaciously against the move, even enlisting the support of the Président du Conseil, Laval, who replied: 'I consider that a nation which makes no special effort in adversity is doomed. In the present troubled times we must repair the breaches in our walls, even if the walls may later be damaged again. I expect you to take all measures necessary for putting your factory in a state to carry out the programmes of work laid down for you by the Comité d'Organisation de l'Automobile' (at Paris).

---

[1] As is known from post-war Germany, there is something to be said—from a purely production point of view—for having one's factories bombed every few decades, and re-erected at state expense, with all contemporary improvements. The Germans had forbidden any photographs of the damage. But Renault insisted that they should be taken secretly. He was thinking of State compensation.

Such was the energy of Louis Renault that he repaired his factory again. And yet again, after the next American air raid on 15 September 1943. Each time he repaired it, he appropriated materials, bricks, cement, steel, a part of which he put aside for peacetime uses. According to M. Dauvergne, who has made a special study of the occupation years, he sequestrated, or otherwise withdrew from German control, the following material which should have been used in German war production:

> 16,000 new tyres
> 100,000 litres of petrol
> 300 tons of lubricating oil
> 1,800 tons of fuel oil
> 200 tons of raw rubber
> 750 tons of chemicals
> 285,000 sq. yards of various materials (coachwork)
> 6,000 pounds of leather[1]

Was Renault a collaborator? Yes; but in his own way. And the other big industrialists were collaborators too.

---

[1] Various methods were also devised for sabotaging vehicles made for the Wehrmacht. One of them was to make the oil dip-sticks with the notch much lower than was correct. Many engines seized up in Russia having run out of oil, and the German drivers were punished.

6 | The Resistance

The events that led up to Louis Renault's end are connected, like everything else in France in these years, with the career and personality of General de Gaulle. The two men never met; but while Renault had barely heard of de Gaulle, the General knew enough about Renault to dislike him. At the Liberation in 1944, great hostility surrounded the business world, which de Gaulle and the left-wing press joined in denouncing, not only for their lack of patriotism, but for having made big profits during the war. As early as 1942, de Gaulle declared in a public speech, 'disaster and betrayal have disqualified most of the owners and men of privilege . . . it is unacceptable to leave intact a social and moral order which has worked against the nation'. Shortly after his return to Paris, in 1945, he was lobbied by a group of businessmen wanting some concession or other. 'I didn't see any of you gentlemen in London,' he is reported to have said. 'You're not in gaol, I see. What more do you want?'

In his autobiography[1] he writes that the disaster of 1940 seemed to most Frenchmen as the collapse, in all domains, of the ruling-class system. People were inclined therefore to consider replacing it by a new one. During the occupation the French masses were exasperated by the collaboration of part of the business world with the occupying power, by the parade of profiteering, and the contrast between the penury in which almost everyone lived and the luxury enjoyed by the few. Within a year the orders and laws promulgated under his authority had brought immense changes to the French economy and the condition of the workers.

His Consultative Assembly in Algiers in 1943, which was supposed to be representative of the nation, was notable for the almost complete absence of the employer class. In its early stages he had tried to enlist, it is true, members of the business community who had what he called 'a good record under the

---

[1] Vol. III.

Occupation'. But by applying his own strict and elevated standards, most of the industrialists were automatically excluded. Even when later he appointed a 'Committee of Employers' Representatives', he consulted no one who had been active in the employers' movement, and chose as chairman Pierre Fournier, a grain merchant scarcely known in French business circles. This was in part due to his uncompromising attitude towards Frenchmen who had not joined the Free French movement; he regarded them all, broadly speaking, as traitors. When the more moderate General Giraud met one of de Gaulle's right-hand men, Leclerc, in Algiers in 1942, the following conversation took place:[1]

Leclerc: Those Frenchmen, civilians as well as soldiers, who did not join de Gaulle in 1940, are traitors. As such, they will be punished.
Giraud: In that case when you get back to France, you'll have to erect a guillotine in every village square.
Leclerc: Precisely!

After the Allied invasion of North Africa, de Gaulle pronounced one of his bitterest speeches against Vichy, demanding not only justice for the 'Vichy traitors', but 'vengeance'. He finished with the ominous words, 'Clemenceau said "The country will know that it is defended." We say, "The country will know that it is avenged."' Some of his lieutenants were even more vindictive. One of them, Paul Rivet, had been director of the Musée de l'Homme, but this contact with the civilizations of the past had not moderated his blood-thirstiness. 'No human force,' he said, 'can prevent the French people from doing justice. They will execute the traitors, if necessary with knives—but execute them they will.' The German S.S. and its French counterpart, the Doriot group and the pro-German Milice, had committed such atrocities in occupied France that the idea of summary execution and the settling of scores without the normal judiciary methods was contemplated by many members of the Resistance long before the invasion of France. That the Germans and their lackeys got what they deserved, no one will deny. It was the manner in which they got it, often involving innocent people, for which the Resistance forces are today criticized in France.

It is perhaps difficult for Englishmen, who have not known

---

[1] Reported by Robert Aron in *L'Histoire de l'épuration.*

civil war since 1640, to understand the degree of violence in France at this time. 'Vichy' was reduced by both sides to a simple formula. To its supporters, it was the most meritorious, the purest expression of French patriotism after the 1940 defeat. To them, Pétain was the saviour of France and the incarnation of the country. One of his Ministers, Pucheu, expressed this devotion—'The greatest honour in the life of a Frenchman today is to have served the Marshal at this, the most difficult moment in French history.'

The antithesis of this was expressed by a Gaullist, General Weiss, whose fury against Pétain was almost pathological. 'How can anyone have confidence in such *total garbage* as Pétain?' he wrote. 'Everyone knows that this blackguard, the greatest in our national history, has been a traitor for the last fifteen years. I hate him with all my soul, and I spit in his face. As a French general, I hate him; as a republican, I hate him; as a citizen of Lorraine, I hate him. . . . If there is any room in your lavatory, you can use it for portraits of the traitor (even this is too good for him) . . . this *canaille*, this Hitler flunkey, this detritus which the public sewers would regurgitate . . .'[1]

De Gaulle's position was not easy because, as the Liberation proceeded, he became aware that the largest part of the Resistance was communist. Since June 1941 and the German invasion of Russia, the communists had taken the greatest risks and suffered the most in France, at the hands of the Gestapo as well as from the Milice. In spite of having rendered themselves ridiculous at the time of the German-Soviet pact, they were now therefore much respected in France. Their representatives had visited de Gaulle clandestinely in London before the Invasion, and he had had to take two of them into the Algiers Consultative Assembly, later to become the government of the French republic. They referred to 'Revolutionary Justice', summary executions and political tribunals. They considered that de Gaulle's Consultative Assembly treated collaborators too lightly (a number of these had been captured after the Allied North African invasion). 'If you don't purge the traitors, we will,' they announced. While from Moscow their leader, Thorez (who had spent the whole war in Russia), invited the country to civil war. 'The people of

---

[1] Ibid.

France,' he cried, 'must take up arms and finish with the traitors, Pétain, Laval and the rest of them.' At Algiers, de Gaulle soon realized that his position would be jeopardized if he did not pay at least lip-service to the communist principles. In fact, he was soon paying more attention to them than to Churchill.

In his autobiography[1] he writes: 'Not that I had any illusions as to the "party's" loyalty. I knew it aimed at seizing total power and that, if I yielded even once it would immediately rise to the attack. But its participation in the resistance, the influence it wielded over the workers, the desire of public opinion, which I myself shared, to see it return to the nation, determined me to give the "party" its place in the task of recovery.'

Malraux says much the same thing:[2] 'General de Gaulle handled the communists carefully because he intended to use every force available to resurrect France (it is significant that there were no strikes between the Liberation and his departure from power). And *they* in turn handled him carefully, because they thought that time was on their side. . . .'

In the communist-influenced Resistance newspaper *Après*, which began to appear in Algiers in 1943, the first 'Collaborators' to be attacked were the 'Trusts'. They were accused of having prepared the defeat of 1940, because they wanted the German army to attack Russia; with France quickly defeated, the Germans could then turn on the Soviets. It claimed that during 1940 the Press (a creature of the 'Trusts') had deliberately encouraged people to leave Paris, in order to create chaos on the roads and hasten the defeat. Had Louis Renault been able to read all this, he might have had some presentiment of what lay ahead. On the other hand, he might easily have said, 'Me? I'm not for the Trusts. I dislike the Trusts,' and regarded himself as not included in the accusation.

From a purely military point of view the Forces Françaises de l'Intérieure, or F.F.I as the communist-controlled Resistance group was called, were far more actively hostile to the Germans in France than the exiguous forces under General de Gaulle. The position of de Gaulle who was in France in 1944 virtually on allied suffrance, was embarrassing and humiliating. Although

---

[1] Vol. III.
[2] *Anti-Memoirs*. Holt, 1968.

nominally leader of the Free French he could not, for nearly four months after the Liberation, exercise any effective government; while he knew that the communists were planning to seize absolute power. They were in a relatively strong position during these months, because the British and the Americans were still well disposed towards Stalin and communism in general. De Gaulle knew that the F.F.I. regarded him as the French Kerensky.

In his speech on 12 September 1944 before eight thousand people at the Palais Chaillot, a fortnight after the Liberation of Paris, he referred to the communists in veiled terms. He said that no latitude would be accorded to any organization which claimed to interfere in legal affairs or the administration independently of the state.' In that part of his autobiography dealing with the Liberation,[1] he writes, 'Armed groups, appearing out of the woods, yielded to the impulse to mete out justice against their persecutors without due process of law. In many places public anger exploded into brutal actions. Naturally, political calculation, professional rivalry and personal reprisals took advantage of the circumstances, so that irregular arrests, arbitrary fines and summary executions added confusion to the chaos resulting from general destitution.' He goes on to say that this risk would have been limited had not the communist party decided to take advantage of the situation to seize power in the provinces as they had tried in Paris. While the regulations of the government required the formation in each department of one sole *Comité de Libération* composed of all movements and parties, countless committees came into being, each claiming to control its municipality, intent on hounding down the guilty and suspect. The wily and well-organized communists working under different names, taking advantage of the sympathies and sense of comradeship acquired in the struggle among all social classes, were not slow to inspire and encourage these illegal groups. On 28 September 1944, his Government issued the following order, 'All house searchings, requisitions and arrests carried out by organizations not officially recognized are illegal; and their authors subject to the full penalties provided by the law.'

That the Allied Governments were well aware of this administrative chaos in France and the danger of the F.F.I. is revealed,

---

[1] Vol. III.

if euphemistically, in this conversation de Gaulle relates he had with Churchill in Paris on 11 November 1944:[1]

Churchill: Allow me to congratulate you on the order which you have established in your country. The demonstration of the French forces was most impressive. Before I left England, some of my colleagues were a little apprehensive about what I might face.
De Gaulle: You mean . . . the F.F.I.?
Churchill: Precisely! But it all went off very well.
De Gaulle: You can rest assured that Frenchmen will always behave well.

Two examples, from many hundreds will illustrate the power which the F.F.I. exercised independently of the Government in the months immediately after the Invasion. They executed Frenchmen, not necessarily for having collaborated, but often because they were rich, or had in some way incurred the hostility of the F.F.I. On 24 August 1944 in Nîmes, the F.F.I. broke into the prison; they shot a number of the inmates, and took out another thirty-four whom they threatened to execute if the composition of the courts for trying collaborators was not in their view satisfactory. If only to save possibly innocent people, de Gaulle's Commissioner and the newly installed Prefect were reduced to parleying with the F.F.I., thereby recognizing them *de facto*. The conditions to which they finally agreed were that the President of the Court should be an F.F.I. man, and that a certain number of Maquis should be on each jury. 'Sometimes,' writes de Gaulle, 'the sessions were disturbed by mob interventions. In several regions there were even riots to snatch the prisoners from the courts. This was the case, for instance, in Nîmes, Mauberge, Bourges, Annecy, Alès and Rodez. . . . I had to urge the Ministers of the Interior and of Justice to vigilance and firmness . . .'[2]

The second example concerns the d'Armagnac family who had a château near Limoges and were prominent landowners. At some point during the German occupation their daughter, who had experience of hospital nursing, was unwise enough (or humane enough) to tend a number of Miliciens who had been wounded in an affray with the Resistance. Not long after the Liberation, she

---

[1] Related in *L'histoire de l'épuration* by Robert Aron.
[2] Vol. III of Memoirs.

was married in the local church. On coming out after the ceremony with her husband and the priest who had married them, all three were shanghaied almost at the church-door. Some days later their corpses were found, she still in her wedding-dress.

Maurice Rolland, Inspecteur Générale de la Magistrature, described these F.F.I. or Maquis elements in his report on 6 November 1944. The euphemism of the official language hardly conceals his true feelings: 'The Maquis recruited were not always the best elements. After having fought valiantly during the Liberation, they have since committed regrettable acts. . . . Surrounded by these Maquis, the representatives of the Government, without practical means of enforcing their wishes, have often had to negotiate with them . . .' De Gaulle says[1], 'The Communists, taking advantage of old local dissensions and the persecutions inflicted by the Vichy agents, had established an anonymous dictatorship in Marseilles which made arrests on its own account and even performed executions without the authorities opposing them decisively.'

Among the forty thousand Frenchmen executed for 'collaboration' during this period,[2] by far the greater number were real fascists and pro-Nazis who had committed atrocities. The manner of their death was often equally frightful. Admiral Platon, one of the most ruthless anti-communist Ministers in Vichy, was first roasted with an oxy-acetylene blow-lamp, then tied between two lorries which slowly tore his body apart.

These matters have been mentioned only to show the climate of opinion in France when, on 24 August 1944, General de Gaulle entered Paris and the ordeal of Louis Renault began.

---

[1] Ibid.
[2] Figures from Robert Aron's *L'Histoire de l'épuration*.

7 | The Scapegoat

Jean-Louis, Renault's son, states that about two years before the Allied invasion of Europe, there were rumours in Paris that de Gaulle had already agreed to nationalize the Renault factories after the war. Representatives of the F.F.I. had visited de Gaulle in London, and stated their conditions for working with the Free French. One of these concerned 'the arch-capitalist, the *saigneur de Billancourt*', whose exemplary dismissals in the late thirties had not been forgotten, and who had, moreover, under Vichy, abrogated the late Matignon Agreements by returning to the old-fashioned notion that a worker should be paid for what he does, and no more. To all good socialists such a man seemed antediluvian.

'Nationalization' as a word had existed at the end of the nineteenth century, but several decades had passed before it was put into practice in France. The railways had come first, just before the war; and now the cataclysm of 1944 was to be used to carry out a number more. Within a matter of months after the Liberation, many banks, mines, insurances, electricity and gas companies were nationalized. And in nationalizing Renault de Gaulle would only be satisfying a demand expressed as early as 1937 by the Trade Unions. In a pamphlet published by the Institut Supérieur Ouvrier, M. Dupiol, referring to the necessary nationalization of 'key industries', described the automobile one as 'eminently ripe for the process'.

Compared with the other big industrialists, Renault was a desirable and easy prey. He was the biggest capitalist in France, owning 98 per cent of his firm, operating in almost water-tight seclusion; while his peers had been wise enough to sell a proportion of their shares and enlist powerful co-directors. He presented a single, they a multiple, target. He had ignored the existence of the Resistance, whereas most of them had been careful to contribute to its funds. De Gaulle and the Resistance would think twice about interfering with a firm like Michelin, two of whose family had died gallantly for the Allied cause. Among the general, apolitical public, Renault had, through his failure or refusal to undertake personal publicity, the reputation of being a hard-faced, ruthless slave-driver who had grown rich on two wars. Lastly, he was disliked by his own class. Far from helping him in his hour of need, the other industrialists would not object to seeing him pilloried, with his automobile empire and all the affiliated industries which had made him independent of them.

On 20 August 1944, with the Allied armies nearly in Paris, Renault went, as was his daily custom, to Billancourt, where he found that work had almost ceased. The signal for the uprising had been given, and many of his workers had joined the insurgents. Those who remained greeted him in silence, but without hostility, at the gates. Meanwhile, the personal attack on him had begun in the clandestine communist newspaper, *L'Humanité*:

JUSTICE FOR THE TRAITORS AND PROFITEERS!

Today we will confine ourselves to the Usines Renault, a particularly unsavoury affair. The entire working-class knows about this great industrial convict prison. Before the 1930 economic crisis, the Usines Renault recruited black labour from North Africa, because it was cheaper than French. Their owner abominated the Trade Unions. After the sabotage of the Popular Front social laws, and the despicable foreign policy which undermined collective security and the Franco-Soviet pact—the sole guarantor of peace for our land—the Usines Renault went on strike. The hand of repression then descended ferociously on the hundreds of strikers who were arrested and condemned in violation of the law, through the influence of Hitler's Fifth Column.

The trusts threw France into a war for which they had made no preparations. Renault was one of the most important vehicle and aeroplane constructors; yet France entered the war without tanks and aeroplanes. Then in 1940 Renault offered to work for the Germans. He shall pay for the lives of Allied soldiers killed by the equipment he sold to the enemy. He shall pay for the hundreds of innocent persons killed in the allied bombardments made necessary by his treason. He shall pay for the French workers delivered to the German hangman!

When Louis Renault went to the factory the following day, the atmosphere was quite different. Some of the workers insulted him to his face, spat, and shook their fists. Meanwhile the rest of the left-wing press of resurgent France, *L'Aurore*, *Combat*, *Libération*, *Franc-Tireur*, had taken up the theme of *L'Humanité*.

Their headlines announced 'Where is Louis Renault?' 'He has taken flight!' 'He is in Madrid!' 'He has accepted asylum in Switzerland!' 'Purification!' cried *L'Humanité*. 'Purification for Renault and his kind!' It then accused de Gaulle of weakness in dealing with the collaborators. 'Renault has not been arrested. He has fled the country! Our new rulers have allowed him to escape! Renault is the owner of 98 per cent of the shares in his firm. He made six billion in his transactions with the Boche. Was he forced to work for them? Here is the answer. When the Allied bombardment damaged his factory, Vichy refused to indemnify him, on the ground that his factories had not been requisitioned by the occupier and could therefore not invoke Force Majeure— because he went to work of his own free will for the Germans. The unanimous opinion of the Resistance is that Louis Renault must pay for the death of our allied soldiers. . . . But alas, there are today in high places influential persons who turn a blind eye. *All such people are doing is to make themselves responsible for disorder.*' (Author's italics.) The last sentence was particularly ominous for de Gaulle.

Renault's family and friends advised him not to return to the factory the following day. They suggested that he should leave Paris until passions had cooled; in no circumstances should he stay at the house in Avenue Foch. In this twilight period when Laval, the head of the Government, had abdicated, and the new régime was not properly installed, there were no forces of public order in Paris. Anything might happen under mob-rule, and the F.F.I., who were occupying public buildings, appeared to be the masters of the city.

For the next week, Renault stayed in the houses of various friends; with his old mistress, Jeanne Hatto; his niece, Mme Lefèvre-Pontalis; with another old friend Mme Dubufe-Morot. He seemed at last to have realized what might lie ahead. He told M. Dauvergne, 'I have no illusions. I now realize that hate means more than my name and work. Looking back, I know that my name belongs to the history of the country. After the first war, I was recognized as having done much for victory . . . now today they say I am unpatriotic. Let them find another industrialist who has done as much for his country as I have. I have the right to be proud at having given my name to France. I will be criticized for not having closed the factory during the war. But I have no regrets. I assured work and pay for my workmen during these four years. My conscience is clear. The envious hate me, I know.' [And he made a particularly significant remark:] 'I succeeded in life because I worked alone. I am now about to fail because I am alone. I know my faults.'[1]

On 1 September he went with his son to see what was happening at the Renault works in Le Mans. But this was equally dangerous, and he was offered shelter by a junior member of his staff, M. le Ferron de Longcamp, who had a château one hundred miles from Paris. Here, M. de Longcamp took a considerable risk, for more violent articles about 'the arch-criminal Renault' were appearing in the Paris Press. He remained loyal to his chief at a time when—as we have seen de Gaulle himself admitted—summary justice was being administered on all sides. The only proviso he made was that there must be nothing secret about Renault's stay. That would be self-incriminatory. Renault remained with him from 6 until 22 September, the day of his arrest.

M. de Longcamp says he became aware during this unpleasant period of a new side to his employer's personality, a 'sensibility and gentleness which I had never suspected'. Renault showed unusual consideration for Mme de Longcamp, saying that she was putting herself out too much on his behalf; for the purely administrative problems of running a house at this time, even procuring food, were enormous. He also expressed concern about the health of their aged cook who was lame and ailing, continually asking how she was, and saying he must give her a good tip. These were not qualities for which he had been known in the past. His speech had become thick, and in his pathetic attempts to articulate he often moved his hands to his mouth as if trying to extract a word. 'If they put me in prison,' he stuttered to M. de Longcamp, 'I'm d . . . d . . . done for!' (*Je suis f . . . f . . . foutu* was the phrase he continually employed.)

At a public meeting on 6 September M. Coste, the Communist Deputy for Billancourt, demanded Renault's arrest for trafficking with the enemy, and brought the charge to the attention of the Commissioner for Justice. Legally, this made a preliminary investigation obligatory. But it is a considerable

---

[1] Quoted in J. Dauvergne's book, *Vie de Louis Renault.*

step to arrest a member of the *Grand Croix de la Légion d'Honneur*. The Commissioner first consulted a number of persons who had worked during the war with Renault to see if a charge could be established. To call a man a 'bloodsucker', a 'warmonger' and a 'Hitlerian lackey' is not enough; concrete evidence is required. But none could be found. During the war Renault had published no pro-German articles; he had not joined Doriot's Légion des Volontaires Français, which had fought with the Germans in Russia; he had entertained no German officers at his house; he had not denounced any of his countrymen to the Gestapo. All he had done was to make lorries and trucks and sell them to the Germans, and that with the approval of the legal Government of France.

Meanwhile de Gaulle, who had been less than three weeks in Paris, had been forced to take communists into his government, if only to avoid a *coup d'état*.[1] Had this taken place, he felt that the Allied High Command, now fully occupied with pursuing the Germans to the Rhine, and in any case still sentimentally pro-Russian, would not have done much to help him. Among the communists he had to accept was Marcel Willart, who demanded and obtained the post of Secrétaire Générale de la Justice; and who immediately announced that among those he would arrest would be 'first and foremost those directors of trusts, organizers and traffickers in defeat, and proprietors of enterprises who have voluntarily worked for the enemy and been enriched by him'. Although de Gaulle had deplored the paying off of old scores by the F.F.I and others, he could not, at least for the moment, state his disapproval too openly. While public passions were so inflamed, he dare not give the impression of being irresolute about collaborators. And the attitude the communists in his Government adopted towards Louis Renault was roughly that of Saint-Juste at the trial of Louis XVI—'If the King is innocent the Revolution is guilty.' A formal order for Renault's interrogation was issued by Willart on 18 September 1944.

On being informed of this Renault, who was still with M. de

---

[1] The figures in the first free elections held a year later explain his predicament—26 per cent communist, 45 per cent socialist, and the right-wing parties only 15 per cent. What then could he have done in September 1944, when the left-wing power was even greater—except play for time?

Longcamp, immediately consulted his lawyer, M. Ribet. He said he had nothing to be ashamed of and would face his accusers. Attempts to persuade him against such an immediate step, to go abroad for a while to Switzerland or Spain, were ignored. He was furious as well as determined; justice would vindicate his honour. It was therefore agreed that he should appear in Paris on 22 September before Juge d'Instruction Martin, who would first establish if there was a prima facie case. It was understood that there would be no question of arrest, only of interrogation. And so it proved that first day, when all the judge required was assurance of his identity. He was then asked to return the following day for the interrogation. He was accompanied on the morning of the 23rd by M. Jean Louis and his valet, M. Clément Pouns, who also drove his car. These two men are the only surviving witnesses of the scene (both Juge Martin and M. Ribet are dead). The interview was short; the judge merely said that Renault was to be placed under arrest in Frèsnes prison 'pending interrogation'. As a concession to his age and eminence, he could be taken there in his own car, and not in the customary 'Black Maria'.

M. Pouns was waiting for them when they came down the steps, and he says that Renault was flanked by two armed guards. Renault sat in the back between the guards, M. Louis in front with M. Pouns. The latter did not know the way to Frèsnes and the guards directed him. When they reached the prison and got out, M. Pouns says that Renault was already manacled. The doors of the prison opened, Renault and his guardians went inside, and the two men, seeing that they could do no more, drove away.

8 | Arrest

In the month after the liberation of Paris, Frèsnes had become full of a completely new set of political prisoners. In the words of Robert Aron,[1] 'almost overnight the prisoners had become the gaolers'. He explains how, since 1939, Frèsnes and prisons like it had been the scene of three political cataclysms. 'First, in the time of Daladier,' he says, 'the prisons were full of communists and pro-Axis elements. Then, after the armistice of 1940, they contained persons suspected by Vichy or the Germans—British and American subjects or sympathizers, Jews, Résistants, Gaullists. Now at the Liberation, all these people were freed and replaced by hundreds of "Collaborators". The professional gaolers,' he says, 'had come to regard this political musical chairs with a certain cynicism. "First, we had the Communists," they said to the new arrivals; "then the English; now it's your turn. We don't really care who you are. We've never really disliked any of you."'

But to the professional gaolers, of whom only a few remained, a new and sinister element was added after the Liberation—self-appointed gaolers. Some of these men were members of the F.F.I, some were unemployed, ready to take on any job, a few were civil criminals masquerading as Résistants, some were hoping to pay off old scores. In those days, there was little time to examine credentials; the prisons were so full that the new authorities were glad to take anyone on as gaoler, if one or two friends could vouch for him. It is understandable, therefore, that the new prisoners looked around apprehensively on arrival, hoping not to see the familiar face of some servant or employee they had once dismissed or otherwise antagonized.

At Frèsnes the new political arrivals were received in the Third Division, which at this time left a good deal to be desired. At the entry, Louis Renault was asked—somewhat to his mystification—the usual questions: name, age, occupation, father's

---

[1] In *L'Histoire de l'épuration*.

Christian name, mother's maiden name, and so on. He had to
hand over his cash and Cartier watch, and was escorted to a
wing presided over by a group of armed men, none of them
wearing uniform. Among his fellow prisoners were—had he cared
to take note—a number of persons as distinguished as himself in
their various walks of life: generals, company directors, politicians, writers, famous actors. There was Abel Hermant of the
Académie Française; the well-known author, Henri Berand;
Admiral Robert; the famous savant, Georges Claude. For a
short time his old acquaintance, the ex-Foreign Minister Flandin,
was on his landing. All these were there, together with a sprink-
ling of the Parisian *monde* who had unwisely entertained German
officers at their houses. It was a fair cross-section of the French
upper-classes.

When Louis Renault entered Frèsnes, he was, at least physically, in good health, wiry, and resilient, although resigned in
manner. The few persons who saw him in the next days—his
wife, M. Louis and his valet, M. Clément Pouns—have been
questioned about the sudden deterioration of his health. M.
Pouns says that to begin with he was in perfect health, talking
volubly and giving instructions about the food and clothes he
wanted them to bring—and then almost overnight he had become a physical wreck, barely able to speak. They all told me
they believe he was physically maltreated. It is true that, for a
man like Renault, who had a horror of physical violence of any
kind, the indignity of being handcuffed and treated like a
common criminal must have had a psychological effect which
would affect his health. But this in itself could hardly account for
the deterioration.

Dr Truchot, the radiologist who later X-rayed Renault's
corpse, says that among the prison staff in Frèsnes was a lay nun,
une bonne soeur, who saw Renault a few days after his arrival
being taken for exercise in the prison courtyard. She noticed that
the gaoler in charge of him was carrying a French *poilu's* helmet.
As Renault walked through the door, this man inverted the
metal helmet and brought it down smartly on his head, with a
curse, '*Va-t-en! Vieux salaud!*' Renault, she says, crumpled up.
This evidence is confirmed by another eye-witness, M. Roger
Charels, a Quaker and prison visitor who states that on 4 October
(after Renault had been in prison twelve days) a young gaoler in

199

Frèsnes indicated Louis Renault to him with the words, 'You see what a state that one's in! He got a good beating up yester-day.'

That the gaolers knew who their prisoner was and were waiting for him is supported by the evidence of Christiane Renault, who was allowed to visit her husband for the first time on 3 October. She found three surly gaolers in civilian clothes armed with sub-machine-guns outside his cell. As soon as she saw Louis Renault, she knew from his expression that he was being physically maltreated, if not tortured. He could hardly speak and communicated largely by signs and through his pleading eyes. She tried to cheer him up, saying that the matter was in the hands of the lawyers, that they hoped for a release within a matter of days. All he could stutter was: 'It'll be too late! It's at night *they* come!'

When the guards heard Mme Renault talking to him quietly they ordered her to speak up, and told her she could stay only ten minutes. But she returned the following day with food because her husband had asked for rice, which was all he could swallow. This time the guards were openly hostile and told her she could not see him because he was in 'solitary confinement'. Whereupon she tried to see the prison governor, to complain about such treatment; she was refused an interview.

The family have since done all they can to trace the nun to whom Dr Truchot refers—without success. Twenty-five years have elapsed since those days, and now we shall never know exactly what happened in the last month of Renault's life. Most of the persons who might throw light on the affair are dead, among them also Juge Martin and Renault's lawyer, Maître Ribet. All my attempts to see Government officials connected in any way with the last days of Renault and the nationalization of the firm were unavailing. (My two letters, for instance, to M. Lacoste, the minister in charge of the nationalization at the time, were not answered.) The French attach great importance to 'legality'—much more than the English do—to the letter of the law and its strict application; for, unlike the English, whose legal system, like their constitution, is not defined but is based on precedents, the French demand everything 'in writing'. Any departure from these clearly defined norms is a heinous crime against French legality.

They are therefore no doubt ashamed now that on 4 October, before Renault had been interrogated, let alone tried, a Government decree was published announcing 'all goods, rights and interests belonging directly or indirectly through third parties to the Usines Renault are to be placed under Government sequestration'. In the eyes of the law, he was still an innocent man, yet his property had already been confiscated. In the days that followed the arrest, Louis Renault was visited by both his wife and M. Pouns. The latter states that he was appalled to find Renault barely able to speak, uttering only the words, 'Don't leave me! Don't leave me!' M. Pouns was also surprised that Renault's lawyer was not allowed to visit him.

On 7 October, Christiane Renault was told at the prison that her husband had been transferred to Ville-Evrard, the prison sanatorium for 'mentally unbalanced' prisoners, 'because he had gone mad'. Even here he was guarded night and day by two armed custodians. She obtained permission to visit him on the 8th, and it was clear the treatment there was no better because he behaved towards her (the words are M. Hubert's), 'like a small, whipped animal cringing and craving the protection of its master'. All he could repeat was, 'It's at night *they* come! They're so cruel!' He would say no more, as if he had been forced to make some pact with his tormentors. He spoke of acute pains in the neck (which would presumably indicate the blow he had received on the head), and of a lumbar injection he had been given. When the guards came to escort his wife away, he hid his head in his hands.

Mme Renault had considerable difficulty in obtaining permission to visit him again on 12 October, when she found him only semi-conscious. She was horrified that he was receiving no proper medical attention, and had not been seen by a doctor. They were, she was certain, letting him die. She was again received by a group of guards at the cell-door, who had evidently received orders that he was not to be removed. Finally, after various attempts to persuade the Juge d'Instruction Martin, who remained curiously obdurate, as if he too were under orders of some kind, she was allowed to call in the family doctor, Dr Marion. He found Renault already in a coma and demanded that he should be immediately transferred to a private hospital. This request was granted, and on 17 October he was removed in a private ambulance to the hospital Saint-Jean-de-Dieu in the rue Oudinot, which was run by monks.[1]

Even on this trip he was accompanied in the ambulance by the guards, who told Mme Renault that if she interfered too much there would 'be trouble for your son too'. Here for several days Louis Renault remained in a coma, until he died on 24 October 1944.

The official diagnosis that death was due to uraemia (excess of urine in the blood) has been contested by medical experts, although it may well be that the harsh treatment he had received had worsened the uraemia. When Louis Renault entered the hospital on 17 October the quantity of urine in the blood was ·6 grams per litre, which is normal for a man of his age; yet he was already in a coma. Every difficulty was put in the way of Mme Renault to bring an outside doctor to see him. This was understandable, because his condition was that of a man suffering more from a cerebral haemorrhage than from uraemia; and there were a number of reasons why the authorities should prefer the official cause of death. If in any civilized country a prisoner is killed in gaol by his warders, the Government has some unpleasant questions to answer.

Although Judge Martin can no longer answer these questions, certain remarks by men who were in positions of authority confirm the overall impression given by the Frèsnes incarceration that decisions about Renault had already been taken. It is most unlikely that his death was openly or officially envisaged; but in this twilight period, before the Government was properly installed and when power resided in a multitude of hands, it would have been easy enough for a chance remark to have been interpreted too literally.

Raoul Dautry has been referred to before as the War Minister, the man who reprimanded Renault in 1939 for inadequate war production. He had passed the war in opposition to Vichy, living quietly in the south of France, and after the Liberation he was recalled by de Gaulle, who made him Minister of Reconstruction. Not long after Renault's death he met his old friend M. Hubert,

---

[1] I visited this hospital in 1968, and spoke to the Father Superior. He says that the only member of the staff who was present at the time is dead, and he knew nothing about the case.

who had been one of Renault's closest associates at the factory. Hubert asked him why Renault had received such harsh treatment and why Dautry, as an influential minister, who had always admired Renault, had done nothing to prevent this miscarriage of justice. All Dautry would reply was 'A head had to fall!' implying that an expiatory offering for the industrialist class was required.

This would be fully in keeping with the character of de Gaulle and his conception of *le chef*. De Gaulle has always believed in attributing full authority for any action to the leaders, never to the subordinates. His own courageous attitude is, 'All right, if my Government makes a mistake, blame me. Shoot me! I take full responsibility.' If heads are to fall, then they shall be those of the leaders. An experiment in socialism, in nationalization, was inevitable; and Renault was a leader and symbol of what was to be supplanted.

Although Renault was placed in his coffin without an autopsy, Mme Renault took the precaution of getting Dr Truchot to take an X-ray through the coffin walls before burial. This revealed— as Dr Truchot later stated officially, publishing the photographs —that Renault had died from a fracture of the vertebrae. In the excited state of public opinion, nothing could be done by the bereaved wife and family. It was not until over ten years after, when passions had cooled, that Mme Renault, interested in establishing that her husband had been murdered, was granted permission for the corpse to be exhumed. But she could not establish this because the vertebrae in question, which Dr Truchot had identified before as having been damaged, had been cut out of the neck with a razor.[1] Moreover, the Juge d'Instruction in charge of this re-examination, could find no contemporary witnesses (the nun, the prison guards, and so on); and the matter was dropped. To M. Pouns was given the disagreeable task of identifying the corpse when the coffin was opened. The body had been partly embalmed and although over ten years had elapsed this was possible. The head, he says, was detached from the body.

Louis Renault was buried in the small churchyard near the property he loved at Herqueville. One of his oldest friends and

---

[1] In an interview with the author, September 1966.

collaborators, M..Sam Guillelmon, pronounced the funeral oration over his tomb: 'Head of the greatest firm in France, which extended the fame of his country throughout the world, Louis Renault worked as hard, if not harder, than the most industrious of his workers—with his head, his hands, by the sweat of his brow in his youth, and, as his firm expanded, with the intellect of a great inventor and organizer.'

9 | Aftermath

'The transfer of the Renault firm into a Régie Nationale had nothing to do with principles; it was a punishment. Its chief result was to place at the disposition of the state the first and finest factory in France.'

The only direct reference to Renault in
General de Gaulle's memoirs

One of the many lessons taught at the Liberation is clear. Persons accused of political offences during a period such as 1940–44, and who are confident of their innocence, should avoid immediate confrontation with their accusers. They should go abroad for some years. This may appear, it will be objected, a confession of guilt. Perhaps—but what is certain is that by the time they return, the public will feel very differently about them. It may be admirable, but it is also foolhardy, to say as Renault did, 'I have done nothing wrong. Justice will prove it.' Self-willed and obdurate to the end, he refused to listen to advice. It was as if everything that had made him great, his authoritarian behaviour, his force of character, his independence and intransigence, expressed as a caricature of these qualities at the end, destroyed him. He knew he had done nothing wrong, and he believed in French justice. But in the aftermath of a war the question of justice often does not arise.

One particular case illustrates this. Long before the war, a clever French pamphleteer named Maurice-Yves Sicard was violently pro-German. He called for friendship with Hitler, and his pronouncements about Anglo-Saxon decadence had a Goebbelsesque ring. He became secretary of Doriot's P.P.F. party, and during the war went with the L.V.F. (a kind of French S.S. in German uniform) to fight on the Russian front. In 1944 he was with Pétain and his entourage in Germany at Sigmarinen, still uttering pro-Nazi statements. About such a collaborator there was clearly no lack of documentary evidence. It is hard in fact to imagine anyone more likely to have been condemned—if not summarily executed by the F.F.I.—at a Gaullist trial. And so Sicard evidently thought himself, because just before the end of the war he decamped to Spain. He was tried *in absentia* by the *Cour de la Justice de la Seine*, and sentenced to forced labour for life.

In 1957, after thirteen years of exile, and some discreet inquiries, he calculated the time was ripe to return. He handed himself over to the French authorities—and was reprieved. Today he lives unmolested in his native land; and in 1964, under the pseudonym of Saint Paulien, he even published a six-hundred page book, *Histoire de la Collaboration*, which is not only an apologia for the Vichy régime and Doriot's French Nazis, but also a vituperative attack on England, de Gaulle, America and Russia. Hitler emerges as a kind of pacifist, hating violence and the destruction of cities, a good man ensnared by the perfidious Anglo-Saxons. Published by L'Esprit Nouveau, it can be had today in any bookshop. 'Many of the author's contentions may be questioned,' say the publishers disingenuously. 'But his sincerity, good faith and the high quality of his historical evidence cannot.'

M. Jean Seruys, the northern industrialist and engineer, relates too, that after the Liberation every industrialist, whoever he was and however gallant he had been in the Resistance, had to pass before a tribunal to be cleared. The reason for this was that everyone connected with big business had bills and receipts in their office showing that at some stage in the four years of occupation he had sold goods or services to the Germans. If Renault could have waited—as Sicard did—he would almost certainly not have been found guilty.

Everyone will recall the trials of prominent Germans after the war. Men like Kesselring and Krupp who managed to escape the gallows in the immediate post-war period were soon reinstated. Krupp's situation had something in common with Renault's; they were the two largest industrialists of their respective countries. The courts condemned Krupp and he had to forfeit his factories; but he avoided the gallows, thanks to a postponement of his trial. The result is that his descendants today are in full possession of their factories, sitting in their offices at the head of affairs again. Renault did not, figuratively speaking, 'avoid the gallows'; unfortunately he was dead. But that the passage of time here, too, changed the attitude of even the French Government which had seized his factories in 1944 is proved by comparing two Government decrees. Their dates are significant. The first is 'Ordonnance No. 45, 16 January 1945', signed by de Gaulle himself; a justification for the confiscation of the Renault factory. The second was promulgated four years later (30 April 1949), and admits, if only by implication, that the act was unjustified.

In the first de Gaulle states:

Though their deliveries to the French army had been very inadequate in the years preceding the war, their deliveries to the German army during the Occupation were of a great importance and were only checked by the repeated raids on the factories at Boulogne-Billancourt and Le Mans by the Allied Air Forces. Furthermore, in June, 1940, Monsieur Renault, who was on a mission in America, hurriedly returned to France in order to put his factories at the disposal of the occupying power. . . . The government . . . has decided to nationalize the factories, and to confiscate Louis Renault's estate and shares . . .[1]

The second document is entitled *'Ordonnance de classement de la procédure suivie contre les Usines Renault'*. It begins by admitting that the information in Ordonnance No. 45 was undoubtedly of a 'contradictory nature and that the Order of January 16 was made without any solid basis, since the preparations for the trial had hardly begun.' It then describes how the Usines Renault were made to work for the 'occupying power':

On June 24, 1940, the German Government ordered the provisional seizure of the factory and German commissioners took over control. They ordered the immediate reopening of the workshops and declared that they were prepared to proceed alone if they did not obtain the co-operation of the French management. The general management was unprepared to take any decision without reference to the Government, which had recently been set up at Vichy, and to General Huntziger, president of the French Armistice Commission. The latter proposed to the Government that the management of the Renault factory be left in Paris with orders to take charge of the production of automobile material demanded by the Germans, for the requirements of the Paris district. The proposal was approved by Vichy and was

---

[1] This and subsequent quotes from the Ordonnances have been taken from *Renault* by Saint Loup.

signed by General Weygand. It became the precedent for the attitude to other factories, notably the Citroën factory, at the beginning of July.

The Ordonnance goes on to say that all documents seized since this time show that the preoccupation of the directors of the Usines Renault was to adapt their programme as far as they could to national (French) requirements. If possible, they modified the programmes laid down by the Germans. But the fact that the Germans reserved the right of granting licences for raw materials meant that, in the last resort, they had effective control.

The Ordonnance further stated that the German authorities laid down rules for what was to be constructed, and that the Usines Renault protested on numerous occasions, asserting that they wished to construct tourist vehicles for the Spanish market, and agricultural tractors. But all these attempts, which were inspired by the desire to safeguard the industrial potential of the factory, its equilibrium and commercial organization, were in vain.

Also Usines Renault satisfied the German Army demand for vehicles only with constant delay. During the four years of occupation, of the 41,909 vehicles ordered in the German programme, only 34,232 were delivered. While in face of the 1,662 vehicles authorized by the Germans for the French civilian market, Usines Renault produced 3,460—that is 1,792 more civilian vehicles than were authorized.[1]

If the comparison of these two 'ordonnances' is still insufficient to prove that the nationalization of the Usines Renault on the grounds of 'Collaboration' was unjustified, the case of Berliet, the other French automobile manufacturer accused of collaboration is the final damning proof.

During the war this firm furnished the German army with vehicles in roughly the same proportions as those furnished by Renault. Berliet was arrested before Renault, on 4 September 1944, and his factories were placed under the provisional régime run by a communist called Mosnier. On 13 September, Berliet's four sons were arrested. In the months before the trial, which took place in 1946, the elder Berliet son, Paul, defended himself

---

[1] See Appendix for a fuller verbatim text.

vigorously during seventy-eight interrogations. In spite of this, at the trial the Berliets were found guilty and sentenced each to two years' imprisonment and sequestration of their factory. It was now that the real fighting spirit of this family emerged. The father, whose sentence had been commuted on account of his age (over eighty) to exile in the south, spent his remaining capital on a series of pamphlets setting forth the illegality of the seizure. One was entitled *Histoire de l'expérience sovietique chez Berliet*, another *Commentaire juridique du procès*. He sometimes posted as many as two hundred of these pamphlets a day to influential people, politicians, other industrialists, newspapers, and so on, for he knew that time was on his side. 'We will wait as long as necessary,' he said, 'to obtain justice.'

By 1947 the communist direction of the Berliet factory had become so inefficient that a strike took place; and at this point, when the Government authorities were beginning to realize they had gone too far, and were sensitive to Berliet's pamphlets, they offered him a sum of several millions for his factories (also, implicitly, to keep him quiet). To his son in prison he wrote, saying that there was to be no bargaining with the Government. Either he (Berliet) was guilty, in which case he lost everything. Or he was not guilty, in which case his factories must be restored to him. They would wait, for years if necessary, until justice was done. On 22 July 1949, over four years after the seizure, on appeal the Conseil d'Etat quashed the verdict, and returned the whole concern to the Berliet family, in whose hands it remains today.

The parallel with Renault is clear here too, although there is one big difference. The Renault firm and family had no one to fight back. Louis Renault had died. Jean-Louis, his son, was aged twenty-one and unversed in these matters. A woman, Christiane Renault, could not do it on her own. François Lehideux had been dismissed from all his duties by his uncle in 1940. If the son had known how to lobby support among the Deputies in those crucial years, as Berliet had—if indeed he or his family *had* any friends among the politicians—Louis Renault's fate might have been very different. As it was, the whole of this vast industrial empire, still in first-class condition, not owing a *sou* to anyone, passed into the hands of the State—by a governmental decree which can be compared with the contemporary seizures in

Communist Eastern Europe. De Gaulle explains this act in his memoirs: '. . . to place by requisition or sequestration at the direct disposal of the State certain public services and private enterprises; the State to absorb any *guilty enrichment* obtained by those who worked for the enemy.'[1] But Renault had not been found guilty. He had never been tried.

The man who was placed in charge of the nationalized Renault factories was Pierre Lefaucheux, an industrialist and engineer himself, with a fine record in the Resistance. When he was installed he made a speech to the workers in which he explained that they would 'henceforth work for the country and them-selves—not to increase the already too great power of one man . . . our aim will be no longer to gain as much money as possible, but to further the interests of the country. . . . I do not love the Germans and their friends any more than you do; therefore we must clear out the bad elements in our midst . . . the atmosphere in this factory has for too long been far from healthy . . .', and he referred to the thirty thousand men he was addressing as 'com-rades'. In an article written about the same time[2] Lefaucheux wrote, 'No State can take over the property of an industrialist for the public good without wounding the principles of liberty to which all Frenchmen are attached, *unless that industrialist has committed a crime against the country* [my italics]. Otherwise, the transfer must be legal and the proprietor fully recompensed.' What crime had Renault committed?

Renault and his family were not recompensed. The corollary is that the seizure of the factory was illegal. Later Lefaucheux was to say, in another article, after he had had some experience of the difficulties encountered in running a large firm, that his earlier views were 'theoretical conceptions' which, after a certain amount of practical experience at the head of Régie Renault, he had had to modify.

At the time of the nationalizations in 1945, public enthusiasm for such measures was great; with Renault went the four largest banks, thirty-four of the biggest insurance companies, electricity and gas companies, and coal mines, all passed by overwhelming

---

[1] Vol. III.
[2] In *Cahiers Politiques*, March 1945.

majorities. Nationalization seemed the cure for all ills, and the opposition to it could never muster more than sixty votes. However, in the three years that followed, popular enthusiasm for nationalization declined, as it began to reveal its inefficiency. Already by 1946 Schumann, the Minister for Finance, was talking about a 'pause' in the process. In fact, successive governments afterwards introduced bills to nationalize the steel industry, radio and television, civil aviation and Paris passenger transport. But only the last proposal was adopted. The nationalized companies still in existence have since been the object of criticism so severe and prolonged that the communists have denounced a 'systematic campaign to discredit all nationalization, and to bring about the return to private ownership'. Had Renault been alive, they might in his case well have proved right. But he had been in his grave too long. And so there his creation remains today, under the name of Régie Nationale des Usines Renault.[1] Quite why the term *Régie* is used, no one seems to know; it is associated in most people's minds with the State tobacco monopoly. But the name of the founder has been retained; surely not out of deference to his memory, but because it stands, as it has stood for over half a century, for all that is best in French industry and craftsmanship.

---

[1] The present Régie Renault must, in all fairness, be given the credit for having doubled the production since 1945; it appears to be the best of all the nationalized industries.

Appendix

This appendix is reproduced in full from *Renault,* by Saint Loup published by the Bodley Head, 1957.

Analysis of blood taken from Monsieur Louis Renault, Room 15, 19 rue Oudinot.
On the prescription of Doctor . . . Professor Marion.
Urea deposit in blood serum: 0 grams 60 per litre.
Died Oct. 24.

LETTER FROM MAITRE RIBET

Batonnier de l'Ordre des Avocats

to

GENERAL DE GAULLE

Re the proposal for the confiscation of the Renault factories.

Copy.   *Paris, 21 November 1944.*

To: GENERAL DE GAULLE,
Head of the Provisional Government of the French Republic.

GENERAL,

A recent communiqué of the Council of Ministers has stated that the Government has decided to confiscate 'The estate belonging to the Renault Company.' The reason given in the official communiqué is that although legal action has been dropped because of the death of Louis Renault, it is true to say that, had he lived, his estate would have been confiscated in the normal course of events after condemnation in the Law Courts.

The Government's decision consequently makes, in its Order, a judgment on a trial which has not been completed and one in which the evidence presented calls for a certain reserve before judgment is pronounced.

Apart from the fact that the memory of Louis Renault has nothing to fear from a full public inquiry and would immediately be cleared of the infamous accusation of treason against his country, it is serious that the Government's decision seriously prejudices the defence of Monsieur de Peyrecave, General Manager of the Renault Company, who has also been accused and is detained at Frèsnes.

What can be the impartiality of the judges who will hear the case if the attitude of the Management of the Company has already been publicly stigmatized by the Executive and if financial sanctions have already been publicly announced?

Already, in October 1941, at the trial of President Daladier, in the High Court, the spokesman of the pseudo-French Government announced over the radio to the astounded French people that it had decided, even before the trial began, to condemn the former head of the French Government, whom I had the honour of defending, to life imprisonment in the Fort du Pourtalet. With reference to this incredible sentence, I wrote a letter of protest to Marshal Pétain and I will quote an essential extract: 'I firmly believe that your decision has transgressed the primary conditions and unchanging principles which must be taken for granted in all civilized societies.'

It may be relevant to recall to you that: (1) An accused cannot be condemned without having been summoned to defend himself; (2) The accused cannot be condemned in any circumstances, before a judgment has been reached by Magistrates specially appointed so to do.

These eternal and basic principles have, at all times, been respected by all régimes which were based on law and order. It is in the interest of France to defend these principles and it is right that if they are temporarily forgotten and some error of a transigent nature is made, that a voice should calmly be raised to recall this fact.

Justice between men of the same nation is the prelude to justice between nations, and it would be difficult if, at the moment when France has to defend her hereditary rights before the International Tribunal, the sacred rights of individuals have been disregarded by her.

It is necessary, sir, that these matters should be drawn to your attention.

The Batonnier de l'Ordre des avocats of the Paris Court of Appeal, Maître Jacques Charpentier, supported my protest, and wrote as follows to the Marshal:

'If examination of the evidence and the trial itself bring the judges to conclusions other than your own, are they to deny the decision of the Head of State? Or are they, on the other hand, to suppress the dictates of conscience and condemn men whom they consider to be innocent? If the sentence is to be such, it will, henceforth, be irreparably discredited.

'It is doubtless the first time in legal history that a directive has been given from above and that the voice of a Head of State has been heard before that of the judges.'

Is it not surprising, General, that these protests which were not directed against you, apply word for word to the decision of your Government?

For four years we have struggled publicly and not without risk, against the violation of basic principles by the pseudo-Government of self-appointed dictators: for four years we have anxiously waited for the return of him in whom our confidence has never wavered and who, in his admirable messages of encouragement, assured us of the re-establishment of republican justice.

This hope has not been betrayed: but in decisions hastily taken, an error may have been made, and it is my duty, with due respect, to point it out to you.

Without doubt, the ministers who have put forward the decree of confiscation to the Government, depending on guilt which has not been proven, have acted in good faith. But what can they know of a trial which is unfinished and which must remain undecided until the jury brings in a verdict?

I am afraid that they have been swayed by the voices of a certain section of public opinion in which impartiality does not seem to be the main virtue.

Consequently, I ask you, in all confidence of the result, to reconsider this abnormal situation and to allow your judges complete independence in coming to a decision and not to assume a guilt which only the jury of the High Court can decide.

Yours faithfully,
Signed: Batonnier Ribet.

Decree No. 45–68, 16 January 1945

FOR THE NATIONALIZATION OF THE RENAULT FACTORIES

Preamble:

Following the Liberation, after four years of occupation, in which a large part of our industrial production was under the control of the enemy and deflected from its normal function, a serious problem was found to exist in the position of the Renault Factories Company Limited and the large industrial combine which it controlled. This was partly caused by the attitude of its management to the invader, and partly by the death of Louis Renault, its principal director and founder, who died just when he had been called upon to account for his actions according to the laws of France.

It is unnecessary to underline the important part played by the Renault Company in the economy of our country and the supreme place it held in our automobile manufacture before the outbreak of hostilities. In 1939 the factories employed more than 36,000 workers and staff and, in the course of the year, delivered 20,000 trucks and

45,000 private cars and vans, engines and munitions, with a turnover considerably greater than two milliard francs. By participation in many other enterprises, either directly or by the intervention of its management, the Company worked out a system of highly developed integration of production and distribution and came to control, directly or indirectly, a vast industrial and commercial system. The control of this powerful combine, with its many branches, which played such a large part in the economic life of the country, was controlled directly by Louis Renault and his immediate colleagues. Consequently, on Louis Renault and the small group of men around him, who controlled both capital and management, rested the major part of the responsibility incurred by the Renault Company, its principal branches and associated industries, who after the Declaration of War, were held responsible to the nation. It is certain that the automobile industry, which is a key industry in war and peace, must have been one of those particularly coveted by the Occupation; it cannot be gainsaid that its productions can most easily and most directly be turned to purely military purposes. If these suppositions explain to a great extent the enemy's particular concentration on the major automobile construction firms, it is still true that the management of these firms must answer for their attitude to the enemy throughout the Occupation and must give an account of their resistance to the enemy management. No such account has been furnished by the Renault Company. Though their deliveries to the French army had been very inadequate in the years preceding the war, their deliveries to the German army during the Occupation were of a great importance and were only checked by the repeated raids on the factories at Boulogne-Billancourt and Le Mans by the Allied Air Forces. Furthermore, in June 1940, Monsieur Renault, who was on a mission in America, hurriedly returned to France in order to put his factories at the disposal of the occupying powers.

In the knowledge of these facts, and the realization of the harm they caused the country, the Government, taking into consideration that legal action has today been closed against the principal member responsible and that the Renault factories were an instrument in the enemy's hands, has decided to nationalize the factories, and to confiscate Louis Renault's estate and shares, to the degree to which the estate and shares played a part in the control of the company's enterprises, by direct participation or by satellites.

The nationalization of the Renault factories is effected by the liquidation of the company and the absorption by the State of its assets and liabilities. In liquidation, the part owned by Louis Renault is confiscated. The relatively insignificant part belonging to other persons will be indemnified. The confiscation of Louis Renault's shares will make it possible for the State to become the principal shareholder in all dependent branches of the Renault factories and to control their activities.

This measure would have no practical value if it were not accompanied by other decisions. This is not only a matter of taking sanctions for past actions, but is also a determination to face a constructive future. The State, having become controller of the confiscated estate, is concerned both with the restoration of the factory and a resumption of the activities of the important industrial combine of the Renault group, its future development and the evolution of its economic and social policies. These problems take on a national aspect and condition the lives of a working population of more than 100,000 and the destiny of one of our most important industries. The State must not only see to it that the factories start work as soon as possible but must plan production according to the needs of the country, and work for the amelioration of its means of production and the conditions of labour. It must take the responsibility of framing a general programme, so as to reconstruct our automobile industry and improve the methods of production, with a programme for the speedy modernization of tooling and the perfection of manufacturing and sales methods in the Renault factory. Clearly the State must set an example in the improvement of the automobile industry, taking into account the state of that industry prior to the war, the lack of financial co-operation between the major constructors, and the repercussions this had on the industry, together with the swift obsolescence of machinery and equipment.

The measures laid down by this Order have for their purpose the organization and exploitation of the assets of the Renault Company Limited with the greatest efficiency. Maximum attention has been given to the organization of State control, which will be substituted for that of the company. It does not seem opportune to have recourse once more to a private company, nor to a Government office working with the usual methods of administrating public accounts. The body responsible for the management of the Renault factories had been set up, taking into account the well-proven methods of workers' participation; in this way the greatest flexibility, indispensable to the working of a large industrial concern, may be combined with the rigorous control necessary in the administration of public property and the desire of the State to run this basically important economic activity in the public interest.

In proposing these measures, the Provisional Government of the French Republic seeks to make its contribution to the moral and material rehabilitation of the country within the war effort of the United Nations, and also to carry out the reforms demanded by the French Resistance and the entire working-class.

There follow the conditions for the seizure of the company, mostly of an administrative character. It is not necessary to burden readers with all details, but we will quote only Article 2, under the first heading:

ARTICLE 2

With the exception of those confiscations decided by the Judicial Authorities, shares other than those in the hands of Monsieur Louis Renault at the time of his death, will receive compensation due to them after the State's liquidation of the Company. The compensation will be calculated on the basis of the last audited accounts under conditions laid down by a ruling of the Public Administration, with reference to the Ministers of Industrial Production, National Economy and the Budget. The attribution of this compensation to those concerned, will be as laid down by decrees agreed between the Ministers of Industrial Production and the Budget.[1]

Signed: DE GAULLE.

The Order in Council of 16 January 1945, authorized the confiscation of the Renault factory on behalf of the nation and declared that no further discussion would be possible concerning the guilt of Louis Renault and the Management of the company during the German occupation, and that their resistance to enemy control could never be proved.

With reference to this, the Public Prosecutor charged the General Manager of the company at the same time as Louis Renault. The conditions were the same, with the one difference, that the General Manager of the company was permitted to exercise his normal right of defence before the Judicial Authority.

We enclose certain extracts from an amendment in his favour, made on 30 April 1949.

EXTRACT FROM THE ORDER OF CLASSIFICATION OF THE PROCEDURES AGAINST THE RENAULT FACTORY

In an Order of Annulment made by a Government Commission on 30 April 1949, an examination of the evidence affirmed that the evidence justifying the Order of 16 January was invalid. This document is too long to be reproduced *in toto*; we give certain comprehensive extracts regarding the relations of the management of the Renault factories with the German Commission.

---

[1] These had not been decided on October 1, 1955.

The Order recognizes first, *that the information has undeniably been of a contradictory nature and that the Order of 16 January was made without any solid basis, since the preparations for the trial had hardly begun.*

The following facts were disclosed in this order:

Louis Renault was sent to America by the Reynaud Government from May to June 1940, to undertake official negotiations for the increase in production. He returned to France immediately on the conclusion of the Armistice.

The Government ordered the evacuation of the factory on 12 June and it was immediately carried out. Only sixty voluntary caretakers were left to look after it. When the enemy armies occupied Paris, the entire factory was requisitioned and put into the hands of the Chief Commandant for Paris; on 24 June 1940, the German Government ordered the provisional seizure of the factory and German commissioners took over control. They ordered the immediate reopening of the workshops and declared that they were prepared to proceed alone if they did not obtain the co-operation of the French management.

The general management was unprepared to take any decision without reference to the Government, which had recently been set up at Vichy, and to General Huntziger, president of the French Armistice Commission. The latter proposed to the Government that the management of the Renault factory be left in Paris with orders to take charge of the production of automobile material, demanded by the Germans, for the requirements of the Paris district. The proposal was approved by Vichy and was signed by General Weygand. It became the precedent for the attitude to other factories, notably to the Citroën factory, at the beginning of July.

On 10 July 1940, Colonel Thoenissen, appointed by the German Command to direct the automobile factories, held a meeting to inform French constructors that peace-time manufactures were to remain in the hands of the French industry and to be administered for their best interests.

All captured documents indicate that the management of the factory was concerned with the adaptation of production to national needs; though the Germans were informed of the programmes, they did not interfere save to direct and modify. However, the Occupation Authorities reserved the right to control sales and reserved the right to cancel sales and contracts.

At the end of August 1940, German plans were more clearly apparent. Many documents at about this time indicate that Louis Renault was worried by the fact that the Germans were requisitioning stocks of rare metals. The German management showed its hand by firm orders after 27 August.

A German order of 20 November 1940, gave factory commissioners extensive powers in the factories, which comprised complete control of documents and dealings, control of the technical staff, the supervision of the carrying out of German orders and the assessment of possibilities of production; this amounted to the complete taking over of the concern.

This taking over was further confirmed at the end of 1943, when, with the agreement of the Government, certain French companies were deputed as 'Patent Firma' (branches of German firms). The Renault Company was given to the Daimler-Benz Company; Prince von Urach, who had been the Commissioner since June 1940, was nominated representative of Daimler-Benz.

On 27 August, 1940, the German commissioners intervened for the first time, giving direct orders regarding programmes to the company. Actually it was on that day that Commissioner Schippert ordered a 50 per cent reduction in the programme laid down.

On 31 August 1940, Commissioners Schippert and von Urach notified Louis Renault that all industrial vehicles in production were to be reserved for the German army. The manufacture of private cars, as well as that of agricultural vehicles and 300-kilo vans, was abandoned. Special instructions were to be given later for the manufacture of gasogenes and electric railway engines. Only production of lorries of 3 tons and $4\frac{1}{2}$ tons was permitted.

On 1 September 1940, the factory was definitely taken over.

To combat these measure, the Management of the Renault Company made a number of protests (notes of 5 and 6 September 1940, to the Syndicate—to Doctor Schippert; on 11, 12, 13 and 14 September to the German commissioners). On almost every day of September and October 1940, the Management of the company sent suggestions and protests to the German commissioners. All these documents were dealt with by experts, but none of the suggestions (export of private cars to Spain, production of agricultural machinery) was accepted. None of these attempts, made in order to safeguard the industrial position of the company, its trade balance and its commercial organization was successful. During the fourth three-monthly period of 1940 the Committee for Automobile Organization (C.O.A.) set up by the law of 11 August 1940, took over control from the Automobile Syndicate. It was the task of this body to maintain relations between the Government, the departments of the Occupation and French constructors. From this time on the Renault Company was responsible to this body.

Research by specialists shows that, after 1942, the execution of orders given to the company every three months was only carried out with constant delays.

In the first two three-monthly periods of 1942 programmes were drawn up for 2,600 and 3,850 trucks respectively. At the end of June 1942, only 2,523 vehicles were completed. The programmes for the two other periods were increased by 2,033 units. Despite the increase, only 2,266 were delivered at the beginning of October. The third period was fixed at 2,115 trucks. There was a delay in delivering 600 of these units.

The programme for the first period of 1943 was drawn up for 3,100 trucks. There was a delay in delivery of 1,093. The speed of production followed a parallel retardation each period, delaying the authorized programme, and in 1944 the German control did not bother to establish any fixed programme.

———

Experts have drawn up a table of results of these activities. Out of a programme laid down for 41,909 vehicles, 34,232 were produced, giving a deficit of 7,677. The audited accounts show that the number of vehicles delivered to the Germans amounted to 34,017, plus 60 agricultural tractors. Sales to French customers were restricted in this period and out of 3,460 sales, only 1,662 were properly authorized, leaving 1,792 unauthorized.

Bibliography

ARGENSON, MARQUIS D', *Pétain et le Pétainisme*, Paris, Editions Créator, 1953

ARON, ROBERT, *Histoire de Vichy*, London, Hachette, 1966

ARON, ROBERT, *De l'Armistice à l'insurrection*, Paris, Gallimard, 1945

ARON, ROBERT, *L'Histoire de l'épuration*, Vol. I, Paris, Fayard, 1967

AUBE, P, and BANDOUIN, Y., *Commission consultative des dommages et des reparations. Ingérances allemandes dans l'activité industrielle (automobiles et cycles)*, Paris, Imprimerie Nationale, 1948

BARRES, M., *L'Ame française*, Paris, Emile-Paul, 1920

BAUDIN, L., *Esquisse de l'économie française sous l'occupation allemande*, Paris, Libraire de Médicis, 1945

BEAUVOIR, SIMONE DE, Prime of Life, Deutsch, 1962; World, 1962

BILLY, A., *L'Epoque contemporaine*, Paris, J. Tallandier, 1956

BOULOGNE, J., *La Vie de Louis Renault*

BOUTHILLIER, Y., *Le Drame de Vichy*, Paris, Plon, 1951

BOUTHILLIER, Y., *L'Action économique en France depuis l'armistice*, Paris, Mâcon, 1941

BOUYER, R., *Le Capitalisme contemporaine, fiction et réalité*, Paris, Centre confédéral d'education ouvrier, 1945

BRADY, R., *Business as a System of Power*, O.U.P., 1943; Columbia University Press, 1943

BROGAN, D. W., *France under the Republic*, Harper, 1940

BROGAN, D. W., *The Development of Modern France* (1870-1939), Hamish Hamilton, 1967

CAILLOT, R., *L'Usine, la terre et la cité*, Paris, Editions Ouvrière, 1958

CAUNTER, C. F., *History and Development of Light Cars*, H.M.S.O., 1957

CHASTENET, J., *La Belle Epoque*, Paris, Fayard, 1951

CHASTENET, J., *Jours inquiets et jours sanglants*, Paris, Hachette, 1957

CHASTENET, J., *La France de M. Fallières*, Paris, Fayard, 1949

CHATELAINE, A., *L'Industrie automobile française*, Paris, A. Colin, 1958

DAUTRY, R., *Métier d'homme* (autobiography), Paris, Plon, 1937

DAUVERGNE, L., *Vie de Louis Renault*, Paris, Table Ronde, 1954

DELAISI, F., *La Banque de France aux mains des 200 familles*, Paris, Comité de vigilance des intellectuelles anti-fascistes, 1936

DETOEUF, A., *Propos de O. L. Barenton*, Paris, Editions du Tambourinaire, 1948

DEYGAS, F.-J., *Les Chars d'assaut*, Paris, C. Lavauzelle, 1937

DRIEU LA ROCHELLE, *Bélouika* (novel), Paris, Gallimard, 1936

DUHAMEL, G., *Scènes de la vie future*, Paris, Mercure de France, 1951

DUNCAN, H. O., *The World on Wheels*, Paris, Duncan, 1926

EARLE, E. M., *Modern France. Problems of the Third and Fourth Republic*, O.U.P., 1951

EHRMANN, H. W., *French Labor from the Popular Front to the Liberation*, O.U.P., 1947

EHRMANN, H. W., *La Politique du patronat français*, Paris, A. Colin, 1959

FORD, HENRY, *My Life and Work*, Doubleday, 1922–26; Heinemann, 1936

FULLER, J. F. C., *Tanks in the Great War, 1914–18*, Dutton, 1920

GAULLE, CHARLES DE, *Salvation*, Vol. III of Memoirs, 1944–46, Weidenfeld & Nicolson, 1960; Simon and Schuster, 1960

GROVER, F. W., *Drieu la Rochelle and the Fiction of Testimony*, C.U.P., 1959

KARSLAKE, K., and POMEROY, L., *From Veteran to Vintage*, Temple Press, 1956

KARSLAKE, K., *Racing Voiturettes*, Motor Racing Publications, 1950

KERNAN, T., *France on Berlin Time*, Lippincott, 1941

LAMBREAUX, ALAIN, *Georges Sorel à Mahatma Gandhi—Nouvelles réflexions sur la violence*

LAROQUE, P., *Les Rapports entre patrons et ouvriers*, Paris, Aubier, 1938

LEAHY, W. D., *I Was There*, Gollancz, 1950; McGraw-Hill, 1950

LE BON, G., *Crowds: A Study of the Popular Mind*, Benn, 1947

LIDDELL HART, B., *A History of the World War, 1914–18*, Faber & Faber, 1934; Little, Brown, 1935

MALRAUX, A., *Anti-Memoirs*, Hamish Hamilton, 1968; Holt, 1968

MERCEDES, G.-J., *My Father, Mr Mercedes*, G. T. Foulis, 1966; Chilton, 1966

MICAUD, C., *La Droite devant l'Allemagne*, Paris, Calmann-Levy, 1945

MONTAGU OF BEAULIEU, LORD, *The Gordon Bennett Races*, Cassell, 1963

MONTAGU OF BEAULIEU, LORD, *Lost Causes of Motoring*, Cassell, 1960

MORAZE, C., *La France bourgeoise*, Paris, A. Colin, 1947

NEVINS, A., and HILL, F. E., *Ford: The Times, the Man, the Company*, Scribner, 1954

NICKOLS, I., and KARSLAKE, K., *Motoring Entente*, Cassell, 1956

NIXON, ST. J. C., *The Antique Automobile*, Cassell, 1956

PERTINAX, *Les Fossoyeurs*, Paris, Sagittaire, 1946

PICKLES, D. M., *France Between the Republics*, Contact, 1946

PIERJANT, J., *L'Industrie automobile*, Paris, Presses Universitaires, 1956

PLATET, J. L., *L'Industrie automobile française depuis la guerre* (doctoral thesis), Paris, Presses Universitaires, 1934

PRELOT, M., *Evolution politique et social sous la 3ᵉ république*, Paris, Ed. Spes., 1939

PROUTEAU, H., *Les Occupations des usines en Italie et en France, 1920–36* (doctoral thesis), Paris, Librairie Technique, 1937

PSICHARI, H., *Usines '42* (novel), Paris, A. Michel, 1946

SAINT LOUP, *Renault*, Bodley Head, 1957

SAULNIER, B. DE, *Histoire de la locomotion terrestre*, Paris, L'Illustration, 1936

SCOTT-MONCRIEFF, D., and others, *Three-Pointed Star*, Cassell, revised edition 1966

SOUVESTRE, P., *L'Histoire de l'automobile*, Paris, Dunod, 1907

TAYLOR, F. W., *The Principles of Scientific Management*, Harper, 1947

VIDAL, J., *Le Mouvement ouvrier français de la commune à la guerre mondiale*, Paris, Bureau d'Editions, 1934

WILSON, C. H., and READER, W. J., *Men and Machines; D. Napier & Sons, 1808–1958*, Weidenfeld & Nicolson, 1958

Articles

France Speaks—Periodical with articles on the degree of French industrialists' collaboration: Vol. I, Nos. 27, 33 and 35

'The Forces of Collaboration' by L. R. Franks, published in *Foreign Affairs*, XXI, 1932–43

'La vie et la grève des ouvriers métallos' by S. Gallois, published in *Révolution Prolétarienne*, 10 June 1936

'L'Infériorité des capitalistes français' by V. Griffuelhes, published in *Le Mouvement Socialiste*, XXVIII, 1910

'Passage au socialisme' by P. Lefaucheux, published in *Les Cahiers Politiques*

'L'Industrie automobile d'après guerre'—an *exposé* by François Lehideux to the Conseil Général des Transports

Article on Louis Renault by André Maurois, published in *Plaisirs de France*, No. 18, March 1936

Chief of the German Mitärverwaltung text by Dr Michel, published in *La France Intérieure*, No. 50, 15 November 1946 and No. 51, 15 December 1946

Strategic Bombing Survey. Renault motor-vehicle plant, Billancourt

Index